TRUSS
AT 10

Sir Anthony Seldon is an educator, historian, writer and commentator. A former headmaster and vice chancellor, he is author or editor of over fifty books on contemporary history, politics and education, including *Johnson at 10*, *The Impossible Office?*, *May at 10*, *Cameron at 10*, *Brown at 10*, *Blair Unbound* and *The Path of Peace*. He's been co-founder of Action for Happiness and the Institute of Contemporary British History, and is founder of the Museum of the Prime Minister.

Jonathan Meakin was educated at Royal Holloway, University of London and at the University of St Andrews. He is a professional researcher and has worked on many publications including *The Cabinet Office, 1916–2016* and *The Impossible Office?*. He has also worked as a researcher on political and historical topics. He has worked at historical sites in Britain and as a volunteer in the United States.

TRUSS AT 10

HOW NOT TO BE PRIME MINISTER

ANTHONY SELDON
WITH JONATHAN MEAKIN

Atlantic Books
London

First published in hardback in Great Britain in 2024 by Atlantic Books, an imprint of Atlantic Books Ltd.

10 9 8 7 6 5 4 3 2 1

A CIP catalogue record for this book is available from the British Library.

Hardback ISBN: 978 1 80546 213 2
Trade paperback ISBN: 978 1 80546 214 9
E-book ISBN: 978 1 80546 215 6

Printed in Great Britain by CPI Group (UK) Ltd, Croydon CR0 4YY

Atlantic Books
An imprint of Atlantic Books Ltd
Ormond House
26–27 Boswell Street
London WC1N 3JZ

www.atlantic-books.co.uk

This book is dedicated to my colleagues, pupils, parents and governors at Epsom College, where I was honoured to serve as Head from February 2023 to August 2024.

CONTENTS

Boris Johnson and Liz Truss were united on little, in truth, except their hostility to Rishi Sunak and hunger for power

DRAMATIS PERSONAE

Liz Truss: Prime Minister (6 September 2022–25 October 2022) Also: MP for South West Norfolk (Conservative, 2010–24), Parliamentary Under-Secretary for the Department of Education (2012–14), Justice Secretary and Lord Chancellor (2016–17), Chief Secretary to the Treasury (2017–19), International Trade Secretary (2019–21), Foreign Secretary (2021–22)

Hugh O'Leary: Husband of Liz Truss (2000–)

Cabinet

Edward Argar: (attending Cabinet) Chief Secretary to the Treasury (14 October 2022–25 October 2022), Paymaster General and Minister for the Cabinet Office (6 September 2022–14 October 2022)

Kemi Badenoch: Secretary of State for International Trade (2022)

Jake Berry: Minister without Portfolio (2022), Chairman of the Conservative Party (2022)

Suella Braverman: Home Secretary (6 September 2022–19 October 2022)

Robert Buckland: Secretary of State for Wales (2022)

Simon Clarke: Secretary of State for Levelling Up, Housing and Communities (2022)

James Cleverly: Foreign Secretary (2022–23)

ix

Thérèse Coffey: Deputy Prime Minister (2022), Health Secretary (2022)

Michelle Donelan: Secretary of State for Digital, Culture, Media and Sport (2022)

Michael Ellis: (attending Cabinet) Attorney General for England and Wales, and Advocate General for Northern Ireland (2022)

Vicky Ford: (attending Cabinet) Minister of State for Development (2022)

James Heappey: (attending Cabinet) Minister of State for the Armed Forces and Veterans (2020–24)

Chris Heaton-Harris: Secretary of State for Northern Ireland (2022)

Jeremy Hunt: Chancellor of the Exchequer (14 October 2022–5 July 2024)

Alister Jack: Secretary of State for Scotland (2019–24)

Ranil Jayawardena: Secretary of State for Environment, Food and Rural Affairs (2022)

Kwasi Kwarteng: Chancellor of the Exchequer (6 September 2022–14 October 2022)

Kit Malthouse: Secretary of State for Education (2022)

Penny Mordaunt: Leader of the House of Commons, Lord President of the Council (2022–24)

Wendy Morton: (attending Cabinet) Chief Whip to the House of Commons (2022)

Chris Philp: (attending Cabinet) Chief Secretary to the Treasury (6 September 2022–14 October 2022), Paymaster General and Minister for the Cabinet Office (14 October 2022–25 October 2022)

Jacob Rees-Mogg: Secretary of State for Business, Energy and Industrial Strategy (2022)

Grant Shapps: Home Secretary (19–25 October 2022)

Alok Sharma: President for COP26 (2021–22)

Chloe Smith: Secretary of State for Work and Pensions (2022)

Graham Stuart: (attending Cabinet) Minister of State for Energy Security and Net Zero (2022–24)

Lord True: Leader of the House of Lords (2022–24)

Tom Tugendhat: (attending Cabinet) Minister of State for Security (2022–24)

Ben Wallace: Secretary of State for Defence (2019–23)

Nadhim Zahawi: Chancellor of the Duchy of Lancaster (2022), Minister for Intergovernmental Relations (2022), Minister for Equalities (2022)

Advisers

Asa Bennett: Speechwriter (2022)

John Bew: Foreign Affairs Adviser to the Prime Minister (2019–24)

David Canzini: Deputy Chief of Staff (October 2022)

Iain Carter: Director of Strategy (2022)

Clare Evans: Director of Operations (2022)

Mark Fullbrook: Chief of Staff (2022)

Jamie Hope: Director of Policy (2022)

Sophie Jarvis: Political Secretary (2022)

Adam Jones: Political Director of Communications (2022)

Sarah Ludlow: Head of Strategic Communications (2022)

Simon McGee: Director of Communications (2022)

Adam Memon: Economic Adviser (2022)

Shabbir Merali: Economic Adviser (2022)

Ruth Porter: Deputy Chief of Staff (2022)

Matthew Sinclair: Chief Economic Adviser (2022)

Jason Stein: Special Adviser (2022)

Members of Parliament

Graham Brady: Chair of the 1922 Committee (2010–24), MP for Altrincham and Sale West (Conservative, 1997–24)

Mark Francois: MP for Rayleigh and Wickford (Conservative 2010–, MP for Rayleigh 2001–), Chair of the ERG (2020–)

Philip Hammond: MP for Runnymede and Weybridge (Conservative, 1997–2019), Foreign Secretary (2014–16), Chancellor of the Exchequer (2016–19)

Sajid Javid: MP for Bromsgrove (Conservative, 2010–24), Home Secretary (2018–19), Chancellor of the Exchequer (2019–20), Health Secretary (2021–22)

John Redwood: MP for Wokingham (Conservative, 1987–24)

Craig Whittaker: MP for Calder Valley (Conservative, 2010–24), Deputy Chief Whip (2022)

Gavin Williamson: MP for South Staffordshire (Conservative, 2010–24, MP for Stone 2024–), Chief Whip (2016–17), Defence Secretary (2017–19), Education Secretary (2019–21)

Officials

Andrew Bailey: Governor of the Bank of England (2020–)

Tim Barrow: National Security Adviser (2022–)

James Bowler: Permanent Secretary to the Treasury (2022)

Simon Case: Cabinet Secretary and Head of the Civil Service (2020–)

Nick Catsaras: Principal Private Secretary to the Prime Minister (2022)

Jon Cunliffe: Deputy Governor for the Bank of England for Financial Stability (2013–23)

Stuart Glassborow: Director to HM Treasury (2022–23)

Richard Hughes: Chair of the Office for Budget Responsibility (2020–)

Catherine (Cat) Little: Acting Permanent Secretary to the Treasury (2022)

Clare Lombardelli: Chief Economic Adviser, Joint Head of the UK Government Economic Service (2018–23)

Antonia Romeo: Permanent Secretary at the Ministry of Justice (2021–)

Beth Russell: Acting Permanent Secretary to the Treasury (2022)

Tom Scholar: Permanent Secretary to the Treasury (2016–22)

Edward Young: Private Secretary to the Sovereign (2017–2023)

PREFACE

She came, she saw, she crashed.

In the three centuries of the history of the British Prime Minister, there has never been a premiership like that of Liz Truss. She had promise: the most experienced incomer in thirty-two years, with high intelligence, a clear plan and the right focus diagnosed: growth. Britain has had short-serving Prime Ministers before. But nowhere else in our long history has a Prime Minister arrived in power, so spectacularly mishandled an ambitious agenda, detonated an economic crisis, reversed their policies and fallen from power *in less than fifty days*. It paved the way for the worst Tory general election result in history in July 2024. We shall not see her like again.

'How could this have happened?' I asked myself, as did so many others. Wasn't Britain supposed to be a 'well-governed nation'? How on earth, I wondered, had the British democratic system, the oldest and most tested in the modern world, thrown up Liz Truss?

And so it was, just ten months after becoming Prime Minister, and nine after leaving it, Liz Truss was standing in front of me and asking, 'Why are you writing a book on me?'

I was taken back by the forcefulness of the question. I didn't know exactly how to respond. But she gave me no opportunity.

'I'm writing my own book, you know.' She looked at me fiercely. 'I'm glad,' I blurted out. And off she strutted.

It was Wednesday, 5 July 2023, at the *Spectator* summer party in Central London and this was the first time I had spoken to Liz Truss.

Since her mesmerizing fall from power some months earlier, I had lost count of the number of people who had asked me, 'Are you going to be writing a book about Liz Truss?' Then the inevitable follow-up: 'I bet it will be a short one!' Well, maybe I should, I thought.

Liz and I may not have met before; but we had history.

She was an admirer of the Institute of Economic Affairs (IEA), which had been established in the 1950s by my father Arthur Seldon. He always insisted, in contrast to his co-founder Ralph Harris, that the IEA stay above party politics: a think tank, not a pressure or spouting tank. It expounded the virtues of the free market and anti-statist thinking that had become her lodestar. Had my father unwittingly helped forge Liz Truss's thinking? Almost certainly.

Fifty years before she came to prominence, another ambitious provincial woman had risen up through the Conservative Party, inspired by the same liberal ideals. Margaret Thatcher had few mentors or historical precedents for the kind of leader she wanted to be, and certainly none of her own sex. But Truss saw in her a pioneer from whom she could draw inspiration, who had gone on to change, as she considered herself destined to do, the entire course of British history.

Truss was born in July 1975 in the city of Oxford where I was a student ending my second year. I had spent my first summer holiday in 1974 working in the Centre for Policy Studies, newly minted by Thatcher to champion free-market ideas. How could one leader get things so right, and the other, so catastrophically wrong?

Another link to Truss was far more recent. Her chief of staff, Mark Fullbrook, had contacted me about my work on how to characterize and optimize successful premierships. He told her about an analysis I had produced in 2017, and when in No. 10, showed her special advisers a BBC film of me talking about it. Here, after forty years of writing about Prime Ministers, was my first opportunity actually to shape a premiership. A week before she entered No. 10 in September 2022, I had published an article in the *New Statesman* outlining the ten dangers that had ensnared previous Prime Ministers, and how she might circumvent them.[1]

Had I in some small part helped create Liz Truss?

It seemed, given her abject failure in office, that she had succumbed to the very dangers I had outlined. But to my dismay and discomfort, she took almost all of my advice on board, by design or, almost certainly, by accident.

'Secure the citadel' by appointing a crack team in Downing Street was advice she followed to an extreme degree by appointing ultra-loyalists. Next up was 'Find your authentic voice early on'. She did indeed. She was not remotely bashful or faltering about what she wanted to do. 'Macro then micro', i.e. stick with the big themes and don't get distracted, was counsel she honoured to the letter. 'Control your time and make others do the detail.' Another tick. In fact, to the consternation of her team, she cancelled endless meetings that she deemed irrelevant. 'Control your Cabinet tightly.' She kicked aides out of meetings and gave dire warnings to her ministers about misbehaviour and leaking. 'Have a big fight with the media early on and win: don't become ensnared in their agenda'. She banished newspapers from her office, squared up to the media… but then lost the big fight. 'Play the part of PM with style.' She did, promptly seeing off Britain's longest-serving monarch and conducting herself diligently through all the events of mourning. 'Seize the big moments and command them.' She didn't just seize the big moment, she made it totally her own and sprayed it in garish colours: the Mini-Budget, the most controversial for forty years, was hers, not the Chancellor's. 'Simplify, and be lean.' She was spare to the point of wasting away: she had one big theme only, growth, and was lean and mean in its pursuit. Finally, 'work with your Chancellor and avoid pointless battles'. She did work closely, all love and harmony – until she sacked him.

I realized I would need a different approach to explain prime ministerial failure to encompass 'outlier' Prime Ministers like Truss (and Johnson). I sought refuge in the more recent 'impossible office' analysis I'd written about in 2021: might that be better at explaining her? Or would Liz Truss defy that approach too?

I decided I would shape the whole chapter structure around the ten fields of this new approach to see if it might explain why her premiership went wrong so quickly and so spectacularly. I would also have to delve far deeper into history than my earlier analysis, right the way back to Walpole's appointment as first Prime Minister in 1721.

I had to write this book. In part to try to understand what went wrong with Truss's bold project, but also to offer a robust and contemporary guide to students and practitioners on how, and how not, to be Prime Minister.

This book, the eighth in the series on Prime Ministers, was written while I unexpectedly found myself back running a school, Epsom College, after the tragic death of the Head. School came first, second and third. The book is dedicated to all at the school.

Anthony Seldon, July 2024

Truss modelled herself on the iconography of Margaret Thatcher, if not her statecraft. Here in Estonia as Foreign Secretary on 30 November 2021

The Sunak team expected Truss to self-implode on the leadership campaign

INTRODUCTION

The office of Prime Minister is the highest position a non-royal can aspire to in the United Kingdom. Since the office was created in April 1721, some 200 million subjects have fretted their ways through Britain's towns and countryside, but only fifty-eight of them arrived at the door of 10 Downing Street to claim the keys.

1 in 4 Million

Put another way, only 1 in every 4 million Britons over those three centuries rose to be PM, and most of them were drawn from a narrow aristocratic elite. Countless politicians aspired to it and some of the very best fell short.[1] For Liz Truss to have been appointed Prime Minister on 6 September 2022 as the last public duty of Queen Elizabeth II was by any standards remarkable. The significance of it was not lost on the younger Elizabeth. Her achievement was unusual for more than not being male or born with a silver spoon in her mouth. Most Prime Ministers had come to office without a very precise programme to enact. Sufficient for many was the premiership itself, content as they were to govern the country responding to, rather than deliberately trying to shape, events. But Truss saw herself in the mould of one of her heroes, Winston Churchill, 'walking with destiny' to fulfil her own historic mission – to save her country from years of torpor and decline.

Once appointed, the top priority for all Prime Ministers is to remain in office. It's difficult to achieve. Barely any since 1900 have left at a moment entirely of their own choosing. But Truss arrived with advantages her recent peers lacked, including extensive Cabinet experience, a full six weeks to prepare for office with top civil service brains on tap and a seemingly impregnable position as Conservative leader – we'll explore that later – on top of her ferociously clear mission. After a run of inconclusive premierships, she believed she was going to buck the trend. She'd arrived and everyone had better watch out.

Her plan was high risk and eminently precise, on paper. In her own words, 'I wanted to concentrate above all on the economy and generating growth. That was my focus until the general election in two years. I knew I'd never have more political capital than at the start. Then, when I won my own election mandate, I would turn my focus for the following five years onto all the other areas like education that badly needed fixing.'[2] She abhorred what had happened to the country under Labour's Tony Blair (1997–2007) and Gordon Brown (2007–10), including granting too much independence to the Bank of England, and the 'furring up' of enterprise and institutions.

As a Cabinet minister under David Cameron (2010–16), Theresa May (2016–19) and Boris Johnson (2019–22), she had watched as, one after the other, they crashed and burned, their missions incomplete. Johnson was the leader she had most enjoyed working for, but she was frustrated he didn't do more to deliver the Brexit dividends. She was not going to make the same mistakes. There would be no pussyfooting, no indecision and no lack of courage: she was going in all guns blazing, like Churchill no less, demanding 'Action this day', or Margaret Thatcher, who early on in her premiership abolished exchange controls in her fight for freedom.

The average length in office of the Prime Minister over the 300 years has been four years and nine months, or 1,734 days. Truss had a decent chance of lasting considerably longer than that. Even sceptics assumed that, after the early departures of Cameron, May and Johnson, and with a significant majority, the Conservative Party wouldn't be so rash as to prematurely unseat a fourth. She may have had few ideological fellow travellers, or MPs who liked her personally, but even her enemies – of which there were many – conceded that she would last at least until the general election at some point in 2024. Given the healthy majority of eighty won by Johnson in December 2019, a Truss victory in 2024, even with a reduced number, didn't seem impossible against an apparently lacklustre Labour leader in Sir Keir Starmer presiding over a still-divided party. But Truss knew that victory would rest on the economy picking up – hence her push for economic growth.

Yet, just forty-nine days later, she and her project had self destructed.

How Unusual was Truss's Brevity?

We know now that hers was the shortest premiership of any British Prime Minister. While seven other premiers since 1721 served less than a year in post, and a further seven less than two years, none had fallen anything like as quickly. Her brevity in post rapidly became a standing joke across the country – the *Daily Star* memorably comparing it to the shelf life of a lettuce. But how unusual was it?

Dig below the surface, and look abroad, and fleeting leaderships are not necessarily unusual.

Last century, the Conservative Stanley Baldwin (1923–24, 1924–29, 1935–37) and Labour's Ramsay MacDonald (1924, 1929–35) served less than a year in their first periods as Prime Minister, in 1923 and 1924 respectively, before coming back for longer stints. They were aged fifty-five and fifty-seven when they first became PM; Liz Truss was ten years their junior. Unlikely though it may seem, no one can rule out her coming back as Prime Minister at some point in the future, expunging forever the unwanted moniker of 'Britain's shortest-serving Prime Minister'. After all, three of the most significant Conservative premiers of the nineteenth century, Robert Peel (1834–35, 1841–46), Benjamin Disraeli (1868, 1874–80) and Lord Salisbury (1885–86, 1886–92, 1895–1902) all served less than a year in their first spells as Prime Minister, at 120, 279 and 220 days respectively. While Peel was the same age as Truss, Disraeli and Salisbury were considerably older and age was more of a handicap back then.

Besides, one might argue, it's parochial to disparage Truss's forty-nine days as absurdly short. Looking abroad, we find American President William Henry Harrison served for only thirty-one days in the White House. He suffered from severe ill health and died in April 1841 following crude medical procedures that included bloodletting (the deliberate loss of blood believed to be restorative). President James Garfield served 199 days before dying in September 1881 from the wounds inflicted by an assassin's bullet at Washington's Potomac & Baltimore railway station seventy-nine days earlier. The President was attended by his Secretary of War, Robert Lincoln, reawakening traumatic memories of the assassination in the same city sixteen years before of his father Abraham. Neither Harrison nor Garfield can be held responsible for the brevity of their tenures; in both cases, however, their doctors might have been.

Truss's stay appears positively leisurely compared to Spain's leading politicians. Of the 102 Spanish Prime Ministers since the office was established in 1823, sixty-six were gone within a year. Nine lasted ten days or less, mostly during the revolutions, civil wars and political upheavals of the nineteenth century.

Elsewhere, though, Europe offers little solace to her. Even Italy, notorious in English minds for serial political instability, saw its shortest-serving post-1945 Prime Minister, Fernando Tambroni, lasting a heroic 116 days[3] in mid-1960 before his supporters abandoned him. Longevity was often elusive among Commonwealth leaders. Four of Canada's twenty-three Prime Ministers since 1867 served less than a year, albeit none as fleetingly as Truss. While Australia has seen six of its thirty-one Prime Ministers since 1901 survive less than a year, three of them came in purely as caretakers. It is to this country that we must look to find a leader who served shorter than Truss. Arthur Fadden stepped up in August 1941 after the stalwart PM Robert Menzies departed, only to resign after six weeks. He later quipped that he had, rather like the Biblical flood, 'reigned for forty days and forty nights'.[4] Some consolation for Truss can also be found in the claim that she is not technically Britain's shortest-serving Prime Minister. In 1746 Lord Bath and in 1757 Lord Waldegrave were appointed First Lord, but neither had enough political support, resigning within a few days. Back then, there was more debate about what constituted a Prime Minister. Lord North (1770–82) refused to be called 'Prime Minister', arguing that 'there is no such thing in the British Constitution', and it was not until Robert Peel in 1846 that the incumbent referred to themselves as 'the Prime Minister'. The term remained constitutionally imprecise until it began to be used in official language at the beginning of the last century.[5] When George I appointed Robert Walpole (1721–42) in April 1721, it was not to the job of 'Prime Minister', an office that did not exist, but to 'First Lord of the Treasury', the name that still appears on the letterbox of the front door of 10 Downing Street, an address into which Walpole moved only in 1735 in his fifteenth year in office.

Truss's blushes might also be spared by acknowledging that many Prime Ministers have faltered early in their premierships – yet they survived, if often as much through luck than judgement. Even several of the nine 'top tier' or great Prime Ministers wobbled badly with early difficulties. Walpole was just over a quarter of the way through his office in June 1727 when he faced his severest challenge, the death of George I and the succession of his son, George II, at a time when the monarch was still the arbiter of the head of government. Walpole had admittedly already served for six years, but it was only by stealth and by milking his astute friendship with the new Queen that he ingratiated himself with the new King. Walpole went on to serve for another fifteen years.

William Pitt the Younger's (1783–1801, 1804–06) early travails arguably eclipsed those of Liz Truss because his position was precarious from day one. When George III invited him to become Prime Minister on 19 December 1783, one wag described it as the 'mince pie administration' as no one expected it to last beyond

Christmas, an analogy deployed by Chair of the 1922 Committee Sir Graham Brady in Truss's final days. Between January and March 1784, the continuation of his premiership was in doubt with many of the big beasts, not least Charles James Fox, Edmund Burke and ex-Prime Minister Lord North, ranged against him. He was defeated in important votes in January, with his support from Cabinet wavering: 'for six weeks, now, the country had had a government, with no power to govern', wrote his biographer William Hague.[6] But Pitt used all his powers of persuasion, parliamentary chicanery and, crucially, patronage to strengthen his ministry and lay the groundwork for a general election. Critically, Pitt retained the confidence of the King, and in March 1784, he felt strong enough to announce the election that resulted in his supporters winning some seventy seats.[7] At last he was secure. Pitt went on to serve another seventeen years as Prime Minister.

Other examples abound, not least Churchill (1940–45, 1951–55), whose position as Prime Minister remained vulnerable after his appointment in May 1940 as the war news darkened and Cabinet discussed whether to continue fighting. Margaret Thatcher's (1979–90) insecure first three years were not finally firmed up till victory in the Falklands War of 1982. Well might Truss rue bowing to advice to U-turn on her economic package, a course her *belle idéale* conspicuously rejected in October 1980. Had she too stood her ground, could she have come through, and like her Conservative predecessors, been in power for many years more?

Alas for her, it did not happen, and she can only cling to her belief that she was betrayed, and that, one day, the great crusade she had started will triumph.

Why Do Prime Ministers Fall?

For the rest of us, we have to make sense of one of the greatest puzzles in prime ministerial history. Why did a PM with a strong parliamentary majority, a credible track record of ministerial experience, and who knew their own mind, fall at such speed? The best place to look for clues is the reasons why other short-serving Prime Ministers fell.

General election defeats are the most frequent cause. Alec Douglas-Home (1963–64) had been at No. 10 for just less than a year when the five-year electoral cycle compelled him to call a general election for 15 October 1964. The Conservatives had previously won convincing victories in 1955 (sixty-seat majority) and 1959 (hundred-seat majority) and looked in a strong position. But Labour had acquired a new dynamism and appeal after Harold Wilson (1964–70, 1974–76) took over as leader in February 1963. The general election eighteen months later proved surprisingly close. Only on the following afternoon was the result known: a Labour victory with a majority of four. At just 363 days at No. 10, Home became the eighth shortest-serving Prime Minister, albeit within a whisker of serving longer.

At two years and 318 days, Gordon Brown is Britain's twenty-first shortest-serving PM. After the May 2010 election, he tried for four days to stay on as head of a coalition government in partnership with the Liberal Democrats. Ultimately he was unsuccessful. He might have surged up the longevity league table had he not backed off calling an early general election in the autumn of 2007. We will never know what might have happened had Brown held his nerve. No doubt the prospect, if he had lost, of becoming one of Britain's shortest-serving Prime Ministers tipped him towards caution. What we do know is that Liz Truss emphatically ruled out any early general election, and that electoral defeat doesn't explain her demise.

Illness, exacerbated by the strains of office, the elusiveness of rest and the unusually high exposure of the PM to germs have been factors in many departures. William Pitt the Elder saw his premiership increasingly bedevilled by illness, including gout and mental health problems felt by contemporaries to border on insanity. Pitt decided in October 1768, having barely governed at all for a year, that he had had enough, resigning on grounds of ill health, the seventeenth shortest-serving Prime Minister at just two years and seventy-six days.

Liberal Henry Campbell-Bannerman (1905–8) led his party to its greatest victory in the 1906 general election, setting the scene for one of its most reforming administrations. Aged sixty-nine when he became Prime Minister, he suffered the death of his wife that August, and a serious heart attack in November of the following year. In March 1908, a concerned Edward VII visited him at No. 10, making it clear that, under all circumstances, a change of premier should be avoided while the King was on holiday. But when Campbell-Bannerman's health deteriorated further, the King summoned Herbert Asquith to Biarritz in the South of France in early April to invite him to take over as Prime Minister. The bedbound Campbell-Bannerman was allowed to remain in Downing Street, where he died two weeks later. 'The doctor going in, and the priest coming out; and as I reflected on the dying Prime Minister, I could only hope that no sound had reached him of the crowd that cheered his successor,' recorded Asquith's wife Margot. Serving two years and 122 days, he was the nineteenth shortest-serving Prime Minister.[8]

Truss certainly did not suffer from physical illness, though some close to her have speculated whether she had a nervous breakdown in her final days in No. 10. This might have impaired her judgement and precipitated her departure, a thesis we examine in this book. We also examine the thesis that her impetuosity was fuelled by excessive caffeine, or even a regular glass of Sauvignon Blanc, her favourite tipple.[9]

What other factors are behind brief premierships? Death in office was responsible for the departures of several including twelfth shortest-serving Prime Minister, the Marquess of Rockingham (1765–66, 1782) in 1782 after a second administration lasting ninety-six days (for a grand total of one year and 113 days), and the thirteenth briefest, the Earl of Wilmington (1742–43) after one year and 119 days. None of the short-servers was more intriguing a character, though, than the man who for nearly 200 years wore the unwanted mantle of Britain's shortest-serving PM, George Canning, who survived just 119 days. One of the great might-have-beens, Canning towered over many of his prime ministerial peers in terms of ability and imagination. A formidable Foreign Secretary during and after the Napoleonic Wars, he was already ailing when George IV invited him in April 1827 to become Prime Minister in succession to Lord Liverpool. With politics riven by the issues of parliamentary reform and Catholic emancipation, and with deep divisions among Britain's governing elite, Canning might have struggled. But fate intervened, and on 8 August, he died of tuberculosis at Chiswick House in West London, where his great Whig political adversary Charles James Fox had died twenty years before.

The Prime Ministers' lives have been constantly in danger throughout history, with Truss under enhanced police protection from the moment it became evident that she was the front runner to succeed Johnson in August 2022. Any number of individuals or groups might want to assassinate the Prime Minister, fired by personal grudges, mental instability or terrorist ideals. The wonder is that only one assassin succeeded in Britain compared to four in the United States, when Spencer Perceval (1809–12) was fatally shot in the lobby of the House of Commons.

So general election defeats, illnesses, sudden death or assassination cannot explain the departure of Truss. But two final explanations for truncated premierships take us closer to an answer. First, some Prime Ministers have had personalities simply unsuited to the demands of the job. Viscount Goderich was one, third shortest-serving Prime Minister at just 144 days. As Frederick John Robinson, he'd been a reasonably successful Cabinet minister, and latterly Chancellor in the 1820s. But in the top job, he proved indecisive, thin-skinned, self-pitying and incapable of generating respect. George IV soon tired of him, supposedly describing him as 'a damned, snivelling, blubbering, blockhead'. Goderich resigned finally in January 1828, and remains the only Prime Minister in history never to have been in office while Parliament was sitting, which then recessed between the summer and mid-January.

Was Liz Truss's personality fatally ill-suited to being Prime Minister? Was she incapable of learning how to do the job? We shall probe in the chapters that follow whether she was wanting in either character or aptitude (or both).

Finally, there are the Prime Ministers who fall through abject failure of their central policy. Neville Chamberlain, a high-quality and proven administrator and politician, had long waited to take the reins from Stanley Baldwin, when he did so in May 1937. He anticipated a long stay, expecting to win the general election due in 1940 and to spend the following years executing his plans for economic and social reform. He and his wife intended to modernize the living accommodation in No. 10 too and make Chequers, the country home in Buckinghamshire the Prime Minister has used since 1921, into a more welcoming residence for visitors. But Chamberlain fatally misread Hitler, believing that he could coax him into being reasonable. When Hitler's actions from late 1938 onwards showed him to be anything but, the ground fell away from under Chamberlain's feet.

Anthony Eden similarly had progressive plans, and had to wait a long time to step up to the top. He had been Churchill's anointed successor since the Second World War but the old leader only finally retired in April 1955. Eden went on, unlike Truss, to win his own mandate in the 1955 general election. But Eden became obsessed with Gamal Abdel Nasser, the President of Egypt, after his nationalization of the Suez Canal in July 1956.

In October 1956, Eden chose military intervention, and sent British forces to seize the canal and destroy Nasser. High among Eden's follies was his deliberate decision to conceal from President Eisenhower and the Americans his secret British, French and Israeli plan to regain the canal. When the troops landed in November, the attack was roundly condemned in the UN General Assembly, Soviet Premier Nikita Khruschev threatened to send soldiers to defend Egypt, and President Eisenhower put pressure on the International Monetary Fund to deny Britain support. In the face of such a uniformly hostile response, Eden promptly declared the military operation over. The U-turn alienated political allies who had told Eden to tough it out. Churchill remarked cuttingly, 'I would never have dared; and if I had dared, I would certainly never have dared stop.'[10]

One can only wonder how far Eden's illness and medication were responsible for his wild and capricious decision-making. As he told Cabinet on 9 January 1957, 'It is now nearly four years since I had a series of bad abdominal operations which left me with a largely artificial inside... During these last five months... I have been obliged to increase the drugs considerably and also increase the stimulants necessary to counteract the drugs'.[11] Former Foreign Secretary and medical doctor Lord Owen speculates that he was taking mind-altering drugs daily during the crisis, including barbiturates, amphetamines and a drug called Drinamyl.[12] The stated reason for Eden's resignation after one year and 279 days, the fourteenth shortest period, was his ill health. But it was the collapse of his central policy that made his continuation in office impossible.

How far was Liz Truss's collapse due to the failure of her central economic policy, and the subsequent U-turn in the face of international financial pressure? Was there indeed an establishment plot to bring her down? In 1924, many Labour supporters believed that the establishment had publicized a clearly fake document purporting to be from Grigory Zinoviev, head of the Communist International in Moscow, to British communists urging them to engage in subversive activities that would be helped by a Labour government. Publication of this alleged letter in the *Daily Mail* four days before the general election of 1924 was for many years believed to have played a significant part in Labour losing that election, meaning that its first Prime Minister, Ramsay MacDonald, was in office for less than a year (a mere 288 days). An independent report conducted by the Foreign Office in 1999 found that any attempt by the establishment, including the intelligence services, to bring down the Labour government was 'unsubstantiated' by the documentation, and 'inherently unlikely'.[13]

Truss and some of her more ardent supporters believe that a similar establishment, or 'deep state', plot was responsible for bringing her down. She told the American Conservative Political Action Conference in 2024 that they had to 'understand how deep the vested interests of the establishment are' and 'how hard they will fight and how unfairly they will fight in order to get their way'.[14] She herself blamed Sir Tom Scholar, the permanent secretary at the Treasury, whom she and Chancellor Kwasi Kwarteng sacked on their first day in power, for encouraging the International Monetary Fund in its damning assessment of the Mini-Budget, resulting in a rush to dump UK government bonds, and the collapse in confidence of the markets. The finger of blame is pointed also at the Treasury and the Bank of England, not least for failing to alert her to the behaviour of pension funds. The Office for Budget Responsibility is also accused of undermining the economic policies. As she wrote in her book *Ten Years to Save the West*, 'the Treasury establishment and the Bank of England were not on my side'.[15] Was this the 'woke' establishment getting revenge against Truss and her right-wing ilk for bringing about Brexit? It is not just those in the political arena who believe there is truth in the accusation: journalist Robert Peston produced a podcast series in early 2024 in which he argued that the Bank of England and the Treasury were in part responsible for her fall.[16] Others see the sinister hand of the supporters of Rishi Sunak, including Michael Gove, Dominic Cummings and a shadowy Tory adviser Dougie Smith, who has been linked to other plots, all intriguing against Truss from day one. Some believe that hostile Conservative MPs alerted their friends in the City of London to sell bonds to undermine the Mini-Budget. We assess whether there is reason for this belief.

Such claims are far from fanciful. When Thatcher became Prime Minister in May 1979, she too was deeply suspicious of the establishment, believing it to be against her breed of free-market economics and wish to slim down the state. Thatcher provides a constant counterpoint to Truss throughout the book. The two Prime Ministers had similarities that were not superficial: both women, from lower middle-class provincial backgrounds, passionate believers in private enterprise and British patriotism. It was a comparison Truss went out of her way to encourage – with photographs and costumes styled on those of the Iron Lady. But one went on to become one of the most formidable Prime Ministers in British history; the other, the opposite. How did that happen? Each of the ten chapters that follow focuses on one of the possible explanations for Truss's failure, recognizing that, as with any catastrophe, the explanation will be multi-causal. At the end of the book, we reach a conclusion about the most telling reasons why she fell, and whether her bold plan for Britain might ever have succeeded.

Writing *Truss at 10*

A historian is only as good as their sources. Aside from two detailed tomes that cover the premiership, and Liz Truss's own volume, other books covering her time at No. 10 have yet to appear. This means that I have had to rely on primary sources, a mixture of in-person interviews providing some 80 per cent of the book's content, a further 15 per cent from contemporary documents including WhatsApp messages, and 5 per cent from contemporary commentary in the media.

Almost all senior Cabinet ministers, Downing Street aides and key figures from across Whitehall and beyond were interviewed for the book, some up to seven times. Verbatim records were made of all the 120 interviews (normally I conduct many more, but this was a short premiership). Many of the interviewees provided supplementary documentary evidence. To try to make the book feel as lifelike as possible – premierships happen in speech far more than in written documents – I have included numerous conversations constructed either from contemporary records or remembered by those present in the room. As always with contemporary history, so much of primary importance is never written down – the conversations, moods, messages and memories that will decreasingly find their way into the archives. All on-the-record quotations have been checked with those who provided them, and the book has been read over in multiple drafts by many researchers and insiders, as with other books in this Prime Minister series, to check for accuracy and completeness.

This book was always going to be about more than just one Prime Minister. It is also a meditation on power, and on the office of Prime Minister, and how and why incumbents, specifically this one, fail to understand either of them. It is also a practical manual on how *not* to be Prime Minister.

Rule Number One: Come to office with loyal MPs and a secure majority. With Hugh on 5 September hearing that she has been elected by a majority of members in the country (though Sunak had won more MPs' support in the first round)

1

SECURE THE POWER BASE

7 July–5 September 2022

'The response to her was tepid. We all noticed; it didn't feel right.'

So said a Conservative MP recollecting the atmosphere among fellow MPs the first time that Liz Truss addressed them as Prime Minister. It was Tuesday 6 September 2022. Her premiership was just hours old and the omens were not good.

'When David Cameron came to speak to us after making the deal to form the Coalition government in 2010, the MPs cheered ecstatically,' recalled another MP. 'They did so again when Boris Johnson first appeared before us after winning the December 2019 general election. Even when Theresa May first met us after seeing our majority wiped out in the 2017 general election, there was far more enthusiasm than there was for Liz Truss. She must've felt it.'

Not since 1945 had an incoming Conservative leader been greeted with such little excitement by their MPs. Indeed, it is doubtful if any new Conservative PM since 1832 had ever had such a sceptical reception. What had happened?

'Many Conservative MPs never accepted the result of the leadership election,' explained the MP. 'They refused to accept that Rishi Sunak had lost. The campaign to unseat Truss started the very day her election was announced.'

Not all expected Liz Truss to emerge as the successor to Boris Johnson as Prime Minister. Not even she herself. Many Tory MPs and a majority of party members in the country never wanted him to go. Yet, in the two months between Johnson announcing his resignation on 7 July, and the announcement of her victory in the leadership competition on 5 September, Truss prevailed. In the process, her premiership was holed below the waterline before it even left the harbour.

Deciding to Run: 7–12 July

'Come back immediately. The atmosphere is worse even than when we last spoke. The mood in the Conservative Party is beyond recovery.' Cabinet minister and Truss loyalist Simon Clarke texted these words to her at 8 a.m. on Thursday 7 July, just hours before Johnson announced his resignation. Most inconveniently, Truss was 7,000 miles away in Indonesia for a G20 meeting in her capacity as Foreign Secretary. In the intense tropical heat, she was in a cold funk. The story began thirty-six hours earlier. Health Secretary Sajid Javid and Chancellor Rishi Sunak had resigned within minutes of each other on Tuesday 5 July, sparking speculation that Johnson would be gone within days. Should Truss leave London at all for her imminent trip while her leadership rivals were making hay? But she was mindful of the damage it could do to her cause if she was seen to be abandoning her duty while Johnson was still trying to resurrect his premiership. So she left – as planned – with a small team on the government's sleek Airbus A321, putting in a stopover at Dubai to refuel. She spoke to Nick Catsaras, her Foreign Office principal private secretary, when the plane touched down in the Gulf, still in two minds about whether to continue further east. Conscious of the positive publicity of her high-profile summit in Bali with Russian Foreign Affairs Minister Sergey Lavrov, given her strong stance on the war in Ukraine, she was torn between duty and the possibility of the premiership.

Tim Barrow, the Foreign Office political director accompanying her on the trip, counselled pressing on too, as did her husband, Hugh O'Leary. 'She always listened carefully and respected [Hugh's] advice,' said an aide. But her close trio of young special advisers, Adam Jones, Jamie Hope and Sophie Jarvis, thought differently after reading the runes in London. For years, these three had loyally served Truss, and it was partly due to their hard work that she was even in contention in the first place. Fraught conversations followed with her team and supporters. She was also talking to her closest ministerial ally, Work and Pensions Secretary Thérèse Coffey, and to her potential rival, Defence Secretary Ben Wallace, who said she should stay. 'She was very careful not to say she was standing, but that she was merely "checking in" with friendly MPs to see how they were feeling,' said aide Sarah Ludlow, accompanying her on the trip.

The exhausted party arrived in Bali in the early hours of Thursday morning where Truss held meetings with the foreign ministers of Indonesia and Australia. All the time, news was coming in from London, where Johnson's premiership was visibly disintegrating by the hour. Truss was tortured by her predicament. Part of her had wanted Johnson to remain. She saw him as a pretty useless Prime Minister, above all in not pushing for the Brexit dividends, but in her heart she didn't feel nearly ready to be PM. 'Are you sure I'm really good enough?' she said to one aide, looking for reassurance rather than an honest opinion. The other part of her was absolutely desperate for him to go, while playing it cool on the surface: 'I'll go for it only when Boris actually resigns,' she stressed by phone to the trio back in London. But the news that he was leaving tipped the balance. 'Liz, wake the f**k up and get back here,' said Adam Jones, the senior of the three. She needed no encouragement, and barked out brusque instructions for her ministerial plane to 'refuel for London'.[1] She had only been on the ground in Bali for a few hours.

She would need a campaign manager if she was to prevail. In a strong field she was far from being the front runner. Her first call was to the man who had been the presiding maestro over Johnson's 2019 general election victory, now working for the Conservative Party. 'I want you to manage my campaign,' she said to Isaac Levido before the plane left the tarmac in Indonesia. 'I'm sorry. I can't do it for you. My contract with the Conservative Party wouldn't allow me,' he told her. To some of her aides this was an ominous sign that the very best didn't want to be associated with her. So she went for Ruth Porter, who had first worked for her as a special adviser in August 2014. Her aides pushed back, wondering whether Porter's experience was suitable. But Truss was adamant. She rated her very highly for her loyalty and capability. Porter promptly left the private sector to head up the campaign.

The plane touched down late on Friday 8 July and she was driven back to her home in Greenwich. Her leadership campaign was non-existent: no money, website, publicity material, office base or lists of potential supporters. This was ground zero. Her nascent team worked at Truss's kitchen table. The star recruit was Jason Stein, a brilliant and mercurial communications aide who had worked on-and-off with Truss since 2017 and who had resigned as Prince

Andrew's PR guru shortly before the infamous *Newsnight* interview with Emily Maitlis in 2019. A video announcing Truss's candidacy was filmed in her garden once it had been cleared of weeds and building debris.[2]

Where was her natural supporter base? Bridges had been burnt with the Remain wing after she emphatically renounced her vote in the EU referendum in her quest to become Brexit Queen. So she reached out for support to right-wing politicians and ardent Brexiteers Iain Duncan Smith, Bill Cash and John Redwood, as well as to financier and Brexiteer Jon Moynihan. 'If you're going to run, I'll help you with the right ideological position,' he told her. He became her campaign's energetic Treasurer and, when she needed money, her fundraiser. Well-liked Thérèse Coffey, Truss's oldest political friend, was tasked to corral MPs. Below them and Stein, Hope specialized on policy, Jones on communications and Jarvis on wooing supporters, at which she was adept. Truss once remarked to her that 'MPs like you. They don't like me. That's why I need you.'[3] Reuben Solomon, formerly of Conservative Campaign Headquarters (CCHQ), worked on digital communications, and Sarah Ludlow completed the band, having joined several months before from PR company Portland Communications. Within days, Truss had a team.

On Monday 11 July, she announced her platform: promoting growth and cutting taxes. From the outset she committed herself to reversing the rise in National Insurance that Sunak had announced as Chancellor in March 2022 and scrapping plans to increase corporation tax.[4] She had her policies. She even had a slogan: 'Trusted to Deliver'. Next up, she secured a base in Westminster's Lord North Street (named after the PM 'who lost America') owned by Tory supporter Lord Greville Howard. The Moynihan money-till began ringing loudly. She had cash. She had momentum. She was in business.

But she wasn't yet in the race. According to the rules announced that Monday by Graham Brady, Chair of the 1922 Committee of Tory backbenchers, candidates had to acquire the backing of twenty MPs by the following day if they were to make it to the first of the two leadership rounds. Eleven candidates announced their intention to run. 'I was holding the pen. It was a real struggle whether we'd get those twenty signatures committed by 4 p.m. on Tuesday,' said loyalist MP Ranil Jayawardena, 'but we did it by 2 p.m.' Coffey was her proposer, right-winger Simon Clarke seconder, 'the idea being to have two Cabinet ministers from different ends of the party'.[5] Prominent among the twenty was her near neighbour in Greenwich, Kwasi Kwarteng, already earmarked for Chancellor, and James Cleverly, who had worked with her closely as junior minister at the Foreign Office.

Round 1: The MPs (12–20 July)

Tuesday 12 July brought big news: the public endorsement of Truss by two of Johnson's staunchest supporters, Culture Secretary Nadine Dorries and Minister of State for Brexit Opportunities Jacob Rees-Mogg. Here was evidence that Johnson himself, destined to be a massive influence on the campaign, might favour her among the candidates. Better still, and in contravention of the protocol that only the PM speaks from the street outside No. 10, they made their announcement with the famous black door in the background. 'Boris had spoken through his two most loyal lieutenants.' However, there was a caveat, a crucial one: 'It was less a positive vote of confidence in her than a move to thwart Rishi,' said a Johnson insider.

'Liz was always opposed to Rishi's higher taxes. [She expounds] proper Conservatism… she's got the character to lead the party and the nation,' intoned Rees-Mogg to waiting journalists. 'I have sat with Liz in Cabinet now for some time. [I'm] very aware that she's probably a stronger Brexiteer than both of us,' he added.[6] Not figures of great political gravitas maybe, but gold dust all the same because of the imprimatur of Johnson. The suggestion was that Truss would be the best candidate to carry the Brexit flag forward.

That mattered because the leadership field was rich with more authentic Brexiteer candidates. A ConservativeHome survey of Tory members published as the contest opened put Penny Mordaunt top on 20 per cent, Kemi Badenoch on 19 per cent, Rishi Sunak on 12 per cent and Suella Braverman on 10 per cent. Fifth and last, and the only one known not to have voted for Brexit, was Liz Truss, scraping in at nearly 10 per cent.[7] The one-time matinee idol on the ConservativeHome website, who had unsettled Johnson so much he'd sent her to the wasteland of the Foreign Office in September 2021, had sunk to the floor. She had work to do.

Three candidates were eliminated before the first hurdle for not reaching the magic number of twenty MP backers. They included two heavyweights: former Chancellor Sajid Javid and long-term Cabinet survivor Grant Shapps, as well as the backbencher Rehman Chishti. Eight made the cut.

One name was conspicuously missing, a figure who had topped an earlier poll in ConservativeHome and would likely have won the race to be leader: Defence Secretary Ben Wallace. He had long circled the job and had been one of the first to advocate Johnson succeeding May. Many MPs and newspapers were impressed by his steadfast support for Ukraine. Indeed, for several months following Russia's invasion of Ukraine, he had been fighting a proxy leadership battle with Johnson and Truss for who could appear the most belligerent.

Wallace's mastery of the defence brief over several years had won him admirers across the party, despite it not usually being a ministerial position that allows the holder much domestic glory. It has never served as a launchpad to No. 10. Many MPs nevertheless saw him as the figure best placed to unite the party. Chancellor Nadhim Zahawi was signed up to be his deputy, a powerful combination. But personal issues troubled the Defence Secretary. He had recently separated from his wife.[8] He worried about the media exposure that his candidature would bring, and the effect on his children of his moving into Downing Street. 'I'm considering it', was the most he would say to those urging him on. When the nominations were announced, his name was conspicuously missing, to the relief of the other candidates. He let it be known that he was putting his family ahead of his personal ambition.

Another prominent name missing was that of Levelling Up Secretary Michael Gove. He realized he didn't have a serious chance after his attempts in 2016 and 2019, but now saw himself as the puppet master. Truss was petrified of what he might do and whether he would try to bring her down, as she was spooked by his former acolyte, Dominic Cummings, whom she'd encountered at the Department for Education where she'd cut her teeth as a minister under Gove from 2012 to 2014. 'At Education she picked up on some causes like Maths and STEM for girls, but she didn't know how to work with officials, other ministers or the Coalition', was one colleague's later verdict. Gove threw his considerable battalions behind the outsider candidate, Kemi Badenoch, who had only entered the Commons at May's 2017 general election.

The first round of voting among MPs followed almost immediately on Wednesday 13 July. The rules, introduced by William Hague in 1998, specified that candidates be eliminated each round until just two remained. Those two would then go forward to the second round to have their mettle tested by rank-and-file members of the Conservative Party. The system opened up the dangerous possibility, as occurred in 2001 with Iain Duncan Smith, that the first choice among MPs was not the figure chosen by the party members at large. It was not a happy precedent.

The bar in the first round at the MPs stage was set at 30 votes. Two fell at this fence: Zahawi received the support of just 25 and Jeremy Hunt 18. Sunak, with 88 votes and Mordaunt with 67 were the clear front runners. They were to hold the top two positions until the last round. Sunak was the person Truss disliked most in the contest. She thought he and the Treasury were dragging their feet over sanctions on those who fuelled the Russian war machine and she called him 'Russhi Sunak' behind his back. Sunak was not the bookies' favourite either, nor that of journalists: 'It is hard – but not impossible – to see how [Mordaunt] does not get onto the final ballot for party members, and current pollings suggest she would then win by a mile,' said the *Guardian* that day.[9] Mordaunt didn't realize how perilous being in the top two was going to prove, or how personal and vicious the campaign would become.

Truss came third in the first ballot with just 50 votes, followed by Badenoch (40), Tom Tugendhat (37) and Braverman (32). She was gloomy when she heard the results: she was exhausted, still not fully recovered from jet lag nor the frenzy of her return. She didn't think she could do it and her mood collapsed. On Thursday 14 July at her official campaign launch, she misread her script, stumbled over words and paused inexplicably mid-sentence. At the end, as her supporters applauded, she appeared momentarily lost and could not the find the exit, which was hidden by standing spectators. She walked in the wrong direction, looking the wrong way, before an aide rescued her. 'Robotic, brain-dead, managing to make Theresa May sound engaging, animated, and personable', was journalist John Crace's gleeful verdict.[10]

Adding to her worries was the defeated Hunt. He urged his supporters to back Sunak, many of whom were already in no mood to let Mordaunt breeze through. Truss's team believed that the 'axis of evil' behind Sunak was vicious, and had been responsible for discrediting Zahawi by leaking information about his financial affairs, including offshore shares in his polling company YouGov.[11] With respected Cabinet minister Brandon Lewis as his campaign chair, Zahawi could have been a strong candidate. But his protracted denial and obfuscation damaged him.[12] Once Zahawi was out, Truss's team believed the Team Sunak trashing operation would soon turn its attention on her.

In the second round on Thursday 14 July, Truss managed to maintain third place and with increased support – from 50 up to 64 votes. But Sunak and Mordaunt increased their votes too, to 101 (up from 88) and 83 votes (up from 67) respectively. Braverman was the one to fall, with just 27 MPs supporting her, with Badenoch (49) and Tugendhat (32) scraping through. The race was on among the five remaining candidates to get Braverman on side. For Truss's team, gaining Braverman's advocacy was deemed an existential challenge. She would bring her hardline Brexit supporters in the European Research Group (ERG) and beyond.

One other big beast was in their sights, though they couldn't get him to declare publicly until the MPs stage was over: ex-Northern Powerhouse Secretary Jake Berry. Having Dorries and Rees-Mogg on side was a huge help given the unrivalled power Johnson still exerted over MPs and members in the country, but further Johnson figures were needed. Close to Johnson personally, Berry had played a pivotal role in his winning the leadership election in 2019. Berry and his backers had thought hard about him running for the leadership as the 'continuity Johnson' candidate before deciding it wouldn't fly. Truss seized on the opportunity. She was still Johnson's Foreign Secretary, and secured a phone call with him to discuss the matter. 'Jake is a great guy and would be a good lieutenant for you,' he told her – hardly a ringing endorsement but serviceable. She was desperate to keep Johnson happy. The truth was that both needed the other in a loveless marriage: she professed affection for him in public while differing wildly on policy; he needed her to keep Sunak down. They both knew the game: he was the king- or queen-maker, she the supplicant. So Berry joining her team was a win for both. Once on board, he educated her team about what 'Boris supporters were after, and how they could hook them'. 'Having Jake was clear, palpable evidence that Boris supported Liz,' said one.

Berry was pivotal too in landing a much bigger fish: the PM-manqué Ben Wallace. He was the number one person every candidate wanted: a nod from him could make or break them. But he had history with Truss, most recently resenting the arriviste Foreign Secretary spouting about military subjects he knew much more about. Wallace knew his support was solid gold, demanding a pledge of 3 per cent plus of GDP going to defence spending. Backing for his candidacy to become Secretary General of NATO, something that would always be difficult because of French and European resistance, was another demand. The haggling went on for days and it was not till the end of the month that he came out in public for her, declaring, 'She stands her ground. Above all, she is straight and means what she says.'[13] No one could accuse him of perjury. It did the trick.

With MPs going back to their constituencies on Fridays, the third round could not be held until Monday 18 July. The Truss team was in panic mode. Kemi Badenoch, the feisty Minister of State for Equalities with firm anti-'woke' beliefs, was seen as the exciting insurgent candidate on the right, and the one around whom momentum was building. Could she edge Truss into fourth place? If that happened, her team worried she might not recover. A planned debate on Channel 4 on Friday 15 July created angst: should she take part? The worry was she would be wooden in front of cameras. Memories of a robotic Theresa May frozen in front of television cameras flashed across their minds. But once the other contenders put their names forward, she had no alternative but to pitch up. Frenzied preparations took place at her Lord North Street HQ.

First out of the blocks in the live debate was Sunak who accused his four opponents of promising unfunded tax cuts that bordered on 'socialism'. Truss was equally pugnacious, building up to what she hoped would be a rousing peroration, only for it to fall short: 'We face grave challenges as a country, the worst economic crisis for a generation [and] an appalling war generated by Russia in Ukraine, after decades of very slow growth...'

'Well, no doubt who lost that one, is there?' wrote Sean O'Grady in the *Independent*. 'An indifferent public speaker at the best of times, she's sadly just as bad as… a few years back. Boris Johnson must be fuming… Liz had herself made up so that she resembled an animatronic waxwork Margaret Thatcher… It didn't work.'[14] Few diverged from that assessment.

Sunak's team decided it was time to knock Mordaunt off her perch; if Sunak faced her in the run-off among party members, he would lose. From 14 to 17 July, Mordaunt duly came under fire. The *Daily Mail* hit her hard for her views on transgender rights, while Truss and Badenoch attacked her in the Channel 4 debate for supporting 'gender self-identification'. Mordaunt damaged herself by denying it, but official documents leaked to *The Sunday Times* on 17 July seemed to prove that she had attempted to remove 'at least one medical requirement' of the process before people can legally transition gender.[15]

The Truss camp opened up another flank of the attack on Mordaunt. International Trade Secretary Anne-Marie Trevelyan, an early Truss supporter, came out on 18 July in a coordinated personal strike: when she had been Mordaunt's ministerial boss at the Department for International Trade, colleagues had 'to pick up the pieces' due to her absences.[16] When Mordaunt's supporters responded with 'well, she would say that, wouldn't she?', the Truss team encouraged David Frost to go on the record saying that when he had been her boss at the Cabinet Office, Mordaunt didn't do the work and he had 'grave reservations' about her being Prime Minister.[17] Mordaunt's team hit back hard suspecting foul play. When she had worked with Frost, he had nothing but praise for her. Trevelyan had deliberately blocked her from gaining any credit, they suspected on the direct instructions of Johnson. But it was too late. 'We did not know whether the Sunak and Truss teams were working together or separately to do her down; what we did know is that they both wanted her out of the way,' said one of her team. The contest was becoming very dirty. These multiple blows were to prove fatal for Mordaunt.

More good news followed for Truss. She had told her team that she would not make job offers to anybody to secure their votes. But Suella Braverman would have to be an exception. On the morning of Thursday 14 July, Truss had phoned her, saying, 'If you stay out of the third ballot, I will make you Home Secretary.' Braverman turned her down but when she was knocked out that night, she called her back: 'I'll come out and back you tonight, if I am given the Home Office, and I will deliver my supporters.' Given the knife edge, Truss felt she had no choice but to accept. Their relationship was difficult. Though both were on the right of the party, they were miles apart on immigration: 'Liz was pretty liberal, whereas for Suella, it was totemic,' said Jason Stein.[18] Truss was to bitterly regret her promise.

She received another boost going into the weekend when former party leader and right-wing cheerleader Iain Duncan Smith came out in support of her. He praised her for being 'strong on Brexit' and implying that other candidates hadn't done as much to deliver on its benefits. This helped to lessen the perception of her as a Remainer. It had been a struggle for her team to get Duncan Smith over the line. Although he was ideologically 100 per cent behind her, not least in her vehement views on China, he was hoping for Foreign or Work and Pensions Secretary, for which she had other plans. Not all previous Conservative leaders supported her: in particular, William

Hague and Michael Howard supported Sunak, while John Major, David Cameron and Theresa May held their counsel.

Truss was nervous about how she'd fare in round three on Monday 18 July, far from sure she'd make it through. This time, however, it was Chair of the Commons Foreign Affairs Select Committee Tom Tugendhat who came fifth and fell off the bottom. Truss was backed by 71, picking up just three of Braverman's 27 votes. First-place Sunak was racing away with 115 votes, Mordaunt stalling in second place on 82, while fourth-placed Badenoch was moving up the ladder and snapping at Truss's heels, with 58.

For the next round, Badenoch was the candidate to beat. A ConservativeHome survey had suggested she would win a vote among party members. The support of Gove helped make her a force to be reckoned with. 'Liz, it would be much better if you backed me so together we can stop Rishi,' she said. Truss, however, would have none of it, believing that she herself had the overwhelming support from the right and that she didn't need Badenoch. All four teams around the surviving candidates were working in overdrive. Any remaining restraints were cast aside in the race for the prize. Each tried to persuade Tugendhat to declare for them with his thirty-one votes. But why should he declare his hand now with the result so unclear? He refused to commit in public. Truss's team watched as they saw the 'Sunak bully boys Gavin Williamson and Julian Smith cornering people in the Chamber, promising promotions, or having ugly words with them. Williamson can be quite brutal,' said one. Wild rumours went round of honours and peerages proffered by all sides.

In the fourth round on Tuesday 19 July, it was Truss who made the breakthrough. The results placed Sunak first with 118 (up 3),

Mordaunt on 92 (up 10) and Truss third on 86 (up 15). Badenoch had been eliminated after achieving just 59 (up 1). For the first time in the race, Truss had momentum. Some of her extra votes came from ten MPs in the Northern Research Group. Founded in 2019 among northern MPs committed to 'levelling up', it had publicly supported Tugendhat until he fell in the third round. But now Berry, its chair, communicated to members that 'Truss best understood the Johnson legacy of winning in the North, and had the right ideas on corporation tax, National Insurance and promoting growth'.[19]

In the twelve days since her return from Indonesia and seven days since the first ballot, Truss had gone from nowhere to a serious contender. The fifth and final round took place on Wednesday 20 July. All three remaining candidates were bidding hard to gain Badenoch's 59 votes. Truss made a great play on the final morning for her Brexit-supporting and 'Red Wall' MPs. The future of the country was decided during these hours. Had Mordaunt hung onto her second place as in the previous four rounds, she would have been in the final two and in all likelihood beaten Sunak. Mordaunt would have been a more measured PM and would probably have led the Conservatives into the general election in 2024. 'I would have pursued a more conservative economic policy to Liz, scrapping tax rises over a longer timeframe and with careful sequencing, but also produced a balanced budget verified by the Office for Budget Responsibility. Immediate tax cuts would have been non-inflationary, like halving VAT on fuel at the pump and increasing low- and middle-income tax thresholds,' she said.[20] There would have been no Truss premiership, no financial meltdown and no Sunak premiership. The history of the party, and country, would have been very different.

Sunak's team preferred Truss to win the final MPs' vote because they judged her easier to beat than Mordaunt in the membership stage. They believed she was fundamentally silly and would self-destruct; as Williamson put it, 'We thought she would implode on the campaign trail: we were right, but wrong about the timing.'[21] Mordaunt's team were convinced that the 'proxy votes' of some of Sunak supporters were switched from him to Truss, so she would come ahead of Mordaunt. Johnson's leadership team had done the same in 2019, urging some of his supporters to vote for Hunt in the final MPs round rather than Gove, because they thought that Hunt would be easier to beat. Ultimately, their plan succeeded and it was Hunt who Johnson faced in the run-off. 'The difference was that we didn't smear and lie about Jeremy Hunt; they went after Liz mercilessly,' said one of Truss's team, the bitterness running deep. 'It was 2019 all over again when the two former Chief Whips, Gavin Williamson and Julian Smith, persuaded people to vote tactically to ensure Boris won. Penny stood no chance against them,' said one pro-Mordaunt MP.

The final result 'was precarious, she could've done much better', recalled Kwarteng. Sunak topped on 137 votes (up 19). Truss for the first time made it into second place with 113 votes (up 27), and Mordaunt, who came third, was eliminated with 105 votes (up 13).

How did Truss's team react to the news? They were all with her in her parliamentary office huddled around the television to listen to Graham Brady of the 1922 Committee deliver the MPs' verdict. The results were announced in alphabetical order by surname. When Truss's result was announced last, there was an odd mood in the room. 'I felt a slight sense of dread when I heard. And I'm sure I was not the only one thinking "Is she really up to it?",' recalled one aide. In Mordaunt's office nearby, there was total despondency and disbelief at her fall. In Sunak's office as captured on a video that his team released that day, there was no reaction when Mordaunt's 105 votes were declared, total silence at Sunak's 137 votes but wild cheering when Truss's 113 votes were announced, palpable proof to the Mordaunt camp that she had fallen victim to Team Sunak's machinations.

Had just five MPs voted the other way Mordaunt would have won. Reeling from the result, she said, 'We must all now work together to unify our party.' No such largesse from Truss who promised 'to hit the ground' as Prime Minister, a statement rapidly amended by her team to include the word 'running'.[22]

Round 2: The Party Members in the Country (21 July–5 September)

Sunak and Truss now went forward to the 'winner takes all' round: a vote by the 172,437 paid-up Tory members. It is thought that over half were aged over sixty, 97 per cent were white, and the majority lived in southern England.[23] This composition is significant because Truss, with her scarcely concealed contempt for Conservative MPs, thought she spoke for ordinary British people, which she conflated in her mind with the party membership.

The competition began the second the MPs' vote was announced, with the first hustings on Thursday 21 July in Westminster, and the first TV debate on the BBC on Monday 25 July. Postal ballots were sent out to arrive between 1 and 5 August, with the polls closing on 2 September. The winner to succeed the still-sitting and still-fuming Boris Johnson as Prime Minister would be announced three days later, on Monday 5 September.

The Commons went into summer recess on Friday 22 July after one of its bitterest sessions. The ritual Tory dogfight was now on to claim Thatcher's mantle.

Truss for some months had been modelling herself as a modern-day Thatcher, not least with her version of the iconic photograph of Thatcher in a British tank with the Union Jack. Even her clothes in the first TV debate bore a striking similarity to Thatcher in an election broadcast in 1979.[24] 'Common sense Thatcherism' was how Sunak described his own economic plan on 21 July.[25] Two days later, Tory grandees Norman Lamont and Malcolm Rifkind attacked Truss's plans, saying that Thatcher would never have approved borrowing to fund £30 billion tax cuts.[26] While both candidates claimed Thatcher's mantle, there could be no doubting that Truss was the Johnson continuity candidate, and that Sunak was despised by Team Johnson.

Ever since Iain Duncan Smith won against Ken Clarke in 2001, and Michael Howard was unopposed in 2003, the conventional wisdom was that the more right wing the candidate, the more likely they were to win among party members. As the contest intensified, both would-be leaders tried to burnish their right-wing credentials, each claiming to be tougher on China and on immigration. Team Sunak had the opponent they wanted. There was all to play for. Huge energy was poured into the competition in the country by both teams. An Opinium poll from 6 to 8 July had put Sunak ahead of Truss. Sunak's team believed they could do it. But on the day the contest officially began, 21 July, much was made of a new poll suggesting that Truss was on course to win. Two days later, Sunak admitted that he was the underdog.[27] From early August, she was regularly polling 60 per cent, with Sunak averaging 35 per cent. Sunak's team clung to their belief that their man was better, and that Truss was stupid and capricious, and that she would self-destruct.

Stage 2 of Truss's strategy was masterminded by veteran campaigner Mark Fullbrook, the long-term business partner of legendary Conservative electoral strategist Lynton Crosby. Ever since Isaac Levido had turned her down, Truss had been searching for a top electoral strategist; Porter had been effective during the early part of the campaign, but Truss now wanted a more established figure, who could better command her team, as chief of staff.

Fullbrook joined the team on 25 July, bringing order and discipline to an amorphous campaign. His focus was politics and messaging. Porter became deputy chief of staff, continuing her work on operations. His strategy was simple: 'Rishi Sunak has only one great claim to having any credibility to win in the country: that he has more Conservative MPs backing him, based on his coming first in the MPs stage. Our whole strategy was set out to prove that is not true, and it is she who has more MPs and support.'[28] 'We made a big, big push at this stage to solidify Boris supporters,' said one aide.

That quest was helped considerably by the naked self-interest of many Conservative MPs. Who would want to declare support for a doomed candidate? Some high-minded politicians aside, most were thinking less of which candidate might best serve the country as Prime Minister than who might best serve their own interests. First out of the blocks in a tightly choreographed sequence of reveals were one-time Thatcher policy chief John Redwood and chair of the ERG Mark Francois on Monday 25 July. By the end of that week, Ben Wallace, Tom Tugendhat, Brandon Lewis and Nadhim Zahawi had endorsed her. Heavyweights all, sending a clear message to the undecided about who to back. Lewis had, at the start of the month, resigned as Northern Ireland Secretary and abandoned Johnson, while Zahawi had remained in the fray to the bitter end as Chancellor.

'It's all about momentum,' said Fullbrook, who followed up these endorsements on Monday 1 August with a piece of careful stage management that redefined the whole competition. The defenestrated Mordaunt abruptly popped up in public to introduce Truss at membership hustings in Exeter saying that she admired her 'authenticity, her determination, her ambition for her country, consistency and sense of duty'.[29] Two days later, Javid declared for her and came out defending her financial plans. This was succour Javid would not forget when, as we shall see, one of Truss's aides made some dismissive remarks about him to a journalist. Then on 12 August, Badenoch came out declaring that Truss was 'a maverick who gets things done'.[30] By mid-August, five of the last eight leadership candidates had declared for her. Apart from herself and Sunak, that meant that only Hunt had come out in public to back Sunak. Nine of Johnson's final Cabinet were supporting her too: Wallace, Javid, Kwarteng, Trevelyan, Coffey, Zahawi, Lewis, Dorries and Rees-Mogg.

They might be endorsing her, but how far was it a marriage of convenience rather than a love-match? At the time, no one cared. They were names, and massive ones. By mid-campaign, the team boasted that she had 162 MPs on side, including twenty-eight current or former Cabinet ministers, fifteen members of the Scottish Parliament and five members of the Welsh Senedd. Team Truss could also claim they had support from six national newspapers: the *Daily Mail*, the *Daily Telegraph* and *Sunday Telegraph*, the *Daily*

Express and *Sunday Express*, and the *Evening Standard*. *The Times* wouldn't be swayed; 'But to be honest, most Conservative members regarded it as a lefty broadsheet of little interest to them,' said one Trussite. Winning over the right-wing press had been regarded as fundamental given their inability to communicate directly with the electorate (neither team was allowed by the rules to know who the Conservative members were). 'I put most store in winning over the *Daily Mail* and *Daily Telegraph*,' said Fullbrook.[31] Ranking next in his hierarchy 'was feeding Guido Fawkes the right information that he would publish on his website. Then, ConservativeHome, albeit no longer possessing the power it once had, and finally, the influential WhatsApp groups.' Truss's 162 MPs were more than Sunak had, if still twenty short of an overall majority. Given the numbers of MPs hedging their bets, or disenchanted by either offer, neither candidate was going to have a majority.

Sunak was toast. He had been outplayed at every point. He could claim no similar list of prominent Cabinet ministers prepared to hitch their wagons to his faltering campaign. Some of those who endorsed him were impressive but, with one exception, they had committed themselves early on while he still stood a good chance: Steve Barclay, Oliver Dowden, George Eustice, Michael Gove, Simon Hart, Dominic Raab and Grant Shapps. The exception was of course Gove, political to his fingertips. When his favoured candidate Badenoch had been knocked out, he faced a dilemma. He loved high office and was far better at it than most other ministers, but he knew that he would never be offered a Cabinet position by Truss. So on 19 August he threw in his lot with the Sunak camp. 'I do not expect to be in government again,' he declared (and who could know at the time how wrong that would prove?). 'But it was the privilege of my life to spend 11 years in the cabinet under three Prime Ministers. I know what the job requires. And Rishi has it.'[32] Even then he was careful not to slam the door, praising Truss as 'tenacious, brave and [with] a huge appetite for policy detail' and 'admirably clear, consistent and principled in the case she has made'. Every word carefully weighed.

Two 'crossed the floor' from Sunak to Truss, the cause of great bitterness: Robert Buckland and Chris Skidmore. Neither were 'A-team' players. None crossed in the opposite direction.[33] A small number held their noses refusing to endorse publicly either candidate, including Alister Jack, Priti Patel and Alok Sharma. Among the 'non-declarers' was the King across the Chilterns, Boris Johnson. He was 'reclusive [and] in a world of his own', according to his team, even though nominally still Prime Minister. The deep gloom that often descends on Prime Ministers on borrowed time had settled on him, and he was wallowing, according to friends, in periodic troughs of self-pity. At his delayed wedding to Carrie Symonds, held at supporter Lord Bamford's stately home Daylesford House in the Cotswolds on Saturday 30 July, his conversation and speech were dominated by why he should still be Prime Minister, and how the crown had been stolen from him. A YouGov poll of Tory members just after the wedding that placed him ahead of Sunak and Truss did nothing to quiet his feelings of betrayal.[34] When asked by MPs who they should support, he would say, with varying degrees of conviction, 'Liz Truss'. But in private, he remained disparaging of her. As long as Sunak remained a serious contender, though, he was in no doubt. Sunak was increasingly and vehemently blamed for the premature end of his premiership. He never blamed himself, naturally. Truss had to win! Hence he and his lieutenants including Zahawi peddled the betrayal thesis far and wide, knowing that it would damage Sunak and benefit Truss. 'Boris understands power better than any of us. He was watching the drama carefully, engineering it all the way,' said one in his camp.

Team Truss had just one blip during this part of the campaign, miraculous given the fear she was accident-prone. On 1 August, she was en route to Exeter by helicopter where she would receive Mordaunt's blessing, while the campaign declared a 'War on Whitehall Waste' to save a claimed £8 billion through adopting 'regional pay boards' for certain grades of civil servant that would 'tailor pay to the cost of living where civil servants actually work'.[35] The plan, which ticked many boxes, including bashing civil servants, seemed clever policy. While discussing it, the team had considered the impact of such a plan on a wider class of public servants such as doctors, nurses, teachers and military personnel, but had ruled it out as politically unacceptable. However, the £8 billion cited on the press release had been calculated in connection with reducing the pay of public servants as a whole, not the intended narrower class of civil servants. 'An oversight of proofing rather than a conscious decision,' one adviser remarked.

Labour and Sunak's team couldn't believe their good fortune, and made all the political capital they could for twenty-four hours until the inevitable U-turn. At Millbank Tower – the new home of the Truss campaign, after leaving Lord North Street in late July – Adam Jones and Jamie Hope decided that the policy was unsalvageable, and called Truss to ask permission to withdraw it. She agreed. A message was sent to the press lobby insisting that 'current levels of public sector pay will absolutely be maintained'.[36]

According to one of her advisers, Truss 'was furious as she had zero tolerance for mistakes'. The finger of blame was firmly pointed at Jones, and, by implication, close teammates Hope and Jarvis. No long-term damage was sustained, though the fallout highlighted existing tensions within Truss's team and her inability or unwillingness to assert her authority. Indeed, like Johnson, she positively revelled in setting off one group against another.

The real ire, though, was not within the team but between the two front runners and their followers. The hostility only grew when it became evident Truss would win. Her team believed that Sunak supporter Oliver Dowden was using the leverage he had possessed as Party Chair to have a say over the party's conduct of the campaign. The accusations did not have to be wholly, or even partially, true to count. What mattered was that the Truss camp believed them to be true. 'They only wanted one candidate left by the end of the membership stage,' said one of her team. How would they make this happen? 'By so intimidating Truss with talk of a thick dossier of her indiscretions, her drinking and even cocaine use by others among her team, that she would lose all credibility, and would throw in her hat rather than face trial by newspapers.' Suspicions of who had compiled the dossier – which never materialized – fell principally on CCHQ insiders. Rumours of her indiscretions, still widely believed, were sourced to this time. The recriminations went further. 'They tried to force through two votes per member to give members the chance to retract their earlier vote for Truss in favour of Sunak,' said one of her supporters. 'So terrible did they think Liz was, all the voters needed was a chance to really examine her, and they would amend their vote,' said another. 'You can't have two votes,' Fullbrook shouted down the telephone to Dowden mid-campaign. The bitterness this generated had an enduring impact.

Team Truss protested that they never engaged in similar tactics or smears. 'We never went for Rishi's tax status, wealth, the US green card, or his wife Akshata Murty's business connections,' one said. But they were not whiter than white. Nadine Dorries, perhaps best known for her neat put-down of David Cameron and George Osborne in 2012 as 'two posh boys who don't know the price of milk', was one of the wider camp free with their comments.[37] She contrasted Truss's £4.50 earrings with Sunak's £3,500 suit, and accused him of 'planning a coup', having earlier 'ruthlessly and metaphorically stabbed Boris Johnson in the back'.[38] 'The stab in the back lie to bring Boris down' was one of the key factors Team Sunak thought responsible for his loss. One card the Truss camp never played was race, even though Sunak's camp thought it a factor at the margins. 'I don't think Tory voters overall are racist. Where I think it might have counted was in a marginal way. Had Rishi's father-in-law been white, wealth might not have become such an issue. So an undertone,' said one highly placed figure on Sunak's campaign.

Truss refused to believe she could win for a long time. 'I'll focus on the campaign, I've won nothing yet,' she regularly told Jason Stein.[39] But then she changed quite suddenly as the realization dawned. 'Am I going to win?' she asked Fullbrook at the Cheltenham hustings on 11 August. 'Yes, you will.' 'Will you bet your life on it?' 'Yes, I will bet my life,' he replied.[40] 'Her whole demeanour changed. She no longer wanted to listen to us but sought the counsel of others,' lamented a member of her old team.

The campaign dragged on for another three weeks, even though most members had voted. At the final hustings in London on 31 August, Truss was introduced by Iain Duncan Smith, while Sunak came on stage with a riff on his position as the trailing candidate:

'Britain loves an underdog.' Final opinion polls gave Sunak some hope, with Truss showing a dramatic loss of support among those who voted Conservative in 2019. Just 31 per cent believed she 'looks like a Prime Minister in waiting' compared to 49 per cent a month earlier, and only 35 per cent thinking her 'competent' in late August down from 55 per cent at the start of the month, a similar fall being shown in those who found her 'likeable'.[41] The final result was declared by Graham Brady in Westminster on Monday 5 September: Truss won 57.4 per cent of the party members' votes to Sunak's 42.6 per cent, a narrower margin than most polls suggested. Just 141,725 had voted, representing 0.3 per cent of the British electorate. This is a telling detail given Truss came to believe that what she heard on the campaign trail was what the British public at large thought. When going up to make her acceptance speech, there was no handshake or word of consolation to her competitor. This was said to be more thoughtlessness than deliberate rudeness, but indicative of her lack of empathy. When preparing her acceptance speech, she had turned to her speechwriter to ask, 'Can we have a bit more about Boris and a bit less about Rishi?' The surprised aide, who had been following precedent in including something positive about the person who had been defeated, asked innocently, 'How much about Rishi?' 'How about nothing about Rishi,' she replied curtly. 'As you will,' he said.[42] Ultimately, she decided to rewrite the speech herself.

The Verdict: Secure the Power Base?

Had she really won? She may have gained more Cabinet ministers and MPs' endorsements than Sunak, but many were sceptical, cynical and even angry. Only fifty MPs had voted for her in the first round, and even that number was approaching the upper limit of the true believers. The 'Truss project' remained a niche idea, supported by a minority of not very influential politicians: none of her ideological soulmates such as Kwarteng, Rees-Mogg, Clarke, Dorries and Jayawardena had deep roots in the parliamentary party. Conservative MPs at large supported her free market, low tax, small state and growth ideals – Tories usually do. But not with her fervour. Nor speed. Nor with her championing these ideals.

Had the rules before the Hague reforms of 1998 still been in operation, with MPs being the ultimate deciders, Sunak would have won and become Prime Minister in July, a fact his team never forgot. She won among members, but members were not her ultimate guarantors of continuation in office. MPs were. They were waiting for her to prove herself. Many were sorry or worse that Wallace, Mordaunt or Sunak hadn't won. Especially Sunak's supporters. She was already walking on very thin ice.

The reasons she won came back to haunt her. Her campaign was much better run than Sunak's, as his team admit. Indeed, they were genuinely surprised that she didn't exhibit the same level of skill in No. 10 that she had in the campaign. Placing the spotlight on her personal journey up from comprehensive school, in contrast to rich public schoolboy Sunak, invited a focus on her personality and intellect, neither of which she was capable of sustaining. Portraying Sunak as the assassin of Johnson, trumpeted not least in the *Daily Mail* and *Mail on Sunday*, won her votes but caused the deep divisions in the party to increase further. The 'betrayal thesis' was concocted on a lie: as shown in *Johnson at 10*, there was plotting by Sunak lieutenants – there are always plots, and talk of plots, at the end of premierships, not the least Thatcher's[43] – but Johnson was brought down by his own political ineptitude and inability to take responsibility.[44] Truss would never have won without the Johnson stamp of approval. Her victory was thus underpinned by a falsity. 'The membership was still in grief about Boris. Like him, she told them what they wanted to hear, big cuts to taxes,' said Gove.[45] But had she also won on a false *prospectus*? Like the Brexit referendum in 2016, had she made promises that could never be completely fulfilled?

Maintaining loyal MPs and a secure majority in Parliament is our first test for a successful premiership. Did Truss meet that criterion? She certainly had a working majority inherited from Johnson. However, she had MPs who were suspending their judgement rather than MPs who were loyal or who liked her. She never had the same legitimacy of a Prime Minister who had won their own mandate. Anyone taking over as Prime Minister in the autumn of 2022, with the Conservative Party in civil war, and the country facing a cost of living crisis at home and war abroad, would need to tread carefully, uniting friends and foes in common cause.

Is that what she did? We now turn to examine Project Truss.

Rule Number Two: Have a clear and realistic plan for government.
Truss arrives in No. 10 as Prime Minister on Tuesday 6 September.
She had a clear plan, but it was not a realistic one

2

HAVE A CLEAR AND REALISTIC PLAN FOR GOVERNMENT

'She is guided by an underlying ideology in a way our last three Conservative Prime Ministers [Cameron, May, Johnson] have not been.'[1] So said Mark Littlewood, Truss's friend since student days at Oxford and fellow traveller on the free-market highway (via brief stopovers at the Lib Dem and pro-EU service stations). Both had risen to the top of their chosen professions: for Truss politics, and for Littlewood, presiding over Britain's oldest and most influential free-market think tank, the Institute of Economic Affairs (IEA). Now the thinker and the doer were poised together to make history.

They were about to hatch the most ambitious and comprehensive programme of economic and institutional reform in Britain since Margaret Thatcher came to power in 1979, and the most wide-ranging package of tax cuts since Ted Heath's 'dash for growth' in 1972.

Successful Premierships Require Clear Agendas

So far, so good. Every premier since the emergence of modern party government in the mid-nineteenth century has had at least some idea of what they would like to do in office. But to be successful the plans have needed to be *realistic*. The most successful Prime Ministers since the office was created in 1721, including William Pitt the Younger, Robert Peel, William Gladstone, David Lloyd George, Clement Attlee and Margaret Thatcher, all knew – to quote Germany's great nineteenth-century chancellor Otto von Bismarck – that politics was 'the art of the possible'.[2]

Had she studied her history, Truss would have known that none of the nine agenda-changing Prime Ministers came to office at the tail end of a long period of one-party ascendancy outside of the exigencies of a world war (Lloyd George in 1916 and Churchill in 1940). She was therefore attempting something never before achieved.

Those who underachieved as PMs either hadn't worked fully through what they wanted to do before they came to office, such as Lord Rosebery and Anthony Eden, or misjudged the politics or the economics, or both, like Ramsay MacDonald and Ted Heath. Some of those who didn't optimize their opportunities may have had considerable achievements to their name, but like Tony Blair moved too slowly when they had the most political capital, while others, like Heath after 1970, moved too quickly.

Prime Ministers who come to power after a general election victory have a greatly enhanced opportunity to articulate and embed a programme worked up over several months or years in opposition. Those like Harold Macmillan, James Callaghan and John Major who inherited mid-term struggled to find the time and opportunity to articulate their own distinctive vision. They also inevitably faced questions about their mandate from the electorate to justify any mid-term change of course. The general election was won in December 2019 on Boris Johnson's manifesto, which was still far from enacted by mid-2022, and here was Truss wanting to take the country off in a radically new direction. Yes, she had presented her platform candidly and repeatedly to MPs and to Conservative members, but not to the electorate on whom the medicine was to be administered.

Truss's ultimate aim was to follow the path of mid-term arrivers Macmillan, Major and Johnson and win her own general election mandate as they did. But she knew that the growing unpopularity of the party meant she would have to go long and not call the general election until the last minute in late 2024, hence upon her personal victory she promised 'a great victory for the Conservative Party in 2024'.[3] She wanted to pass her economic plan as soon as possible, to give the maximum chance for positive impact before voters made up their minds.

Too many Prime Ministers have arrived at No. 10 with 'at best a shopping list, at worst a collection of slogans', as Harold Wilson's biographer Ben Pimlott memorably put it, of his return to Downing Street in March 1974.[4] Alas, slogans are what the British public has tended to receive instead of defined agendas from its Prime Ministers in the intervening fifty years. They arrive on the doorstep of No. 10 for their ritual first speech as the nation's leader bursting with high-minded ideals. To Thatcher in 1979, it was St Francis of Assisi's 'Where there is discord, may we bring harmony.' To Major in 1990: 'A country that is at ease with itself.' 'A mandate to bring this nation together, to unite us,' was Blair's offering in 1997. Brown was inspired by his school motto in 2007 to pledge that 'I will try my utmost'. When Cameron won his own majority for the Conservatives in 2015, he promised, 'We can make Britain a place where a good life is in reach for everyone who is willing to work and do the right thing.' May had a tighter mission in 2016, to fight 'burning injustices'.

Johnson's vision included 'uniting our country' and 'answering at last the plea of the forgotten people', as well as defying 'the doubters, the doomsters, the gloomsters'. They all, or mostly all, did their best to live up to the aspirations that they articulated. Thatcher largely sidestepped her uplifting motto, replacing it with an agenda that soon became known as 'Thatcherism', defined as 'a mixture of free markets, financial discipline, firm control over public expenditure, tax cuts, nationalism, "Victorian Values"… privatisation, and a dash of populism' by her long-serving Chancellor, Nigel Lawson.[5]

With Truss, there was no pussyfooting around. She was going to give the country her agenda with both barrels from day one.

Personal and Political Journey: 1975–2012

Sunak's team tried to besmirch Truss during the leadership contest for flip-flopping: the Liberal Democrat who became a Conservative, and the Remainer who became an ardent Brexiteer. Such jibes miss the strong core running through her thinking. 'She is, and always has been, a market liberal with a deep suspicion of entrenched, vested interests. She instinctively believes the state has a greater propensity to do harm than to do good,' as Littlewood puts it.[6]

The 'Truss project' was an amalgam of several different elements that she encountered at Oxford and beyond. These ideas motivated her to go into politics, and underpinned her actions. They were blended with an exceptionally high degree of ambition and self-belief, as a politician and a minister.[7]

Margaret Thatcher was the first serving Prime Minister whose name she heard spoken as a young child. Thatcher had moved into Downing Street in May 1979 when Truss was three and she quit when Truss was fifteen. The young Truss was captivated by her boldness and ideology.

Free markets, deregulation and liberal economics were all in the ascendant in the 1980s. By the end of the decade, the Soviet Union would be on the verge of collapse, and with it, its grip over Eastern Europe. In China, Deng Xiaoping's free-market reforms initiated the process of economic transformation from Mao's communist state. In the United States, President Ronald Reagan's economic liberalism had proven a success. In the UK, the Labour Party had begun to jettison the left-wing socialist prescriptions of its leader, Michael Foot (1980–83), in favour of embracing growth and the market. The three predictions that my father Arthur Seldon had outlined at the beginning of the decade, that the Soviet Union would not last till the end of the century, that Labour 'as we know it' would never govern again and that China would embrace capitalism, all appeared to be coming true.[8] The atmosphere for Truss was intoxicating.

The 1990s saw the march of economic liberalism continue apace. In January 1990 in Moscow's Pushkin Square, McDonald's opened a branch attracting a record 38,000 customers on the first day. President Clinton told America 'the era of big government is over'.[9] The European Union created a Single Market in 1993 to boost free trade between member nations. In contrast to her admiration for Thatcher, however, Truss found little to admire in her successor John Major, Prime Minister during Truss's A-levels and undergraduate years. By the time Major fell to Labour in May 1997, when Truss was twenty-one, her world view had largely been formed. Despite Tony Blair's abandoning 'Clause IV' of the Labour Party constitution that committed it to nationalization, and his embrace of business, Truss disliked the new government's granting of so much independence to the Bank of England in 1997 and the statist direction of Blair and Brown's economic policies.[10]

Real world events excited her more than reading philosophical or economic literature. An autodidact, she discounts the idea that she was influenced by anyone or anything: 'Frankly the influence of the IEA on me has been much overstated,' she said.[11] She lacked the intellectual curiosity of Thatcher or the incisive mind of Cameron who achieved a first class degree in PPE at Oxford, the same subject she studied, and she lacked his ability to see nuance and to judge character. History was not her thing: 'She had no sense of it at all or interest in it. I didn't think she read much. I remember she once tried quoting Harold Macmillan, but butchered the point,' recalls Kwasi Kwarteng.[12] Her intellect was governed rather by mathematical reasoning and logic, and she loved to test the ability of others against hers by setting them arithmetical challenges at job interviews. Art, drama, classical music and religion passed her by. She never watched TV. She knew about books rather than read them, her favourite for a while being *What it Takes: The Way to the White House* by Pulitzer Prize-winning journalist Richard Ben Cramer, an account of the post-Reagan 1988 presidential campaign focusing on the six principal candidates: George Bush, Bob Dole, Michael Dukakis, Richard Gephardt, Gary Hart and Joe Biden. The latter was the only one she would encounter, albeit in unhappy circumstances. Reading about the razzle-dazzle of American electoral politics enchanted her far more than the dry, but often more grounded, political memoirs of British politicians, whose pages she would flick through in search of inspiration.

After university she had spells as a chartered management accountant, working at Royal Dutch Shell and then Cable & Wireless. But politics is what really interested her. She became deputy director of the centre-right think tank Reform in 2008, authoring several reports, including *The Value of Mathematics*. Two years later, she entered Parliament in May 2010 as MP for South West Norfolk, and soon established the Free Enterprise Group that attracted a diverse list of some thirty Thatcherite-leaning MPs including Coffey, Javid, Kwarteng and Zahawi. The group enabled her first foray into publishing, co-writing *After the Coalition* (2011) and *Britannia Unchained* (2012). The former advocated reducing the top rate of tax to 40 pence in the pound ('George [Osborne] only reduced it in 2012 to 45p – we wanted him to go further,' she said).[13] Their aim was to influence the content of the Conservative manifesto at the 2015 general election in a pro-capitalist direction. In this, they were unsuccessful. The manifesto was built around the concepts of security and continuity, rather than tax cutting and deregulation.

Kwarteng quickly became her ideological soulmate among the 2010 entrants to Parliament. The same age as Truss, he had attended Eton College before Cambridge where he achieved a double first and then a PhD in economic history. *War and Gold*, his most thoughtful book, was published in 2014. It looked at the history of financial crises, particularly in the twentieth and twenty-first centuries.[14] Surprisingly, Kwarteng is an advocate of balancing the books and his favourite Chancellor is Neville Chamberlain, who championed that approach.[15] Truss, for all her liking of Kwarteng and admiration for his intellect, did not agree. By 2022, her ambition was effectively to become her own Chancellor. If she was to make it to the very top, 'she would want to be heavily involved in economic policy from the centre and would need a Chancellor who was willing to accept that,' said her economic adviser at No. 10 Shabbir Merali.[16] 'Very few Chancellors would have stood for it, but he was happy to do so: every other conversation was him saying that Rishi was a bad Chancellor because he would argue all the time with the PM; "I won't be like that," he would say,' said one of Kwarteng's economic advisers.[17]

Ministerial Career: 2012–22

Truss zipped up the ministerial ladder. But she never felt particularly secure on the rungs, nor was she to win many admirers for her pirouettes as she reached the top. Rumours were common that she was to be dismissed at the next reshuffle. Cameron provided her first break in September 2012 when, aged thirty-seven, she was appointed a junior minister at Gove's Department for Education with responsibilities including childcare. Despite the promotion, she never made it into Team Gove and was denigrated by Cummings, his special adviser, as a 'human hand grenade' who 'caused chaos instead of getting things done'.[18] Cameron wasn't put off – he had his own battles with Cummings. But he needed seasoned women to promote and the field wasn't vast. In July 2014, he thus offered Truss her first senior post as Environment Secretary, bringing the proportion of women in Cabinet up to a historic one third.

'I think it's bloody disgraceful what the Prime Minister has done to you,' outgoing Environment Secretary Owen Paterson told her on her appointment. 'You've been in parliament for three nanoseconds. You know about education… But here you find yourself dummied into DEFRA where you have no background at all.'[19] Hyperactive on a series of initiatives, she failed to convince either the farming or the environmental lobby that she fully understood her brief. She took time out for the June 2016 referendum to campaign for Remain. 'Her views on Brexit were nicely balanced. She could see the economic advantages of staying in, and the transactional dislocation of leaving, which I think decided it for her,' said Adam Jones. 'But once it happened, she embraced it wholeheartedly, wrapping herself in the flag and setting herself up as the Brexit darling.'[20]

Cameron's replacement Theresa May had fresh ideas for her, promptly appointing her Justice Secretary and the first ever female Lord Chancellor in July 2016. 'At the Ministry of Justice, I saw close up how bad the institutions were, and how little accountability there is,' she recalled.[21] Truss fought hard and courageously to increase the number of prison officers after a series of cuts, but fell foul of the legal profession when in November she was accused of failing to support the judiciary after three High Court judges incensed the *Daily Mail* sufficiently for it to run the headline 'Enemies of the People'. Their crime? Ruling against the government on whether the process of leaving the EU could be triggered without Parliament's agreement. Furious calls from across the spectrum were made to No. 10 for Truss to resign for failing to exercise her constitutional position as defender of the judiciary. May didn't like the noise the row created, nor did her team. And they weren't impressed by what they saw as her serial leaking. 'You could tell when Liz was responsible for a leak because she'd always be painted in a favourable light,' said one May acolyte.[22]

May had had enough, and Truss, to her fury, was demoted to the position of Chief Secretary to the Treasury in 2017, allowing her to attend Cabinet, but no longer as a full member. For the first time, she'd experienced a reversal in her upward momentum. It hurt her deeply and unleashed an inner rage. May had no idea what she had done. The defiant Truss was going to show her critics the kind of person she was. 'As Chief Secretary... I aim to be the disruptor-in-chief; I want to challenge those who aim to block change, stop development and restrict success. I want to challenge the caution that strangles risk-takers and go-getters,' she wrote in her favourite daily newspaper, the *Daily Telegraph*, a month after her appointment.[23] The next day, fortified by a new speechwriter, she gave her most vigorous address yet, calling for liberation at last from state shackles 'from the grainbelt of our agricultural heartlands to the brainbelt bursting out around our great universities... From the port cities to the inland empires... free enterprise... breaks down monopolies, hierarchies and outdated practices. It destroys barriers, and erodes inequality.' Then, in the most ringing section, she extolled free enterprise as 'good for our nation of Airbnb-ing, Deliveroo-eating, Uber-riding freedom fighters'.[24]

But Truss ran up against the hidebound (as she saw it) Chancellor of the Exchequer, Philip Hammond. Hammond's view was that his second in command should be like the cerebral David Gauke whom she had replaced. 'I didn't dislike her, as I most definitely did her predecessor as PM. She was quick, analytical and intelligent, if not profound. I thought I could work with her,'[25] Hammond said. But she had difficulty understanding why her views were not immediately taken up by others. 'She absolutely hated it when others didn't take her opinions seriously.'[26] So wary did Hammond's Treasury become of her that she was excluded from sensitive discussions, which made her even angrier, and which she blamed, unfairly as it happened, on the senior official in the department, Tom Scholar. This would later have devastating consequences. Once again, rumours circulated that details from documents from her office quickly found their way into the newspapers.

Being at the Treasury allowed her to range widely across every area of government policy, a luxury afforded to ministers in no other department. 'She was actively engaged well beyond the brief, having great interest in ideas and evidence,' said Shabbir Merali, who joined as her economic adviser in February 2018.[27] Littlewood was one of several thinkers she was talking to as she set up a covert operation to challenge Treasury orthodoxy. For a while, she was fascinated by *The Captured Economy*, a book by two US liberal economists, Brink Lindsey and Steven Teles, who advanced the populist argument that rich individuals and businesses had rewritten the rules of the US economy, 'capturing' the regulatory system and using it to squeeze out the competition.

Truss's low tax, low spending, anti-institution agenda, if still inchoate, was beginning to crystallize. So too was her conviction that she might be destined for the very top, on a mission to put the country back on track after years of decline. By the end of the year, she became a regular presence on Instagram and Twitter, and her team began looking for ostentatious photo opportunities – perhaps peaking during her time as Trade Secretary with the photograph of her on a Brompton bike, holding a Union Jack umbrella, with Sydney's iconic bridge and opera house in the background. Guided by her adviser Adam Jones, her communications improved markedly, becoming more strategically minded and impactful.

Few things piqued Truss's curiosity more than the monthly Cabinet popularity ratings on the ConservativeHome website. 'She would be absolutely glued to it, mesmerized by it,' said an aide. She would love to see her ranking against her colleagues rise and fall, and she became intrigued by the actions she could take to maximize the opportunities of the former. But currying favour with her colleagues, essential if she was to have a reasonable prospect of becoming leader, did not always rank high. In June 2018, she devoted a speech to tax and spending cuts that contained the intentionally provocative phrase 'it's not macho just to demand more money'.[28] Prudent policy maybe, but bad diplomacy. It was seen as a direct snub to Defence Secretary Gavin Williamson, who had been 'waging a relentless political campaign' to increase defence funding, not a man who any savvy aspirant for the top office would want to antagonize.[29] Her words managed to annoy ministers at large too, including Gove, Javid and Hunt. Not smart, but part of her seemed positively to rejoice in aggravating colleagues.[30]

When May's enfeebled premiership spluttered to an end in July 2019, Truss flirted with the idea of standing in the leadership contest. When she was told that it would go nowhere, however, she threw in her lot with Johnson, only to be livid when, rather than being issued with one of the great offices of state, she was appointed International Trade Secretary. Partly out of guilt, partly to shut her up, Johnson added an extra portfolio of Minister for Women and Equalities on Amber Rudd's resignation in September 2019. It was at Trade that she forged a significant bond with her permanent secretary Antonia Romeo.

Truss threw herself into her new portfolio, bursting to prove her Brexit credentials in a party in which the cause was riding high. No one minister in the government was doing more to exploit Brexit opportunities, pressing free-trade negotiations way beyond what fellow ministers thought possible or desirable, irritating Environment and Rural Affairs Secretary George Eustice, Gove and Sunak in the process. Midway through her time in the department, her team began to notice a subtle shift in her mindset. 'Always a politician who could read things a long way ahead, she started to become more ideological after a year, and rather than judging everything on evidence, she increasingly approached new issues with preconceived views,' said one.

Jet-setting Liz criss-crossed the world with trips to the United States, New Zealand, Australia and Japan in search of new trade deals. She could not be faulted for industry in post, though her dreams of a US trade deal did not transpire. Still, her unguarded comments on these trips aroused the attention of No. 10, with her nemesis Cummings furious at her verbal incontinence, her preening and her chaotic *modus operandi*. His departure in the autumn of 2020 helped save her ministerial career. Even though Johnson remained unimpressed with her performance, and scornful of her personally, it didn't stop him making her Foreign Secretary in September 2021 when Dominic Raab was removed after holidaying during the botched Western departure from Afghanistan. She would either implode or explode, he thought.

Johnson's intention was to remove from domestic politics a bumptious rival whom he found increasingly irritating. But if he thought he was burying her, he was quickly disabused because she showed far more aplomb in post than anyone had anticipated. Indeed, her Foreign Secretaryship gives pause to those who would dismiss her as a lightweight, incapable of making a success of high office. At her best, she could be impressive, as shown in her uncompromising stance on Xi's China, her pressing at the UN for the release of Nazanin Zaghari-Ratcliffe from custody in Iran (which eventually transpired in March 2022) and her launching what would become the Windsor Framework for Northern Ireland. The process was concluded in March 2023, but was built on her Northern Ireland Protocol Bill, which eased customs checks on goods from Great Britain. She recognized early on that the key to finding a way through was enlisting the support of EU Commission President Ursula von der Leyen, and negotiating directly with her.

Truss certainly made her mark as Foreign Secretary, not least in her forceful stance on Ukraine. Before the Russian invasion in February 2022, she pressed successfully for the release of Western intelligence on Russia's military plans, and she travelled to Moscow to talk to Foreign Affairs Minister Lavrov. She strongly pushed for Ukraine to be supplied with NLAW anti-tank missiles (weapons that would prove their worth on the battlefield). After the invasion she lobbied hard for the G7 to place unforgiving sanctions on Russia, and for them only to be lifted in the event of a total Russian withdrawal. In Britain, she helped to force through very swift legislative changes that created sweeping sanctions against Russia (including the sanctioning of individuals based on US, EU and Canadian sanctions – a process called 'mirroring'). The credibility she gained on the international stage, even with PM Johnson and Defence Secretary Wallace in the same lane, won her new admirers at home and abroad.

Her diplomatic success owed much to her willingness to listen to civil servants, despite the fact that she came to despise the collective civil service on ideological and temperamental grounds. Chief among them were Nick Catsaras, her principal private secretary at the Foreign Office whom she persuaded to come to No. 10 with her, Political Director Tim Barrow whom she elevated to National Security Adviser once she was PM, and Permanent Under-Secretary Philip Barton whom she left in post to work with whoever she appointed as Foreign Secretary. 'Find me reasons to contest official advice', had been a regular Truss mantra in her journey up the ministerial ladder. It suited her. Once in Downing Street would she still be able to trust civil servants who proffered good advice on topics about which she knew little, as she had done at the Foreign Office?

Truss might have shaped up to be one of the better Conservative Foreign Secretaries of recent years. But with only ten months in office, her stay was too short to assess properly. It had been sufficient, though, to add another component to the Truss agenda: international crusader for liberty. 'The free world has taken its eye off the ball,' she declared in a landmark speech at the foreign policy institute Chatham House in December 2021 called 'Building the Network of Liberty'. The West, she said, had lulled itself into complacency because of 'strategic drift. Defence spending fell. Countries became strategically dependent on cheap gas or reliant on others [i.e. China] for vital technology like 5G.' In its place, Truss proposed a 'network of liberty [to] advance the frontiers of freedom' with all 'freedom-loving nations' abandoning 'protectionism and isolationism' and building 'security links' in common cause.[31] 'This new view of the world was very Manichean,' said Adam Jones. 'Countries were either good or evil, for or against us, pro-freedom or enemies.'[32] Her 'network of liberty' strategic framing was all about trying to bring 'contested countries' into the orbit of the West, rather than let them drift towards Russia, China or Iran. In aspiration, if not vaulting language, it echoed President John F. Kennedy's celebrated inaugural speech in January 1961, about the need to 'meet any hardship' to ensure 'the success of liberty'.

It echoed too, intentionally, the world view of her hero Margaret Thatcher. It was on a visit to Estonia in 2021 that she was photographed in a tank, in conscious mimicry and homage to Thatcher's iconic photograph from 1986 taken in another state, West Germany, close to the frontline of the Soviet Union.

Policy Beliefs

Unlike many incoming Prime Ministers, Truss had the significant advantage of a worked-through ideological underpinning. She was going to be pro-Brexit, pro-global free trade, pro-liberty and capital, and pro-Britain being a major force in the world. She knew, and the world knew, what she stood for.

Truss's world view had four key planks.

Her Atlanticist foreign policy was her first. To an extent that was to irk Washington, she placed a close relationship with the United States at the heart of her overseas vision. She looked back to the strong relationships between Thatcher and Reagan, Major and George H. W. Bush, and Blair with both Bill Clinton and George W. Bush. The question was left in the air whether President Biden's vision of the United States' relationship with the United Kingdom and the world at large would be the same. To Truss, Britain should be a moral exemplar. Unlike the divisive insurgency wars of Afghanistan and Iraq, the forthright response to the Russian invasion of Ukraine offered the promise of a new era of transatlantic cooperation and Western unity, even if much of the optimism about the future of the Ukraine conflict turned out to have been misplaced.

Thatcher inspired the second plank. Truss's tax-cutting, public-spending reductions and state-shrinking outlook owed much to her understanding of Thatcher. But it was the man who was US President at the time of her political awakening, Ronald Reagan, who had more direct influence on her policies. At Mansion House in a speech in 2019, she paid tribute to him: 'President Reagan was clear that in order to defend freedom you cannot afford to stay silent.'[33]

During the leadership campaign on 15 August, Reagan's celebrated speechwriter Peggy Noonan came to see Truss in Lord North Street. 'Don't be distracted by detail, bureaucracy or the news cycle. Go for the big picture,' Noonan counselled her. 'I'm not interested in having a small vision,' Truss replied, enthralled at having this living link to her idol talking to her in her own office.[34] 'She and her economic advisers were absolute followers of Ronald Reagan,' said Kwarteng. 'They really did believe that if you cut tax, it would lead directly to a supply-side revolution and growth.'[35] The question was whether this economic philosophy would deliver the expected benefits as quickly as she hoped.

Thatcher's influence on Truss transcended the mere ideological. She told Philip Hammond that 'if you are a woman in British politics, you have to be ruthlessly single-minded or you'll get nothing done. That is the lesson I learned from Margaret Thatcher.'[36] It may not have been the best lesson. To Hammond, who worked with her for two years at the Treasury, she believed that she had to set her own agenda and wouldn't deviate from it, because if she bent, 'it would be seen as displaying weakness and [she] would be finished'.

Her reading of Thatcher was partial, as Thatcher's biographer Charles Moore observed: 'Mrs Thatcher would work intensely hard to ensure she grasped every aspect of her brief and had a strong sense of context and history. She was then very good at explaining what she was trying to do. I'm not certain Liz Truss had those same qualities.'[37] Truss alighted in particular on the Thatcher trait of announcing at the beginning of a meeting what she thought. 'Liz would say "I think XYZ" and then wouldn't listen. But Thatcher did listen, and had the confidence to absorb contrary viewpoints,' observed Hammond.[38]

Truss didn't fret over her interpretation of Thatcher. If she travelled Thatcher-lite, so be it. She was not the only one to claim the Thatcher mantle in a Conservative Party that had so lost its common sense of mission that Thatcher idolatry was almost the only shared belief. 'Sunak and Truss have declared themselves Thatcherites. For Sunak, that means adhering to fiscal conservativism to tackle inflation; for Truss, it means cutting taxes to go for growth. Each claims that their Thatcherism is the true Thatcherism,' as journalist Tom McTague crisply put it.[39]

The third plank was libertarianism, which owed much to the ideas emanating from the international Mont Pelerin Society founded in 1947, with Friedrich Hayek and Milton Friedman as its two great luminaries, and the Institute of Economic Affairs founded in 1955 its champion in the UK.[40] Under Mark Littlewood's leadership, the IEA continued its move away from the academic scholarship that characterized its early years and became close to a certain breed of right-wing politician, promoting specific causes such as Brexit, climate change scepticism and opposition to 'the nanny state'.

Truss was instinctively libertarian, disliking attempts by the government to rule on 'private matters' such as smoking, drinking and sexual mores.

Singapore-on-Thames characterized Truss's low tax, low regulation vision for Global Britain, unshackled from meddling from Brussels, though she didn't use that term herself. It differed from the vision of Brexit Britain favoured by Nigel Farage, the Leave campaign and some of the tribal figures who were by then closing in on her. Their Brexit was nationalistic and isolationist, with immigration cuts at the heart. Singapore-on-Thames in contrast was an internationalist vision: after all, 40 per cent of

Singapore's population are foreigners, with the state benefiting from high levels of immigration. Truss was not an all-out 'little Englander' and her liberal views on immigration would, in time, cause conflict within her own government.

Her core team was never ideologically at one. Free-marketeer Ruth Porter had worked at the IEA, and libertarian Sophie Jarvis at sister think tank the Adam Smith Institute. But Truss called her policy aide Jamie Hope a 'political mercenary' for his pragmatism and referred to Adam Jones as a 'centrist dad.'[41] As the prospect of No. 10 came into view, a new cast of liberal thinkers arrived, and came to influence, if not her instincts, then the confidence with which she articulated them. 'My views were pretty much formed already, and on the campaign trail, I found I needed to be not only the front room public figure but also the back room person producing the ideas,' she recalled.[42]

Matthew Elliott, chief executive of Vote Leave and founder of the TaxPayers' Alliance, started to be seen much more frequently from July 2022. So did fellow Brexiteer and venture capitalist Jon Moynihan, who 'was always pushing the anti-green agenda on Liz', according to an aide, who added, 'She wanted his money for the campaign, but not his views on the environment.' She gave him a peerage in her resignation honours list, along with Elliott and Porter. Matt Sinclair, who had run the TaxPayers' Alliance, came in mid-campaign 'out of a blue sky' as her chief economic adviser, on Elliott's advice. This disconcerted her team, who complained that 'the boss didn't know him' and, more importantly, 'he never understood Liz'. From the same political stable were two politicians, both fervent free-marketeers and Brexiteers, Thatcher's former head of policy and Cabinet minister John Redwood and Jacob Rees-Mogg. While Nadine Dorries' involvement waned after their Downing Street declarations for Truss, Rees-Mogg was to wax into a constant and insistent voice in her ear.

The fourth and final plank had always been present in her mind. This was a sense of anti-establishmentism and a suspicion of the 'blob', the combined forces of the establishment and 'deep state' that she and others like her saw as obstructive towards bold inclinations and liberal policy. Into this group Truss placed not just the civil service, but also the Treasury, with its orthodox, anti-growth mindset, and the Bank of England, the Office for Budget Responsibility and the International Monetary Fund. 'She always thought the establishment was there to resist what practical politicians like herself were trying to do,' said one adviser.

Figures like Elliot, Littlewood, Moynihan, Redwood, Rees-Mogg, Clarke and Kwarteng shared a secret understanding: that Truss's grasp of the subtleties of market economics, while deeply held, was superficial, and they were there to stiffen her resolve when she found herself up against the agents of the 'deep state'. They were there to keep her honest and straight: 'We can expect to see a whirlwind of activity and announcements from the very first minutes of her entering Downing Street... The overall direction of travel in the Truss administration will be crystal clear – to move power and money away from the state bureaucracy and into the hands of ordinary men and women,' wrote Littlewood just hours before she became Prime Minister. They were her minders, a secret cabal to protect her from the forces of darkness, the secret state.[43] She of course contests this, and believes her suspicions about institutions had been long acquired in office. Maybe, her Praetorian Guard might say, but look at how she crumbled when she came up against the forces of the 'deep state' once in power.

Four Weeks to Power: 8 August–5 September 2022

Truss was nervous throughout the campaign, initially doubting whether she could win, then doubting whether she was really up to being Prime Minister. At a staff meeting on Friday 29 July, she was tetchy. When it was suggested that she needed to think more about Downing Street, she snapped, 'Look, I've not won anything yet. I'm going to keep my focus on the campaign. Get on with your jobs.' But then everything changed.

In early August, Mark Fullbrook suddenly announced, 'This is the endpoint of the campaign. There is very little that we can do now. Most members have made up their minds and voted.' An aide recalls Fullbrook telling Truss, 'I don't want you out on the stump any more, Liz. You need to be switching to the transition process and working out what you will do for the country.' She paused but then accepted the verdict.

The family atmosphere among Truss's team that had endured from the moment she had returned from Bali now began to break up. Realizing they were standing on the precipice of power, her team became locked into a bitter struggle for the possession of her soul. On the one side, her young team who had bonded together during her time at International Trade and the Foreign Office, focused around Jones, Hope and Jarvis. With the exception of the last, who was like a daughter to Truss and shared her anti-China zeal, they were more pragmatic and centrist than she was. On the other side were the joint campaign directors Fullbrook and Porter who claimed seniority and Truss's own preferment, and who had a closer affinity with her vision to recast the self-serving British establishment. To Jones et al., Truss was selling out by throwing in her lot with Porter and Fullbrook, and the people they brought in like Sinclair. 'She said that we were not sufficiently on mission, nor experienced enough, nor true believers. So we were sidelined,' said one. 'But we were the people who challenged her, and the others did not. We knew how to get the best out of her,' explained another.

Not aligned to either camp stood communications specialist Jason Stein, who, apart from Porter, had been with Truss the longest. An ingenious loner, he had been behind many of the initiatives that had made Truss into a national figure, and possessed a grip over her that none other could match. 'It was a Rasputin-like hold. He would pump her up, dance with her, get inside her mind, and he gave her a confidence no one else could before the big media occasions,' said one aide.

Without Stein, she would not have emerged as the prominent figure that she was. But could she go on any further with him? To some, he was divisive and resented others coming into his space and claiming her attention, above all with the big prize coming into sight. His animosity focused on Fullbrook. Matters came to a head on Friday 12 August. Travelling in the back of the car with her, he was furious when he heard that she had decided to keep Fullbrook on as chief of staff if she became Prime Minister. 'He's no good as campaign manager, a con man, and he'll probably end your premiership,' he blurted out. 'Thank you, Jason. I've made my decision,' she said before getting out of the car. Stein was left behind to ponder. 'Wow. You're a brave kid,' said the security policeman in the car with them. 'I've done this job for a long time and I've never heard anyone speak to a Secretary of State like that.' Later that day, Truss sidled up to him, saying, 'I want you to know, Jason, that I like you a lot. But I am very angry with you. I'm not going to let go of Mark. We're going to have to sort this out.' She then gave him a long hug and left.[44]

That night the leadership circus moved on to Manchester. Fullbrook sought out Stein and tried to smooth things over. 'I know you can't stand me, but let's make a deal for the sake of Liz. I won't mess you about if you don't mess me about.' Fullbrook was not reassured by his response. 'Mark saw Jason as a political terrorist, a mini-Cummings whose method was to belittle and undermine others; definitely not a team player,' said an aide. The next morning at breakfast, Truss told Stein, 'I've got serious concerns about you coming into Downing Street, Jason, and that you won't be able to work with Mark.' For the time being, the difference was patched up. But it did not augur well for when she became Prime Minister.

Truss had been in turmoil about who she'd place at the heart of her premiership. Like Boris Johnson, she loved mystery and to have conflicting circles of advisers. Originally, Truss set her heart on David Frost having a big role beside her. A former Foreign Office diplomat who became Johnson's chief negotiator during the Brexit negotiations, he resigned from his Cabinet in December 2021 with ambitions to succeed Johnson himself. Frost was revered on the Brexiteer wing of the party and in the right-wing television and press. Following his trashing of Mordaunt in the MPs stage of the contest, he became a commanding figure early on in Truss's campaign before overreaching himself. He wanted to be her right-hand man in No. 10 as Deputy Prime Minister (DPM). His ambition caused consternation among the team, and he shortly after disappeared. Truss had already earmarked her closest parliamentary ally Coffey as DPM, and fell back on Fullbrook as chief of staff. Campaigning was Fullbrook's strength, while Porter was to emerge for a time as

Truss's key figure over policy. Stein saw himself left out in the cold. This situation was exacerbated by Truss changing her phone number for security reasons partway through the campaign, because it was suspected of being hacked by the Russian security services.[45] Though utterly unavoidable, it cut her off yet further from her stalwarts, who complained they could no longer get hold of her. A subsequent change of phone was deemed necessary, and thereafter access to her was only through Fullbrook and Porter. Realizing he would never get anywhere with Fullbrook, and fearing that Porter was forming 'an unholy alliance with him', he turned to the latter. 'You should quit now,' Stein told Porter. 'I can't quit. I've worked my whole life for this,' she told him.[46]

Porter set to work at once to ensure that Truss was meeting the right people. Over the weekend of 6–7 August, a select group of economists was invited to her home in Greenwich. 'You should hear from these free-market people,' Truss was told by Sinclair, one of the figures behind the meeting. 'Our understanding is that it was devised as an egg-on for Liz, to stiffen her resolve,' said Shabbir Merali, her economic adviser. Littlewood and fellow economist Julian Jessop were present at the tutorial, as was Rees-Mogg, hoping to be her Chancellor. Did she need this turbocharging? Even some of her most ardent ideological supporters had reservations: 'Their radicalism gave fresh tinder to something that was already burning too brightly within Liz,' said Simon Clarke.[47] The ideas flew around the room. A few days later, the idea of scrapping the cap on bankers' bonuses was mentioned. 'Let's go for it!' Reducing the 45p tax rate? 'Long overdue.' 'How about replacing all direct taxes with a flat 20p rate of income tax?' 'Great idea, Jacob.' This last proposal was nicknamed 'Estonia' (a reference to a similar policy adopted there) and Rees-

Mogg 'estimated it would cost £41 billion'. 'I'd long been attracted to the idea of flat rate taxes,' Truss said later.[48]

'These ideas might have been fine if it had been a blue skies airing of a hundred things that we might do together at some point. But these guys were deadly serious,' recalled one adviser. He watched with horror as those present vied with each other to produce the most radical and outlandish ideas, none more so than Rees-Mogg. 'What is the number one problem with the UK energy system?' he asked. Silence. 'Not enough nuclear power,' he said, answering his own question. 'We need more small reactors in the UK.' 'How would you do it?' one asked. 'We should get a nuclear submarine to dock at Liverpool and plug it into the grid. That would show people it was safe.' Shock. Simon Case quietly interjected, 'I fear that's a non-starter: the submarines are needed on operations.' 'No one even laughed. It was totally pie in the sky. I thought they should've been blowing up these ideas rather than legitimizing them,' said another present. After they left, her young aides rounded on her: 'Liz, this is totally mad. You're not really serious about these ideas, are you?' 'I was worried,' Kwarteng later said. 'Liz was losing her perspective. She was beating Rishi Sunak, vanquishing establishment sceptics William Hague, Michael Howard and *The Times*. And she thought she had done it by talking about the folly of "abacus economics" [a term for 'Treasury orthodoxy', or the Treasury's obsession with balancing the books, in contrast to more ambitious deficit spending]. She believed she had a mandate and was now going to go for it.'

At this point, mid-August, another group came into her orbit. 'Let me know how we can help you think about the transition', was the message sent to both candidates by Simon Case, Cabinet Secretary and head of the civil service, soon after Truss and Sunak were declared winners of the MPs stage on 20 July. Truss had mixed thoughts on reading it. She hadn't formed a high opinion of Case during the Johnson years and 'thought he was a creature of Dominic Cummings', Johnson's once powerful political strategist, an insider recalled. She had already decided with Kwarteng to sack Tom Scholar, the permanent secretary at the Treasury, and had thoughts of moving Case on too. Could the head of Whitehall, which she believed had done so much damage holding back the country, really help her, she pondered? From the outset, Case worked supremely hard to be helpful and personable: dealing with Prime Ministers (and would-be Prime Ministers) was a particular forte. 'Within a few weeks, if not days, his skill on the transition and advice on how the Cabinet Office machinery worked ensured she quickly came to rely [on him],' said an aide. 'Simon was fully aware of the deep suspicion towards the civil service, and from the outset was going to lean over backwards to show she had no grounds for her concerns,' said an insider. They quickly developed a strong personal chemistry: 'Her dependency on him was evident: he was operating as if he was already Cabinet secretary to the Prime Minister,' said another.

Helping Truss set up her transition team base at the Foreign Secretary's country residence at Chevening was one of his early tricks. 'It was absolutely awful, no catering, poor Wi-Fi and incredibly hot in the summer weather,' said one of Truss's team. But it was a lot better and more secluded than trying to work from offices in London with the constant presence of the media, which had decided that she was the heir apparent. So from the week starting Monday 8 August, she set up camp at Chevening, and it was there, until the team departed on Friday 2 September, that the blueprint for her premiership was hammered out.

Down to Kent trooped the cream of the civil service, with one exception: the shortly to be defenestrated Tom Scholar. The Treasury's Cat Little, Philip Duffy and Beth Russell were the most frequent attenders. They did voice caution, but Truss was not taking the criticisms on board. 'You can't do it all now,' the officials said to her. 'But what she heard them say was "you can't do it *at all*", which was not what they were saying,' recalled one present.

Fully mindful of the public comments Truss had made about her dislike of the Treasury and its views, the civil servants trod carefully. 'To a man and woman, they were eager to show that they were on side and ready to deliver whatever she wanted,' said one present. 'It was a bit strange for them, giving advice to the Foreign Secretary and not to the Chancellor Rishi Sunak, even if the Cabinet secretary had authorized it. They were building relationships, demonstrating technical competence and showing they could be impartial,' said a Treasury official. 'At the end of the meetings, I could see their faces were in shock. Kwasi seemed to share the horror, but then fell in with it,' said one observer, charged with overseeing liaison with the civil service. The talks had been initiated by Truss's team because they knew they were winning; no such process took place for Sunak's team, who realized it would be a wasted effort.

At the conclusion of one meeting, towards the end of August, Hope passed a note to a senior Cabinet Office official: 'No way you can do this politically. It would mean not hitting the 20k increase to the police force, massive real terms cuts to the NHS, breaking the "triple lock" on pensions, not delivering on the AUKUS pact [trilateral security agreement with the USA and Australia], schools falling in, the Defence Secretary and Home Secretary resigning.' For good measure, he added, 'It's f**king mental.' 'I agree,' the official wrote covertly back to him.

Those who had concerns, however, kept them to themselves, and few even asked probing questions in the meetings. Participants at Chevening were either too afraid of censure and ridicule, or high on the sugar rush of seeing ideas long advocated now rising to the top. Consequently, the conversations became circular and the atmosphere one of self-reinforcing groupthink.

Tax cuts were going to be at the core of Project Truss, as promised in the campaign. The economic and political climate would allow nothing else. But were the conditions still right for speedy and radical change? High spending during the Covid pandemic meant gross government debt in September 2022 had risen to an alarming 100.2 per cent of GDP, while productivity growth and business investment were sluggish.[49] On top of all this, the cost of living crisis was beginning to make itself felt, with the price of fuel rising by 40 per cent in August 2022. In his Budget back in March, Sunak had raised income tax, National Insurance contributions and corporation tax, resulting in 'the biggest overall UK tax burden since the 1960s'.[50] Tax cuts dominated the leadership campaign, with even Sunak saying that he would cut the basic rate of income tax by the end of the next Parliament. The principal Budget questions for Truss's team thus were: where should the tax cuts fall, how would they be balanced by spending cuts, and how could the confidence of the markets be maintained?

The politicians who came down to the meetings at Chevening, many eager for top positions in the Treasury, jockeyed for Truss's ear and for who could be the most radical. One of the hot plugs suggested that the government should remove all barriers to rich Russians coming to London to boost the economy. Rees-Mogg advocated abolishing inheritance tax and removing tax relief on civil servants working from home, a proposal that gained traction until it was pulled late in the day.[51] His angling to be Chancellor never stood a hope. She had settled on Kwarteng, who may have been less of a true believer, but whom she trusted after years of friendship. She thought, correctly, that he would be easier to push around than any one of the other opinionated tall men. Rees-Mogg's influence was to wane during August: she was told either he or his team were leaking when some of his more extreme ideas failed to gain traction, and he was excluded from some late meetings. She was fond of Simon Clarke, who pressed strongly for 'investment zones', which chimed with her. John Redwood was a figure early on at Chevening until he made it clear that he didn't want to become a minister for personal financial reasons, so was replaced by Chris Philp, who was to succeed Clarke as Chief Secretary to the Treasury in September.

Truss's chief economic adviser Matt Sinclair represented the views of economists Mark Littlewood, Julian Jessop and Gerard Lyons at the meetings. Equally, he was the voice of Matthew Elliott and Jon Moynihan who were not physically present, but whose influence was never far away, the former on operational matters and the latter on ideology and structures. Sinclair pressed hard on freezing alcohol and stamp duties, and reducing income tax, and observers felt he might have had a role in radicalizing Kwarteng, but he never won Truss's full confidence. As she kept reminding them, she needed no one telling her what she should do. She had made up her own mind and didn't need to be told to be radical. 'Her inner conviction was always telling her let's go further, further, further. It all came from her,' said one present. 'It was all Liz. She had a very clear programme in her mind from day one. We had to deliver. No excuses,' recalled Clarke.

Time pressed down on Truss. Every day that passed was bringing her closer to Downing Street, but she didn't feel her agenda was anything like ready. 'She had a manic restless energy all the time. "We have only two years left in this Parliament. We have to act now. Now! We have to be bold!"', was her constant refrain, according to a political ally who was there. But unlike Gordon Brown taking over in similar circumstances, she never contemplated a snap election to gain a personal mandate, as she knew she'd be trounced. 'She wanted to have the very maximum time to deliver the changes she thought the country needed,' Fullbrook said. Some speculated if the haste stemmed in part from a deep inner anxiety, a doubt whether she really had it in her to be Prime Minister. 'She felt she had to make her mark early on to prove to herself that she really could do it,' said one. An official who worked closely with her concurs. 'Her strategy was to go really hard to get as much done as she possibly could, and then hunker down. She knew she had a highly divided party and no personal mandate. She wanted to do it all before her political capital dwindled altogether.'

She knew that the state of the Conservative Party was precarious. Johnson's great election victory in 2019 had united them under the slogan 'Get Brexit Done'. But beyond that single issue, the manifesto was thin. He had delivered little on the nebulous concept of 'Levelling Up' and there was no chance of an 'Australian-style points system' for immigration.[52] Failure exacerbated division and blame. The party was also still nursing deep wounds since the 2016 referendum, divided on their views of Europe, on immigration, and between the 'One Nation' tradition Tories and the more free market-inclined MPs. 'It was impossible to manage. There was no clear sense of what the party wanted to do any longer. I basically thought that the best way to handle it was just to get on and do things', she said.[53]

Mid-August was when Truss fatefully decided that the financial measures, including tax cuts, announced within days of her becoming Prime Minister would not include spending cuts to balance them. Cuts would be announced later in the autumn, as part of the Medium-Term Fiscal Plan. 'When it came to finding cuts in spending to offset the tax reductions, she really wasn't interested in doing the easy thing. She seemed to enjoy the risk of it all, the bravado,' said one witness.

The Circle Narrows

Truss was continuing to change inwardly, according to those who had known her for several years, becoming tetchier, more distrustful and imperious. Never comfortable with challenge, she was now even more intolerant and suspicious of those who queried her judgement. An illustration of this came when the possibility of Suella Braverman as Home Secretary arose in conversation. 'Surely not!' said one of her team, bursting out laughing. Truss marched the aide out into the garden. 'It's not your place to offer advice on who I'm going to have in my Cabinet. You're lucky to be on the team. Stay in your lane,' she shouted. People noticed that her trait of humiliating her team in front of others became more pronounced. 'She couldn't abide any contention. It was either all in with her, or all out. A very peculiar personality type,' said an aide.

As the days passed, she grew ready to embrace radicalism. Her three core initial priorities – reverse the corporation tax rise, pause the green tax on energy and cancel the rise in National Insurance contributions – no longer sufficed. For a few days, she became fixated on the bankers' bonus issue. 'Yes, it may be fiscally neutral, but it is still careless politics,' Jones warned her. This provoked some healthy, if forthright, disagreement.

'On Sunday 14 August we were suddenly told to down tools; [that] there will be no further meetings on transition with us, no more work for now,' recalled Ranil Jayawardena, the MP Truss had charged with directing the transition.[54] It was no longer just aides being shown the door; ministerial big-hitters like Clarke and Philp were too. Their sin? Arguing that tax cuts had to be at least partially offset by cuts in spending. 'Whenever we mentioned it, Liz was manic – "no, no, no" – and made it very clear to us it was not something she was going to do,' said one present. 'There were a number of possible options worked up, but these were not taken forwards,' said Chris Philp. 'I think that if the tax plans had at least been partly funded on the spending side as I argued, then the reaction of the financial markets would have been different.'[55]

They were not the only people talking about it; Kwarteng had been equally concerned. Truss was absolutely clear she wasn't going to include savings. 'I've been Chief Secretary to the Treasury. It's a whole world of pain if you talk about cuts, especially in a campaign. Let's just go for it,' she told him. 'But why are we trying to do it all now? We have a Budget in the spring,' he asked her in private at Chevening. She rounded on him. 'Look, we've only got two years.' Taking his political life into his own hands, he reminded her that Thatcher had bided her time for two years until 1981 before her defining Budget. 'At that, Liz freaked out,' he said. So he tempered his line, knowing the case he was putting forward enraged her. Did he wonder whether her promise of the Chancellorship might be jeopardized if he persisted? 'I should've put my foot down harder,' he admitted later.[56]

Gerard Lyons, the economist who had been advising Mordaunt till she was knocked out, had mixed feelings about Truss, but in a call with her mid-August, he gave similar warnings. He endorsed reversing the corporation tax and National Insurance increases, telling her, 'Reversing them is necessary to prevent the economy falling into the recession that many economists are predicting.' But he expressed the need for great caution if the larger prize of freeing up the economy was not to be put at risk. Then at pivotal meetings at Chevening on Monday 29 August and Saturday 3 September, he went into more detail. At that 3 September meeting, Truss, flanked by Kwarteng and Sinclair, met with Lyons and economists Julian Jessop and Andrew Lilico. The economists were supportive of her growth agenda, but in a note Lyons and Jessop submitted beforehand that was leaked to the *Guardian* and the *Financial Times*, they warned that 'the markets are in a febrile state… very wary of your interventions – you must tread very carefully. If immediate economic policy announcements are handled badly, then a market crash is possible.'[57] They expanded on their concerns at the meeting: the pound had weakened, foreign holdings of gilts and UK equities were high, expectations were low. The need for keeping the markets on side was paramount. At the meetings, the economists thought that Truss asked the most pertinent questions and seemed most on top of the material, but they worried about her overconfidence.[58] This was not the 'blob' talking to them, but blue-blooded economists. The warning, on the cusp of Downing Street, could not have been clearer.

They were alarmed that she might spoil the best opportunity to enact free-market policies for many years by bad delivery. In a note that Lyons sent to Kwarteng at the end of August, he warned, 'You need someone to mark your homework.' Specifically, this meant having the Office for Budget Responsibility (OBR), set up by Chancellor George Osborne in 2010, commenting on the financial measures. Lyons knew that the OBR epitomized everything that Truss and Kwarteng deplored about the establishment, but believed the volatile state of the markets made its involvement inevitable.

In Truss's view, the OBR, the Treasury and the Bank of England formed 'an axis of evil'. During the campaign, she had been open about her criticism of the Bank and its Governor, Andrew Bailey, for not doing more to tackle inflation. Menacing threats about how she would curtail the Bank and even change its mandate peaked in early August. Jon Moynihan was the most vocal of her ear-whisperers in this quest. 'Everyone in the City is telling me to sack the Governor,' she told one startled economist in August who was surprised the prime ministerial candidate did not seem to know she wouldn't have the power to do this. It was left to Labour's shadow Chancellor Rachel Reeves to point out the obvious: it was 'deeply irresponsible' for her to threaten to change the Bank's mandate and attack the Governor on the brink of a recession, which 'creates huge uncertainty that will hold back vital investment'.[59] The tone changed in mid-August. Truss and Kwarteng realized that talking about changes to the Bank's mandate was not good for the distressed pound, and they 'should be hugging the Bank of England closely instead', as one of the Bank's senior leaders put it. Kwarteng would duly announce on his first day as Chancellor his 'full support for the independent Bank of England'.[60] Bank-bashing in public was off the table, but they doubled down on criticizing the OBR and Treasury orthodoxy. Moynihan was the 'captain or chief of the institutionbashers', with Elliott, Rees-Mogg, Philp, Littlewood and Sinclair key players in the team. Kwarteng was 'on the bench', according to one aide. This description misses the point: the team captain was always Truss herself. The opposition to Truss orthodoxy never stood a chance.

'The final two weeks of August were pivotal,' recalled Clarke. 'With an unassailable polling lead and most votes already safely cast by party members, Liz settled in at Chevening for a blizzard of meetings. Here her distaste for "abacus economics", always present, won over caution,' he concluded.[61] 'Spending cuts are not something I am going to do in the fiscal event,' she told her team, referring to what would become the Mini-Budget announced on 23 September. She hadn't listened to the economists, but maybe she would listen to her ministerial backers. They joined together and sent her a note on 30 August summarizing the tax and spending cut options, which included the idea of uncoupling increases in welfare benefits from inflation from April 2023. '[We] need to maintain the confidence of the bond markets in our fiscal plans or we will find ourselves paying higher interest rates on new gilt issues… In order to navigate the choices available, we need to have some kind of medium-term fiscal rules within which to operate to maintain the confidence of the bond markets,' it said.

'Drop these ideas. We are not interested in running with them,' Sinclair told one adviser over the phone. In case they hadn't got the message, Truss underlined it for them herself. 'We don't need to talk about all this,' she told them when they persisted that cuts must appear as part of the planned fiscal event. When the fiscal measures went disastrously wrong, there was a rush to rewrite history, hence these quotations from contemporary documents.

Energy Price Angst

By this point Truss could not avoid talking about the astronomic rise in fuel prices and the cost of living crisis. Initially, she was not inclined to subsidize energy bills. Then, abruptly, she changed her mind. What had happened? Why did she change her mind on energy support but display total rigidity on plans for the fiscal event that was so perturbing some of her team?

'Liz was very concerned in July and early August about the costs of any energy intervention, and Rishi coming after her for fiscal irresponsibility,' said one of them. But the August forecasts of a massive energy price spike in the year ahead changed her tune. 'She felt she had to do something because she wouldn't survive, she thought that no Prime Minister would, if everything went south. She changed from being very hawkish about reducing state spending to spending a lot of money to fix this,' said Alex Boyd, who had advised Truss in International Trade and the Foreign Office and was now working for her on energy.[62]

News that she was looking for some form of intervention had an unintended consequence. 'It created great interest in the markets,' said one of the Bank of England's senior leaders. 'Once it became clear Sunak wouldn't win, the markets became very volatile. Everything hinged on what an energy support package might mean. If handouts and rebates, inflation would increase; if a cap, it would be counter-inflationary.' Throughout August, the Bank's Monetary Policy Committee monitored her thinking and every utterance forensically. 'She was being very coy about it, and it led to questions about whether she really had a plan,' he added.

But what to do? Simon Case, drawing on his experience of crisis management when working in No. 10 and the Cabinet Office, stepped in and became a decisive figure. 'He was very conscious of the risks and dangers, and was working on them closely with Kwasi,' said one of Truss's team. On 4 August, Case convened a meeting in 70 Whitehall, the home of the Cabinet Office, on the challenges in the energy market following the invasion of Ukraine, the ensuing sanctions cutting gas supplies, and the hot European summer putting pressure on hydroelectric power and nuclear reactors that were running short of cooling water.[63] Various solutions were debated then and in the following days including delinking gas and electricity prices. The free-marketeers argued that no intervention remained the best option and they became increasingly irritated by the time and energy Truss and Kwarteng were putting into the issue rather than into the economic proposals.

During the dry August days, hours were eaten up as her team listened to presentations from officials with charts showing the likely impact of price increases. 'At its worst, pubs, shops and independent traders would have to cease trading – hugely sobering,' said one aide. Truss settled on a price cap, Case's favoured option, with the government paying the difference. The resistance she encountered from the Department for Business, Energy and Industrial Strategy in particular confirmed all her prejudices about the civil service. 'She bulldozed her way through huge internal lethargy: we would never have had it in place without her personal bloody-mindedness,' said one observer. Much of the heavy lifting was done by official Madelaine McTernan, latterly director general of the Vaccine Taskforce, whom Case drafted in to drive the work. Ofgem's confirmation on 26 August that bills would rise to more than £3,500 a year injected further adrenaline into the system.[64] Predictions that the average household bill would jump to £6,000 a year, driving inflation to 15 per cent, created further anxiety.[65]

Truss was under pressure from two quarters: Littlewood, the economist who preferred to do nothing or to have minimal intervention, and Jones and Hope pressing her to go as far as fiscally possible. She rejected the Labour solution of a windfall tax or means testing. She knew that there could be no new taxes and accepted the argument that generous help would get the country through and would not be nearly as expensive as the naysayers predicted. The unpredictability of the forward curve on energy prices caused much anguish when it came to settling on what the level of support should be: officials suggested somewhere between £2,000 and £3,000, and she decided to split the difference, rejecting advice from the Treasury that it should last for six months only. 'I want to give people some security and not have them worrying about the future. It will last two years,' she declared to one adviser. With the leadership contest still in full flow, she was reluctant to come out about the energy price cap in public, concealing it in an interview with George Parker of the *Financial Times*.[66] 'She felt at the time she had to conceal what she was about to reveal if she became PM, but felt that the markets would be able to absorb the cost of the package,' an aide recalled.

Truss was in her element, pushing for long-term contracts with the major gas suppliers – the Qataris, Norwegians and Americans. Discussions that opened at Chevening continued into No. 10 before petering out. But the Energy Price Guarantee, announced by Truss to the House of Commons on Thursday 8 September, two days after becoming PM, went ahead. She announced plans to freeze energy bills at an average of £2,500 a year for two years as part of a package of support for homes and businesses.

The Verdict: Have a Clear and Realistic Plan?

How did Truss fare on this second requirement for a successful premiership? Truss's plan for government was not fully complete when she became Prime Minister on Tuesday 6 September. She signed off the details of her Energy Price Guarantee late on the Wednesday evening before announcing it in the House of Commons the next day. But many of her hopes – to secure long-term gas contracts and to provide long-term energy security through nuclear, fracking and onshore wind sources – were not completed and remained in planning. Freeing up onshore wind had been a particular passion, with her desire to ensure a much quicker connection to the national grid. But her ambition to balance the spending on the Energy Price Guarantee with energy reforms to make a once in a generation shift in energy supply were, like so many of her plans, to come to nothing.

Her economic agenda more generally was still incomplete when she became Prime Minister. She had wanted to see a huge supply-side injection of enterprise into the economy, with significant investment in roads and other connections to allow the economy to move faster. Planning permission would be reformed, removing 'green' obligations to spur building.[67] 'Investment zones' were a particular passion that would have a combination of low tax, tax relief and low regulation. 'More, we want more,' she would regularly say. When aides explained that such zones would suck economic activity from nearby areas, her response was, 'Let's see, press ahead.'

How to kickstart economic growth was the priority above everything else. There was little discussion of any departure from existing foreign and defence policy, and reforms in areas such as health, education and social care were barely considered. 'I intended coming round to them towards the end of the Parliament in the run-up to the general election,' she said.[68] Everything was swallowed up in her ambition to fire up the economy. The plan for the fiscal event was broadly in place when she moved into Downing Street. It would focus on supply-side reform, reverse the planned rises in National Insurance contributions and corporation tax, and include tax cuts still to be agreed. While some of the wilder reveries of Rees-Mogg et al. had been discarded, the decisions on the abolition of the 45p rate of income tax and the cap on bankers' bonuses had not yet been taken. But the fateful decisions to exclude the OBR and to postpone announcing cuts in spending had.

The verdict? Truss came to power with a bold plan, a benefit many recent Prime Ministers did not have. But it was not realistic to launch it in the way she did, or at the time she did, or with some of the content she did. She could have involved the OBR, who might have provided some much-needed scepticism. As it was, the atmosphere led to a cycle of self-reinforcing groupthink as confidence and daring led to arrogance and, ultimately, hubris. Some of those alongside her overplay the extent of their contemporary warnings. But the written evidence from the time is clear. She was explicitly warned of the risks of what she was doing. She has no one else to blame but herself.

Rule Number Three: The Prime Minister must appoint a loyal and capable team. Here at her first cabinet with Coffey and Rees-Mogg on Wednesday 7 September

3

APPOINT THE BEST CABINET/TEAM

1–7 September 2022

Truss needed to appoint the strongest and most representative Cabinet possible if she was to have any chance of negotiating the perilous waters ahead. Achieving this is the third requirement for a successful premiership. The office of Prime Minister lacks executive power: it lies in the hands of the Cabinet ministers who carry out the work of government on behalf of the PM. If the Prime Minister does not appoint, motivate and work with the best, they will underperform. 'Prime Ministers must govern with others', was the thesis of the supreme post-war specialist on the Cabinet, George W. Jones: 'They depend upon the support or at least tacit compliance of their fellow ministers to achieve their goals. This cooperation is not automatic and must be won.'[1] Who better than Liz Truss to know this? She had served under Cameron, May and Johnson, and had ringside seats in each of their departures. Incredibly, she was the first Prime Minister since Eden in 1955 to serve in Cabinet under three PMs (Baldwin, Chamberlain and Churchill in Eden's case). Did she, we may ask, learn anything from experience and history?

The Prime Minister has to be both manager of their team as well as the captain on the pitch. 'Hero Prime Ministers' who try to do too much themselves, like Chamberlain in the Munich Crisis or

Eden during the Suez Crisis, and who become detached from their Cabinets, become unstuck. This is what happened to Blair over Iraq, or Thatcher over the poll tax at the end of her premiership. Spurned Cabinets will eventually bite the Prime Minister. Hero premiers never end well.

The PM and Cabinet in History

The modern Cabinet did not exist when Robert Walpole became the first Prime Minister in 1721. Heads of departments including the Treasury and the Southern and Northern Departments (out of which would be formed the Home Office and the Foreign Office) owed their appointment and allegiance to the monarch and discussed department business directly with them. The monarch could also seek advice from the Privy Council, which included notables such as the Lord Chancellor and the Archbishop of Canterbury, but which lacked any sense of collective responsibility.

During the eighteenth century, the sense of a decision-making Cabinet operating with the Prime Minister and responsible for its own decisions grew, though unevenly and uncertainly. In February 1746, in protest at George II's taking political advice from non-ministers, and in opposition to his unilateral appointments, Prime Minister Henry Pelham (1743–54), his senior Cabinet ministers and dozens of junior ministers resigned over the course of a few days (Pelham resumed office shortly after at the King's request). This helped to create the doctrine that the Cabinet was *collectively* responsible for the direction of policy. In 1782, the fall of Lord North saw the resignation of all his ministers too, enshrining the custom that a discredited ministry resigned entirely with the PM.[2]

Pitt the Younger after 1783 began to utilize the Cabinet as a valuable resource, promoting a crop of talented young politicians, who would ultimately dominate British politics for decades.

Up until the twentieth century, the system of Cabinet, though increasingly underpinned by convention and tradition, retained the gentlemanly amateurism of its early days. Minutes were not taken at all, though Prime Ministers dutifully recorded Cabinet proceedings in their letters to the monarch. On occasion, Cabinet met and ministers would leave the meeting without a clear idea of what had been decided.[3]

David Lloyd George (1916–22) effectively created the modern premiership with his creation of the Cabinet Secretariat (which became the Cabinet Office) and the position of Cabinet secretary in December 1916, and from this point onwards, Cabinet became more organised and was underpinned by a stronger bureaucracy. From now on, Cabinet minutes were taken, agendas circulated and proper process added to what had been, for the first 200 years of the role of Prime Minister, an unabashedly fluid system.

At the same time, the size and ambition of government expanded enormously into economic, healthcare and social policy areas. Suddenly, the Prime Minister had to be a chief executive at the head, not just of politics and Parliament, but also a burgeoning administration in Whitehall.

Clement Attlee (1945–51) set the standard. A master at appointing and sacking, he had a slew of war-blooded ministers from Churchill's Coalition government to slot into the right positions, including Ernest Bevin at the Foreign Office, Hugh Dalton at the Treasury and Herbert Morrison as Leader of the House. He was equally good at spotting fresh talent, like Nye Bevan, whom he appointed to oversee the creation of the NHS. The uncharismatic and retiring Attlee proved to be without equal at Cabinet management, holding it together through the period of the biggest domestic policy activism of the twentieth century.

Harold Wilson after 1964 was accomplished too at promoting talent, appointing Cabinet ministers of the calibre of Roy Jenkins to the Home Office, James Callaghan to the Treasury and Denis Healey to the Ministry of Defence. Wilson fell far short of Attlee, though, at managing Cabinet and spent huge political resources trying to do so often at the cost of clarity of direction.

Truss's lodestar Thatcher appointed a broad-based Cabinet in May 1979, recognizing that she was not yet politically strong enough to fill it with true believers in her free-market philosophy. She waited over two years before dismissing 'wets', including Lord Soames, Mark Carlisle and Ian Gilmour, in a reshuffle in late 1981. In their place came figures ideologically close to her, such as Nigel Lawson as Energy Secretary, Norman Tebbit as Employment Secretary and her philosophical soulmate Keith Joseph at Education. For the next seven years, until she began to lose her grip over the Cabinet, she was in command of her team.

Cabinet Selection

Did Truss spend time pondering her idol's statecraft? If she did, there is little evidence that it informed her decisions.

By 15 August, recognizing that she was going to win, she began to focus on who she would choose as her Chancellor. One arch supporter had convinced himself that he was the ideal fit. He would become the Nigel Lawson figure who, for six years after 1983 until they fell out, had been Thatcher's agenda-changing Chancellor. Jacob Rees-Mogg saw himself as heir to Lawson, his intellectual equal and as zealous a champion of the free market. He imagined Kwasi Kwarteng would continue as Business, Energy and Industrial Strategy Secretary (with perhaps the title of Deputy Prime Minister to boost his esteem). He launched into his suit with the passion of Malvolio wooing Olivia. Truss's Foreign Office special advisers, playing the parts of Fabian and Feste, were horrified that she might appoint him, especially after the, to their mind, ludicrous ideas he had postulated at Chevening. 'All of us inside the tent knew Jacob could never be Chancellor: you only had to hear his flat rate tax and other mad ideas to realize his thinking was politically toxic,' said one.

Truss either did not notice or did not care what her minions thought. She had already decided that she had absolutely no intention of appointing Rees-Mogg. She wanted to be Chancellor in all but name and to receive the credit for the success of the measures, not to appoint an intellectual loudmouth with his own ideas who would play to the gallery. So she decided to sideline him, doing so in a particularly brutal way. She and Ruth Porter had established two work streams at Chevening: an economy strand and an energy support package strand. One morning in August, he arrived at Chevening and was surprised to learn an economy meeting was about to begin. Truss intercepted him. 'Jacob, this is a meeting that we didn't need you at,' she said. Those present noticed him wince. A figure of immense dignity as well as sensitivity, they noticed how subdued he was for the rest of the day as the truth sunk in that he would not be handed the prize he desperately sought.

Truss, of course, had long had her ideal candidate in mind. Kwarteng was her long-term friend and Greenwich neighbour and he shared many of her beliefs. She knew he would ultimately always yield to her. 'She asked me around 18 July as she and Rishi got into the final two,' he said later. 'We had written two books and collaborated together. It was always the understanding.'[4] If it was, no one else was in on the understanding, and not everyone was pleased. Cabinet Secretary Simon Case for one. He was 'pretty frank' with Truss about the risks of appointing him. 'I know Kwasi Kwarteng well,' she told him, implying that she had his measure. Her reassurance didn't totally convince the sceptics, recorded an insider. To succeed Kwarteng as Business Secretary she wanted Simon Clarke, although he felt unable to take the post for personal reasons, so she had to think again. Clarke was appointed to Levelling Up Secretary, swapped with Rees-Mogg who took the Business portfolio while keeping responsibility for Brexit opportunities to assuage his Treasury disappointment – a not inconsiderable empire.

These positions were all decided by Monday 22 August. The Cabinet Office sent down to Chevening the celebrated 'whiteboard' on which recent Prime Ministers and their teams have planned reshuffles. 'Oh my goodness, the whiteboard exercise was grim,' Truss later said.[5] 'The fact they sent it down to us two weeks before the result was a clear indication to us that the civil service thought we would win,' said Fullbrook.[6] With the board came Whitehall's software programme, which the team refused to use because it had been written by a member of Cummings' team. 'We were not going to put our most secret stuff somewhere where that man could read our innermost thoughts,' said an aide. Truss's fear and hatred of Cummings permeated across her close advisers.

Only one position was already pledged before the board was even erected. No sooner had Truss made the offer of Home Secretary to

Suella Braverman in mid-July than she regretted it. In addition to her Foreign Office team's objections to the appointment she now had to cope with disapproval from Fullbrook as well. Fullbrook pressed her to rescind the offer on the grounds that Braverman was not loyal and would, he believed, brief against her. 'I'm sorry, Mark, but it was decided before you joined the team,' she confessed to him. As the big day approached, Truss herself became increasingly anxious about the decision, wanting to make her Justice Secretary instead, and putting Brandon Lewis in as Home Secretary. Braverman would have none of it: Truss's attempt to renege on their deal did nothing to improve their relationship.

For her Cabinet-making, Truss leaned on a very small team. Apart from Fullbrook, the key influence was Coffey. She listened to Coffey. 'A former PM had told her that the one lesson she should know is that she cannot trust another politician 100 per cent. She told him he was wrong. She trusted Thérèse Coffey absolutely 100 per cent,' one recalled. Always earmarked for Deputy Prime Minister, Truss wanted her to combine the role with that of Chief Whip. 'Liz had a strong sense that the Chief Whip should be a woman, given the issues that had plagued Boris and ultimately led to his downfall. She was right in this regard. It was symbolically important,' said Stein.[7] So when Coffey flatly turned her old friend down, Truss had to move quickly because time was short and the Chief Whip would be integral to the reshuffle. She rued her failure to persuade Iain Duncan Smith to do it. But he wanted a bigger job, not unreasonably having been party leader twenty years earlier, and she was getting desperate. Worrying that she wouldn't find someone in time, she alighted on Wendy Morton who had been a junior whip, won plaudits for her work on Truss's campaign and had an impeccable back story, being both state educated and representing a West Midlands constituency. Concerns she was relatively inexperienced and considered by some to be too gentle for the post were swept aside. 'Liz wanted to appoint someone who, after the Johnson years, would tackle the behavioural issues and set a new tone,' said one Truss parliamentary ally.

But had Truss gone too far the other way? In recent history the Chief Whip has often been a bruiser, especially with the Conservative Party being so fractious. Without a touch of fear and menace, it wasn't clear that this Chief Whip was going to be able to ensure control. Truss was aware of these concerns, and instituted a number of changes, including announcing that the whips were to be moved back to 12 Downing Street where they hadn't worked for twenty-one years (having been relocated to the less prestigious and non-adjacent 9 Downing Street in 2001), and though the Chief Whip was only attending Cabinet (rather than a full member) Truss ensured that Morton became a member of her inner circle.

Nadhim Zahawi, eliminated after the first round of the MPs' ballots, was next. As Johnson's serving Chancellor, he was the highest ranking candidate for a job. He had made himself useful to Truss in her quest to secure long-term energy supplies; in Fullbrook, his former campaign manager, he had a strong ally too. She wanted to utilize his personal-management and organizational skills as a fixer across-the-board, facilitating government relations. So she slotted him into the Cabinet as Chancellor of the Duchy of Lancaster to allow him to range widely.

Mordaunt, eliminated after the fifth and final round of the MPs stage and with a demonstrably wide following among MPs and party membership, had wanted either to return as Defence Secretary or be promoted to one of the great offices of state, but Truss didn't want to move Wallace, least of all in the midst of the war in Ukraine, and the other spots of Foreign Secretary, Home Secretary and Chancellor were taken. Mordaunt wasn't considered a friend, and Truss, loving her power, was in no mood to accommodate the wishes of the one-time front runner who had fallen only five MP votes short of her crown. Mordaunt was offered Party Chair or Northern Ireland Secretary, both of which she declined, reluctantly accepting instead Leader of the Commons.

In contrast, Truss liked Kemi Badenoch, who had been eliminated after the fourth round, but she had to make do with International Trade Secretary. Tom Tugendhat, eliminated after the third round, had been offered Foreign Secretary at the start of the competition if he backed her. He declined, only to come back to her some days later having changed his mind. Not the loyalty I require, Truss felt. 'So he got a much smaller thank you from her: he had had his opportunity,' said a member of the team dismissively. He had to make do as Minister for Security.

That left the job Iain Duncan Smith wanted: Foreign Secretary. James Cleverly had been one of Truss's Ministers of State at the Foreign Office. She liked and trusted him, so she gave him the nod, to the irritation of some of the staff, who complained, 'You are selling it too cheaply without getting anything back.' 'She had loved being Foreign Secretary and it meant a lot to offer it to him,' said an aide.

She made up the rest of the Cabinet by rewarding loyalists: Brandon Lewis to Justice Secretary, Ranil Jayawardena to Environment Secretary, Anne-Marie Trevelyan to Transport Secretary, Chris Philp to Chief Secretary to the Treasury, and Jake Berry became Minister without Portfolio and Party Chair. Johnson loyalists Alister Jack was retained at the Scotland Office and Kit Malthouse at Education.

Coffey on top of Deputy Prime Minister was given Health, an extraordinarily naïve move. The department was under considerable duress and demanded a full-time and experienced Cabinet minister. The DPM equally required a full-time incumbent. Both Coffey and Truss were responsible for the folly of her taking on both posts; as a result, a proficient politician managed neither DPM nor Health well.

The name that most stood out to contemporaries was Michael Ellis, who was appointed to the non-Cabinet (but attending) post of Attorney General. Why was this odd? Because he was the most senior Sunak supporter during the campaign to be given a job. 'He was selected because we deemed him an honourable person, and it sent a message to the Sunak camp that all was not lost. We only needed one in that message,' said a senior figure in Truss's team. Job done, they thought. Or was it? Sunak ally Robert Jenrick, who had been Johnson's Housing Secretary, was also given a junior post that Truss regarded as 'the key olive branch to the Sunak side', according to one close to Truss. But Chris Skidmore, who had jumped across to Truss during the party membership stage, was not but was asked to head up a review into Net Zero instead.

Truss decreed, not least because she considered Sunak's team to have been so vicious in the final two weeks of the campaign, that there would be no further reaching out. 'She regarded Rishi as screwing her in the campaign, alongside his team, and she was seething,' said one of her side. She was never going to offer a job to Michael Gove; Sunak's principal lieutenants Oliver Dowden, Dominic Raab, Julian Smith and Gavin Williamson were also overlooked. As was Sunak himself, having made it clear he wouldn't accept any position. Truss's personal dislike of him ran very deep. Of all the members of Team Sunak, she came closest to appointing Raab, her predecessor as

Foreign Secretary, but 'Dom had made some disobliging comments about her and she worried that Labour would make great play of it, so he was passed over,' said an aide. A series of Johnson's ministers were told that their services were no longer required: Steve Barclay as Health Secretary, Greg Clark as Levelling Up Secretary and George Eustice as Environment Secretary. Proven senior Cabinet ministers Jeremy Hunt and Sajid Javid were bypassed. Simon Hart was removed as Welsh Secretary to be replaced by Robert Buckland.

The rationale was justified by harking back to her two female predecessors as Prime Minister. 'She thought Thatcher had made a clear mistake by appointing enemies to her Cabinet and then having to get rid of them,' said an insider, which speaks of Truss's misreading of the history of early Thatcher. From Theresa May's experience in July 2016 when she appointed a broad-based Cabinet including both strong Brexiteers and Remainers, she also took a lesson. The three years of in-fighting that followed, never more so than at the infamous 'Chequers summit' in July 2018 for crunch Brexit talks, were cited as showing the futility of a broad-based Cabinet. But the analogy breaks down because the world Truss faced in September 2022 was so totally different to the one May faced after July 2018. Rather, Truss's attitude was 'I've got to the top now'. Some confidants like junior minister Daniel Johnson advised her to go for a narrow-based Cabinet: 'I thought she had so little time to make an impact, she needed to work just with loyalists,' he said. 'But I was wrong.'[8] She didn't need anyone to tell her what to do after her years of being patronized, as she saw it, by public school men. 'I've beaten my enemies, I've beaten the f**king establishment. I'm not going to bother to build bridges,' was her attitude, as described by a member of the team. 'Having won she felt emboldened to do whatever she wanted: Liz habitually turned the dial up to 11, in the hope she'd get 70–80 per cent of what she wanted,' but now, 'she decided to take on most of the economic establishment, half the Tory party without the secure base to do it,' said Adam Jones.[9]

Sophie Jarvis had her first row with Truss over her Cabinet-making. 'You haven't got a majority of eighty,' she told her. 'You've got to bring people with you.'

'I am not going to have any "wets" in Cabinet,' Truss replied (harking back to Thatcher's mistrusted centre-left ministers).

'You can't call them "wets", Liz. You've got to form the government that will last.'

'Sorry. Let's just f**king go for it,' was her tart response.

In opting for such a narrow Cabinet, Truss had gone against the advice from senior politicians. One of these was Mordaunt. 'I completely understand, Penny, what you're saying about my building a broad team,' Truss had reassured her over the phone in late July when they discussed Mordaunt pledging her support.[10] Mordaunt urged Truss to offer middle-ranking appointments to two Sunak supporters: Laura Farris and Kevin Hollinrake. Neither made the cut. Jayawardena, initially charged with overseeing the transition, was another to advocate breadth, suggesting figures such as Gillian Keegan, Damian Hinds and Greg Hands. 'But to Liz, her attitude was "you are either for me or against me"', a witness said. Jayawardena could get nowhere, and before long, Porter and Coffey had taken over.

Truss herself completely denies that she made an error in having a narrow Cabinet; indeed, that it even *was* a narrow Cabinet. One senior Cabinet loyalist said, 'It was much broader than the Rishi Sunak Cabinet that followed. She gave jobs to those who had fought against her: Suella, Penny, Kemi and Tom. Rishi made it clear he wouldn't accept a job. She appointed people on the left like Vicky Ford. She brought in people like Robert Jenrick, Michael Ellis and Vicky Prentis.' They asked, 'How can anyone say she appointed an ultra-loyal Cabinet when so few stood by her? The way they behaved was extraordinary.'

Even at the time, contemporary commentators foresaw trouble. 'MPs are seething about her decision to appoint only friends and supporters to Cabinet, and to leave out so many experienced substantial figures,' reported Andrew Marr on LBC.[11] 'Perhaps the best way of illustrating the loss of experience is @trussliz will be the only person who's continuously served in Cabinet for the last six years,' commented Gavin Barwell, May's latter chief of staff, on Twitter.[12] Without realizing it, she was compounding her problem of paper-thin support among backbenchers by alienating large swathes of the party's great and good. She even managed to upset the minnows, by leaving to Coffey and Morton junior ministerial hiring and firing. 'It was silly of Liz not to squeeze every ounce of goodwill out of people by being the one to appoint them, so things got off to a bad start on literally day one,' said a loyal MP.[13]

Coffey and Morton successfully lobbied to bring in some names who would add breadth as Ministers of State, including Victoria Prentis in Work and Welfare and Mark Spencer in Food, Farming and Fisheries. 'The criticisms that she was not inclusive are unfair,' Morton later said, agreeing with Truss.[14] She and Coffey would put up a series of names on the whiteboard for her to say 'I like that, I don't like that'. The process frustrated her. She barely knew her MPs at that personal level, and did not have a good sense of who would be a good appointment and who not. She did not have the experience of

Blair or Cameron, who had had years to lead and get to know their MPs (while also leading their party into an election and meeting candidates). She also suffered because she had no natural allies or supporters. Who was a 'Trussite'? Virtually no one.

Most indeed found it hard to empathize with her. The Brexiteers were sceptical because she had backed Remain until switching with fervour to the Leave camp after the referendum, while Remainers mistrusted her for that very reason. Moderate and centrist MPs thought she was unsound and apt to play to the gallery; an unpredictable firebrand in the eyes of some, to others a figure of ridicule.

Fullbrook masterminded the choreography of reshuffle appointments, with many being seen by Truss in her office the day before the formal handover. Those who were successful were presented with a letter picking out two or three initial objectives. Simon Case remarked that it was the smoothest transition he had seen in his time in Whitehall. It was remarkable for another reason: Palace sources confirm that approving the list of her Cabinet was Queen Elizabeth II's final act as head of state before she died.

Cabinet and No. 10 Management

But it wasn't a smoothly functioning Cabinet, for all its being packed with allies. Cabinet management is a skill Prime Ministers must possess, with the ability to chair meetings efficiently, to handle big egos, to ensure business is properly transacted and ministers are taken along.

Truss arrived with some firm ideas about how she was going to run Cabinet. She had a particular dislike of leaking, born some say of deep experience. So she whittled down the numbers of special advisers and officials permitted to be in attendance, and banned even her own communications team. Even at the time, this struck many people as distinctly odd. When, days later, the first leak happened, 'she was extremely cross', said an official.

Altogether, she presided over six Cabinets: on 7, 9 and 23 September, and 11, 18 and 25 October. Officials noticed little change in her style, which was adequate if not sparkling or even commanding. But from the beginning there were ministers round the Cabinet table, including Mordaunt, who were bitter, felt they had been deceived and had seen their advice to appoint moderates ignored. Braverman was never convinced by Truss – they did not see eye-to-eye on cutting immigration, which was *the* central priority for Braverman – nor was Wallace – with whom she'd clashed over Ukraine. Even among the inner circle of Kwarteng, Coffey, Clarke and Rees-Mogg, there were divisions. The first three were sceptical of her inflexibility and unwillingness to listen to advice, most especially over the Mini-Budget. The seeds were sown for rancorous divisions.

However, all looked promising at her first Cabinet on the morning of Wednesday 7 September. 'She was very clear and very businesslike. She wanted everything done very properly,' said an official. She knew that her time was short, and she had to change the direction and performance of the government if she was to win the general election in 2024. Cabinet ministers had been presented with letters listing their immediate priorities; these were updated, revised and distributed again two weeks later. One aide recalled that the process of preparing them was 'incredibly painful', and that Truss was 'obsessed with getting these right', asking for five redrafts for some of them. She wanted her Cabinet ministers to have clear instructions and to get on with their jobs. 'As Prime Minister, I didn't want to micromanage,' she said.[15]

While some Cabinet ministers were grateful for the clarity of direction in their letters of appointment, others contested their instructions. Braverman wanted Truss to qualify the priority she was given to support growth 'through legal immigration' by underlining the aim 'to reduce immigration in the medium term'. Wallace had different objections, requesting that Truss 'remove references to the MoD facilitating return flights for illegal immigrants', making it clear he did not want 'defence capabilities and real estate used for this purpose'.

The appointment letters reveal Truss's focus on the Mini-Budget and energy support package. She had ambitions across government, to be sure, albeit much of it retreads from earlier administrations, but these were totally subordinated to her ambitions for growth. Her plan for the Treasury stated that 'Our most significant challenge is the historical and present weakness in economic growth. You should be radical and establish an immediate two-year plan, supported by a medium-term plan to boost UK productivity and target an increase trend growth to 2.5 per cent a year.' The details included the need to 'turbocharge the City' and 'reduce the overall tax burden on businesses and households', while stressing the need to 'maintain a firm grip on public spending'.

From Cameron, she also took the idea of a small, high-powered No. 10, although, as an official commented, 'I'm not sure she ever really understood how it operated under him, or any other Prime Minister.' She wanted everyone to be smart and wearing ties, and she wanted to distance herself from the shambolic informality of the Johnson years. His staff were unceremoniously dumped, with foreign affairs specialist and historian John Bew and aide Charlotte Owen two of the few survivors. One position she sought to fill was Downing Street permanent secretary. Nick Catsaras pushed her hard on it, knowing that he wouldn't himself be in for the long run, and that he lacked the Treasury experience he thought vital to the role – the late Jeremy Heywood, who was ex-Treasury and had been Downing Street permanent secretary under Cameron before becoming Cabinet Secretary, was the model he had in mind. In James Bowler, who had worked happily with Truss as her permanent secretary at International Trade, Catsaras thought he had found the ideal candidate. But when Bowler turned it down for personal reasons, 'no suitable alternative could be found, and the idea petered out', said an aide. Simon Case, who had never been greatly enamoured with the idea, went on to do the job de facto, a role at which he did well.

'She invested enormous energy into thinking about No. 10, where everyone was to work, and how she wanted it to operate,' said an official overseeing the transition. The floor plans went through several iterations as she was never satisfied: 'It really mattered to her,' said an aide. No. 10, built in the seventeenth century as a house and modified higgledy-piggledy ever since, doesn't have a designated study for the Prime Minister to use. So she chopped and changed her mind about where she would work, ending up deciding, as had Major, that she'd use the large oblong Cabinet Room as her office. In Downing Street, proximity to the PM is power. The most sought-after space is the room through the double doors at the end of the Cabinet Room, sometimes called 'the den' in which most Prime Ministers from Blair to Johnson had worked. It was in here that Fullbrook, Porter, Catsaras and Jones were crammed, along with the Prime Minister's diary secretary and the ever-present duty clerk.

'We've blown up the No. 10 floor plan,' an aide said. *Spectator* journalist Katy Balls wrote that 'slimming down doesn't just set an example to other departments; it's also intended to create higher accountability'.[16] Almost every Prime Minister arrives in Downing Street thinking that their predecessors had no idea, and that they know how to do it.[17] Truss was no exception, and had a clear vision for No. 10, articulated at the time by Adam Jones: 'Liz doesn't want a presidential-style No. 10. She wants it to be lean, professional and relentlessly focused on delivery, policy-making and legislating. You'll see fewer prime-ministerial visits, fewer events in No. 10, and in its place more meetings on the economy, on energy and the things people really care about.'[18] As in all matters connected with her premiership, her ambitions were never fully realized.

The Private Office, historically the beating heart of Downing Street and staffed by civil servants, was to be her key power centre in the building. With a trio of stellar officials in Catsaras (principal private secretary), Ollie Ilott (deputy) and Simon Billett (foreign affairs), this was her nerve centre, keeping control of her diary, meetings, paper flow and visits. Initially deeply suspicious, she created an unnecessary fuss when she saw an official who worked for Gove in the office. However, she soon learned to trust her officials. Not officials at large, of course, but those she knew.

If her Private Office had a weakness, it was Truss turning her back on appointing Treasury officials to the top two positions. Another historical anomaly: top positions in the Cabinet Office were thinly staffed by Treasury people. When the Mini-Budget hit the fan, it showed.

Other units within No. 10 she emasculated or moved. The Delivery Unit, data team and Legislative Affairs were all banished elsewhere, making way for a pruned communications team which came back into No. 10. This also made way for a brand new economic unit under Matt Sinclair, designed to help Truss and Kwarteng 'take on Treasury orthodoxy'. The Policy Unit, which had survived for fifty years since its creation in 1974, was all but disbanded because she thought it confusing for Whitehall to have instructions from both it and the Private Office. 'In her mind, she wanted No. 10 full of special advisers working for her, as she had had at the Foreign Office,' said an official.

However, from the beginning, Truss's No. 10 team suffered from organisational weakness. For example, Truss would not have a daily meeting with her team until David Canzini started to organise them towards the end of her premiership. She later wrote that she did not feel that the number of staff available in Downing Street was commensurate with the status of the office. She was surprised to have only about a hundred staff directly working for her, in contrast to having thousands when in charge of a department.[19]

For all her not inconsiderable forethought, and the quality of many individuals within No. 10, it never worked very well under her. Some of the issues were picked up on at the time. 'Everyone around Liz is quite young… I worry that they're not ready for the challenges ahead,' a Cabinet minister told the *Financial Times*.[20] Henry Hill on ConservativeHome worried that her smaller No. 10 would give too much power to the Treasury and other departments, and increase 'the likelihood of media landmines'.[21] More serious concerns were her lack of trust and secrecy, which inclined her to split jobs. Inevitably, this led to confusion. Adam Jones was political director of communications and Simon McGee official head of comms, with Jason Stein given a floating role. Policy was split between Jamie Hope and Matt Sinclair. Sophie Jarvis was political secretary, but Truss sought political advice from others including Ruth Porter, whose overlapping field with Mark Fullbrook as chief of staff was never clearly defined. They were all young apart from Fullbrook. There was no commanding figure like Jonathan Powell or Sally Morgan under Blair, nor Ed Llewellyn under Cameron, nor Gavin Barwell under May. There was no one to check her or put her in place. She had the No. 10 she wanted and perhaps deserved.

Sacking of the Treasury Permanent Secretary

The Prime Minister is head of the executive, and in that capacity, needs to ensure that Whitehall is working to execute government policy. The way the Prime Minister treats the civil service, as any leader with their employees, is widely noted. Any unfair blame and capricious dismissals do not inspire confidence.

The official with principal responsibility for public spending and balancing the nation's books under Truss was Tom Scholar, permanent secretary at the Treasury since July 2016. He had been Downing Street principal private secretary to Gordon Brown, then the Treasury's second permanent secretary, then the Prime Minister's adviser for European and global issues. He was regarded by many in Whitehall as indispensable, by ministers as a reassuring symbol of continuity, and by markets as a guarantor of the credibility of government policy – the mandarin's mandarin who would, had he applied for it, have been the obvious choice for Cabinet secretary in 2020 ahead of Case.

The relationship between the PM and the chief official in the Treasury is always of paramount importance. No civil servant apart from the Cabinet secretary is more senior and, given the paucity of economic advice at the Prime Minister's personal disposal, none so important over the economy. Although the permanent secretary works directly with the Chancellor, the Prime Minister needs to feel comfortable with the incumbent. Harold Macmillan thus appointed the congenial Frank Lee in 1960, Thatcher for the same reasons Peter Middleton in 1983, while Brown and Cameron were more than content with Scholar's predecessor, Nick Macpherson. There is no history of an incoming administration immediately replacing the Treasury permanent secretary.

But Truss was not comfortable with Scholar. She was prone to noticing slights and not forgetting them. Bad blood dated back to the time when she was Chief Secretary to the Treasury between 2017 and 2019. Chancellor Philip Hammond reportedly found her to be rather tiresome. 'She would turn up at his meetings with notes, and then spout. We would listen politely, and then he would tell her "I don't think that we will do that, Liz",' recalled a minister. Soon, the Private Office got into the habit of excluding her from important conversations, relying on the ploy of sending round a note to say 'no junior ministers for this meeting'. Officials and ministers testify to Scholar's personal courtesy and mildness of manner, but she saw him as patronizing and aloof, and responsible for her and her prescriptions being marginalized.

He epitomized everything she disliked about Treasury orthodoxy. 'She thought Scholar presided over an entire culture where the Treasury would say "no" as a reflex response and be the enemy of growth by adhering rigidly to "abacus economics" and book-balancing,' said a personal aide. It wasn't a blanket disgust: she liked some Treasury officials, notably James Bowler, before she made him her permanent secretary at International Trade, and his deputy, Anthony Segal-Knowles.

Scholar was also a marked man from his time as the Prime Minister's Europe adviser during the negotiations for a new deal with the EU before the 2016 referendum. 'He was never forgiven, it is said, by Truss… for not getting more from the EU in those pre-2016 talks,' wrote conservative political commentator Iain Martin.[22] Detractors blamed him for 'Project Fear' and 'for Turbo-charging Philip Hammond's plans for a soft Brexit'.[23] Not hated and mistrusted as much by Brexiteers, maybe, as May's chief EU adviser Olly Robbins. But close.

Truss's sights were fixed on Scholar even while she was Foreign Secretary: 'He's not the right person to run the Treasury,' colleagues would hear her mutter periodically. During haggling over Foreign Office funding with the Treasury, Truss was sometimes heard to remark that Sunak and Scholar were personally frustrating what should have been a straightforward process. But for all this, Truss is adamant that 'the decision to replace Tom Scholar was Kwasi's. I felt it had to be his choice [to choose his own people].'[24] According to Kwarteng, they made up their mind to sack him the moment Johnson announced his resignation. 'We decided this at Greenwich in her house. Our understanding was he would go quite quickly,' he said.[25] The figure they set their heart on as his successor, if she ever became Prime Minister, was the permanent secretary when she first went to International Trade, Antonia Romeo. She was Truss's type of woman, her type of can-do official.

The anti-Scholar mood came out into the open when it became clear at Chevening that Truss would win the leadership contest. Articles started appearing in the press alleging that he was arrogant, kept her out of Budget discussions and wouldn't let her see key papers. Mid-August, a long profile in the *Daily Telegraph* talked about his work for Gordon Brown, while unsavoury allegations appeared elsewhere that he had been working from South America during the pandemic, which were subsequently proven to be untrue.[26] The 'useless' Governor of the Bank of England, Andrew Bailey, was targeted too, as well as a host of other high priests of the 'blob' that Truss was convinced was ruining Britain's economy. 'They thought they couldn't chop out both Andrew Bailey and Tom Scholar, so they went for the latter,' surmised one who was present at the Chevening talks. Truss wanted a public defenestration, and she wanted it immediately. 'It was a mixture of simple revenge, a statement that she was going to be radical, and a signal to civil servants that they [her government] were not going to let themselves be frustrated by them,' said a former Treasury and Bank of England official. 'Liz really had it in for the civil service, with plans to cut numbers back very significantly,' said an aide. 'They intended the sacking to send a message to the "blob": "Beware, no one is safe." It was a classic action – take out one person and the others will fall into place,' said Fullbrook.[27] A rifle shot was to be the opening salvo.

Permanent secretaries in other departments had been dismissed by incoming governments before, but never this quickly or as brutally. Truss left it to Kwarteng to pull the trigger. He wanted to tell Scholar 'I love the Treasury, but there's one thing I need to have: my own permanent secretary', recalled an official. She was nervous he would bottle it: 'She was petrified he would go native, be too nice, and end up not doing it,' they added. Kwarteng summoned Scholar into his office at 7.30 p.m. on the day Truss became Prime Minister, Tuesday

6 September. There in the Chancellor's office, new to Kwarteng but deeply familiar to his guest, the new incumbent declared, 'I'll get straight to the point. You have seen in the leadership campaign criticism of the economic orthodoxy of the Treasury. You are the embodiment of that orthodoxy. So I need to see fresh leadership at the Treasury.' Scholar was shocked. The two men had had a cordial relationship over several years dating back to when Kwarteng had worked for Hammond for nine months. He had spoken to Scholar briefly at a routine meeting the week before, with no hint of what was coming. Kwarteng later recalled telling Scholar that he knew his father, the former permanent secretary Michael Scholar, and that 'it is nothing to do with you personally. You have been a great public servant.'[28]

Scholar, who had had his five-year contract renewed only the previous year, stood his ground. 'You have a huge amount to do with a Budget by the end of September and big ideas. It will take a lot of work here. My job leading the Treasury is to do what you and the Prime Minister want. I'm confident we can do it for you,' he replied, trying to gauge the response, 'but if, after the Budget, the relationship is not working for you, then we can have another talk.' Kwarteng says Scholar tried to bargain for a while but he was not going to budge on the decision.[29] Kwarteng gave the impression that he was distinctly uncomfortable and was operating under instructions. 'We've got nowhere to go on this,' he eventually said to Scholar, desperate for the agonizing discussion to be over. One of the most consequential conversations between the Chancellor and their permanent secretary in history had lasted just twenty minutes.

After collecting himself, Scholar made a record of the meeting and left the Treasury. He only spoke to the Chancellor's private office the following day. None of them had seen it coming. Scholar knew that with his open-ended employment contract the Chancellor was unable to dismiss him altogether, so it was a question of whether he would accept or not. He knew too that there was only one possible outcome, given that the Prime Minister endorsed it. So the next morning, he sent a message to Kwarteng's private secretary to say that he had accepted and that it should be announced immediately. The response came back: 'Leave it till Friday. We have the energy support package on Thursday, and they wouldn't want you to go giving the impression you were leaving as you disagreed with it.' Scholar responded, 'Friday will be fine.' But when it became obvious later that day that the Queen was dying and there would be a prolonged period when there could be no announcements, the plan was accelerated. A statement was released on the afternoon of Thursday 8 September.

The sacking was cheered by the right: 'A cause for celebration…[he was] a malign influence of Treasury orthodoxy at play,' wrote former minister Theodore Agnew in *The Times*, citing Scholar's passive resistance to creating a Treasury office in the North of England and botching Bounce Back loans during the Covid pandemic.[30] The establishment hit back at 'a new level of the growing trend of blaming the civil servants', in the words of the former head of the civil service Lord Kerslake.[31] 'Sacking him makes no sense. His experience would have been invaluable in the coming months,' wrote Scholar's predecessor Nick Macpherson.[32] Even the most senior living civil servant, former Cabinet Secretary Lord Butler, felt compelled to take up his pen: 'It'll weaken them, but it'll also corrupt our system'.[33] Well, they would say that wouldn't they, Truss acolytes responded.

With Scholar gone, and no one yet to replace him, Truss and Kwarteng had a problem. No other figure had the depth of his experience, knowledge of gilt markets, or contacts across the financial sector, including the Bank of England. It all added to the uncertainty over how the economy might respond to the Mini-Budget. 'None of us asked the critical question: do we really understand the knock-on of losing him?' admitted a top Truss adviser. Officials who were already reticent about offering opinions that might not be congenial became even more guarded.

Meanwhile, the mood in the Treasury was 'shellshocked' and 'distracted', with many genuinely upset that a civil servant of his renown could be dispatched so peremptorily and so cruelly. Scholar, it was widely asserted, had always provided honest analysis, even when it was uncomfortable, and now he had paid the price – why take the risk? 'The atmosphere was very toxic and one in which people who provided criticism of their programme was seen as threatening,' one of Truss's advisers later admitted. Within the Treasury, the two most senior officials, Cat Little and Beth Russell, were promptly appointed acting permanent secretaries, working flat out to ensure that disruption and diminution in quality of advice was minimized.

Truss had no option but to rely more on Case, whose efficiency in making Scholar disappear quietly from the scene greatly impressed her. Thoughts of dismissing him too evaporated. From then until the end of her time in office, she was in debt to him. A premiership that opened with a determination to be free of civil servants and orthodox Tories was to end with her being utterly reliant upon three officials and a centrist politician.

The day Scholar departed, Truss had just forty-two days left in Downing Street before she announced her own departure.

The Verdict: Appoint the Best Cabinet?

Truss failed the test of appointing the best Cabinet more roundly than almost any other. She didn't appoint or nurture a Cabinet that would lead her government and rally around her. She didn't appoint a team in Downing Street to support and challenge her. And her precipitous first action as head of the executive branch demoralized Whitehall when she needed its support. 'We thought the system would work better because Scholar had gone,' said the Trussite minister who had advised her to go for an ultra-loyal Cabinet. 'We were wrong. It didn't.'

Rule Number Four: Prime Ministers must command the big events. Truss seems overwhelmed by the death of the Queen. Rather than seizing the opportunity to settle the nation, she did the opposite. Here she is reading at the funeral on Monday 19 September

4

COMMAND THE BIG EVENTS

7–19 September 2022

Prime ministerial performance is partly judged on how well the incumbent rises to major events. It is no coincidence that all the top rank Prime Ministers from Robert Walpole to Margaret Thatcher were able to command rather than be overwhelmed by their shocks and distractions. It is a mark of a great leader to turn a reversal or upset into a gain.

Several of the top tier Prime Ministers including Pitt the Younger, Lloyd George and Churchill were in office at times of major wars; others, like Gladstone and Attlee, during eras of major social change that they were able to channel and shape. It begs the question: do great leaders make history, or rather, are they made by major historical events? The answer perhaps is both.

It's certainly true that poor-performing Prime Ministers succumb to the great historic crises of the times. Famously, Lord North was unable to provide a commanding response to the revolutionary uprising in the thirteen British colonies in North America, and, like George III, was quite overwhelmed by events. Though, given the popularity of the American rebellion, and Britain's isolation on the world stage, it is hard to see how even the most resourceful Prime Minister could have won that war for Britain. Neither Asquith nor

Chamberlain provided the quality of leadership required in the First and Second World Wars.

The majority of the fifty-eight Prime Ministers since 1721 have served at moments of relative calm and never had the opportunity to be tested in moments of extreme danger and challenge. Good leadership is often characterized by personal calm, clear-headed decision-making and moral example. Contrast Eden's frenetic and brittle response to the Suez Crisis with the measured sangfroid demonstrated by his successor Macmillan, who dismissed the resignation of his Chancellor (and two Treasury ministers) in 1958 as 'a little local difficulty', before setting off on a Commonwealth tour and letting the crisis dissipate. Prime Ministers have to know when the time is right to make light of a crisis. Most famously, Callaghan misjudged the national mood amid widespread industrial action when, returning from a conference in Guadalupe, he testily responded to a journalist's question about the crisis at home with 'I don't think that other people in the world would share the view that there is mounting chaos.' The *Sun* responded to his nonchalant response with the headline 'Crisis? What crisis?', a phrase that has coloured the entire perception of his three-year premiership.[1]

Unfortunately, Liz Truss had two significant moments to master, both coming at the very start of her premiership. The first was the energy crisis, the second was the death of Queen Elizabeth II. The latter made her the first Prime Minister to handle the death of a monarch since Churchill seventy years before. If she misplayed the first, she would have faced her own 'winter of discontent', as Callaghan did; misplay the second, and she would have become a figure of national ridicule.

The Energy Crisis: 5–8 September

Soaring gas prices during the Ukraine War had been a regular talking point during the leadership election in July and August. At first, Truss said very deliberately that she would not favour any package of energy support, uttering her much-analysed words to the *Financial Times* in August that 'there would be no further handouts'. But then she changed her mind. Why?

The confidential briefing overseen by Simon Case in 70 Whitehall in early August had spooked her. Some advisers told her to hold her nerve. 'We don't need to offer any package, Liz,' one said. But others on the right argued differently. 'In August, there was a very real threat that the crisis would turn into a catastrophe,' economic adviser Julian Jessop wrote later, 'with some estimates that the average household [energy] bill would jump to £6,000 a year, driving inflation to 20 per cent.'[2] 'She and Kwasi decided from very early in the campaign to intervene, but she couldn't say so publicly till the end,' said one of Truss's senior advisers. As she had ruled out means testing and a windfall tax on the energy companies, it would have to be a price guarantee, and those who queried the cost would be ignored. 'There was more than a touch of Boris and financial cakeism about Liz at times,' remarked one senior adviser, referring to what *Financial Times* journalist Gideon Rachman described as Johnson's 'notion that it is possible to govern without making hard choices'.[3] 'She was adamant it was going to be a decisive intervention to kill the problem, hard and fast at the very beginning,' recalls a minister.

Truss's senior economic team became progressively alarmed, though, at the sheer scale of intervention she was proposing. On Friday 2 September, Kwarteng and Philp held an emergency meeting.

They estimated that her envisaged package could cost as much as £150 billion. For context, public expenditure over 2021–22 *in total* was £1,185 billion, so £150 billion was over 10 per cent of that cost, a greater figure than the budget of Education and Defence combined.[4]

They frantically looked at ideas to mitigate the sum. Philp's idea was a 5 per cent surcharge on customers' energy bills to be in force for twenty years to recoup at least some of the cost of the intervention. When they put it to Truss, she responded sceptically, 'That sounds to me like a new tax. We should absolutely not be doing that.' 'But it will help reassure the bond market,' Kwarteng interjected. 'No, no, no,' she retorted. According to one of her incoming ministers, 'Liz was not willing to give even five or ten minutes to listen to our concerns. She ruled them out totally.'

On Monday 5 September, the day her victory over Sunak was announced at the Queen Elizabeth II Centre, she spent her last hours before becoming Prime Minister at Admiralty House. This is the eighteenth-century building facing Horse Guards Parade, where Prime Ministers decamp when Downing Street is out of action (as it was during the 1958–60 renovation or when it needed to be repaired after the IRA's 1991 mortar attack). The scene was mayhem with staff meeting each other often for the first time, and a small team huddled around the whiteboard with details of the reshuffle still to be finalized. At 4.15 p.m. a high-level meeting was convened to finalize the details of the energy support package. 'She was contemptuous of any attempt to mitigate the expense,' said one present. Then she announced out of the blue that she would set the price-ceiling for a typical home at £2,500, not £3,000, 'a £10 billion plus decision taken on her own in less than thirty seconds', said another. The meeting ended tensely.

Kwarteng seized a last opportunity to convince her to moderate the energy proposals, asking her to have a discussion in the courtyard outside the building so they could converse in confidence. 'I urged her again to claw back the huge spend over twenty years. But she categorically said "no". I told her that the OBR would've scored it as a net [debt] zero if we had done so, but she wasn't listening to me,' he said.[5] Seriously worried now, he sought out Porter to try to enlist her support. 'Sorry. Liz wants a full-on intervention,' Porter told him emphatically. Her tone suggested to the Chancellor-elect that the conversation was over.

'I should have stood up to Liz more,' he later said. 'My mistake was to tell her "you've won the election fight. We're now here to do what you want."' He ascribed his reluctance to all his reading about 'the destructive spats between Chancellors and the Prime Minister': 'I'd read books on the Chancellors by Edmund Dell and Roy Jenkins, I'd devoured the Lawson memoirs and I had seen close up the totally destructive and dysfunctional relationship between Rishi Sunak and Boris Johnson, which was much worse than that between Philip Hammond and Theresa May, and I had formed the view the Chancellor should defer to the Prime Minister.'[6] Truss was no longer listening to him and Philp but was leaning more to her political team, particularly Hope and Jones, who reminded her that Sunak had borrowed £400 billion during Covid without unsettling the markets, and that, given the gravity of the energy price crisis, markets would probably be equally relaxed about her new measures. She also reassured herself that the UK fiscal position was basically sound with a lower debt-to-GDP ratio than most developed countries. 'She didn't need to listen to advisers on any side: she had made up her own mind that she was in the right,' said an aide.

That evening, she slipped away for a victory party at the Deliveroo headquarters in the City of London, circling the room for thirty minutes before returning to Admiralty House, even though she had planned to be there for two hours. In the small flat at the top of the building, recently vacated by Johnson's chief of staff Steve Barclay, she sat down for a few drinks and takeaway pizza with her family, senior staff and old Foreign Office team: husband Hugh and daughters Frances and Liberty, Coffey, Fullbrook, Hope, Jarvis and Jones. 'Time for bed,' Fullbrook said before midnight, 'we have a big day tomorrow.'

The energy support package was still not finalized on Tuesday 6 September, which proved an unusually fraught day for the incoming Prime Minister. Appointments and initial statements usually fill the head of the new PM at this stage; instead, Truss was having to think about a major policy announcement and a severely ailing monarch. Truss rose early that morning to pore over the package's final details and her appointments.

Her team were itching for Johnson and his staff to quit Downing Street (it had been nine weeks since he'd announced his resignation) so they could move in. After an emotional farewell breakfast with his close supporters in No. 10's Pillared Drawing Room, Johnson emerged onto Downing Street at 7.30 a.m. to give his speech to the waiting media. Bar a swipe at how the 1922 Committee 'changed the rules halfway through', his words were more gracious than his angry resignation speech in July. He promised to support his successor 'every step of the way' before being driven to RAF Northolt to board a plane to Aberdeen. In Aberdeen he boarded a helicopter to Balmoral, arriving at 11 a.m. and leaving just before midday. The Queen had travelled to Balmoral in July for her regular summer break. But all was not well for the ninety-six-year-old monarch. During the Platinum Jubilee celebrations in June, she was notably absent from some of the major events. On Friday 2 September, it was announced that she would miss the Braemar Highland Gathering for only the fifth time in seventy years due to 'mobility issues'. That was also the explanation for why she remained at Balmoral and did not return to London to appoint the new Prime Minister. Asking both leaders to make a 1,000-mile round journey on such a day was not a decision that she had taken lightly.

Truss had left Admiralty House for RAF Northolt herself soon after 9 a.m. with Hugh by her side, as well as Principal Private Secretary Catsaras, who was moving with her from the Foreign Office, and Jones in the second car. As they drove through the streets of West London, surrounded by police outriders on motorcycles, Catsaras was in contact with the office about her timetable, while Jones worked on her forthcoming statements. The weather was deteriorating and there were concerns about her plane landing at Aberdeen and the onward helicopter journey. The absolute safety of the incoming Prime Minister was paramount. Truss's despised 'deep state' was not going to take any risks with her safety, least of all at a time of such economic and political turbulence.

At 12.25 p.m., only slightly behind schedule, her party arrived at Balmoral. Truss was greeted at the royal residence's door by Edward Young, private secretary to the Queen, who in the days before had been forging a close relationship with Catsaras: together with Case as Cabinet Secretary, the three officials formed the 'golden triangle' at the heart of the British Constitution.[7] The Palace was anxious to avoid a repetition of the unfamiliarity with the Prime Minister's principal private secretary that had occurred when Johnson had suddenly kicked out the very capable Peter Hill in favour of the unsuspecting but proficient Martin Reynolds, with whom he had worked closely when Foreign Secretary. It still rankled with the Palace that, a month after Johnson succeeded in 2019, the Queen, on his direct advice that she was bound to follow, ordered Parliament to be prorogued, advice that was later ruled unlawful. Had a more familiar relationship between the principals been in place, the damage might have been mitigated.

At 12.52 p.m., the Palace released confirmation that Truss had been appointed Prime Minister, with a photograph of her meeting the Queen. 'Her Majesty was on sparkling form,' said one present. A few days earlier, knowing that the audience was coming up but before the winner in the leadership election had been announced, she told a courtier, 'I'm going to be bouncing into the room to greet them.' After the audience was over, Young requested a personal meeting with Truss. Unlike Buckingham Palace and Windsor Castle, there is no private room for them nearby to use, so they had to ask for the library (where the waiting party were having tea) to be cleared; he then explained that the Queen might not live much longer. 'It was a shock: I mean, I knew us travelling up to Balmoral was not good news, but I hadn't anticipated the speed,' said Truss.[8]

Reeling from what she had been told, while giving nothing away to her team, Truss underwent the same journey in reverse, helicopter, plane, police-escorted car journey back to Downing Street. All the way home she was worrying about her speech. 'It's going to be a bloody difficult first six months. We've got to hit the ground running. There's no time to bed in and admire the furniture,' she said to her team, while also constantly probing for reassurance. '"Am I doing the right thing? Am I framing it the right way? Have I practised the speech enough?"' recalled an aide.

At 4.55 p.m., with rain bucketing down and the Downing Street lectern covered by an unsightly black bag, Catsaras and Jones were in conversation with Truss's team about whether she should give her initial speech from inside No. 10. The potential for bad headlines from an incoming Prime Minister trying to make herself heard over a downpour while getting drenched was very real in everyone's minds (and one that subsequent Prime Ministers ought to have borne in mind). 'Absolutely not', was Truss's response. The police were asked to put in some extra loops over Thames bridges on the route back from RAF Northolt to eat up time, given that for security reasons the Prime Minister's convoy is never allowed to stop except for collection or dropping off. All the while, her team inside No. 10 watched the aerial footage of the convoy wending its way through the rain on Sky News, powerless to change the weather. Sitting in the back of her car with Hugh, Truss tried to focus her attention on the speech she was shortly to deliver. At 5 p.m. came a break in the rain. 'Waiting for it to stop was the most stressful moment of my life,' said Clare Evans, her new head of operations. 'But then suddenly there was a break in the clouds, and we urgently called for the car to swiftly deliver her to Downing Street where she was able to have her much-anticipated moment in the glorious sunshine.'[9]

Her six-minute speech encapsulated her entire ambition for government. It opened with a passage of necessary obeisance: her paying 'tribute to my predecessor, Boris Johnson' who 'delivered Brexit, the Covid vaccine, and stood up to Russian aggression. History will see him as a hugely consequential Prime Minister.' She then outlined the three priorities that would have defined 'Trussism', had such a word ever emerged. First, 'grow the economy through tax cuts and reform', which lay at the heart of her thinking. Second, 'take action to help with energy bills and to secure our future energy supply'. Third, 'put our health service on a firm footing'. In the short term, this meant reducing waiting lists, but in the long term, she had ideas for root-and-branch reform of the NHS.[10] She was driving the first goal, and the second, and she intended Coffey to galvanize the third.

All incoming Prime Ministers, in a tradition dating back to the early post-war years, are clapped in by staff standing on either side of the long corridor from the front hall all the way down to the Cabinet Room at the other end. The PM is traditionally greeted at the front door by the country's most senior civil servant, in her instance Case, who escorts them into the Cabinet Room where they are told about the 'letters-of-last-resort' to be dispatched in sealed envelopes to the four Royal Navy nuclear submarine commanders in the event of a nuclear war. The Prime Minister indicates their intention in a handwritten letter that is then sealed. The average deployment of a British Vanguard-class nuclear submarine is estimated to be five and a half months, which raises the possibility that Truss's letters never found their way on board a submarine before they were destroyed and superseded by Rishi Sunak's letters six weeks later (though it also leaves open a remote chance that Truss's writ continued in a submarine safe under the ocean for many months after the end of her short-lived government).[11] In her bellicose mood, she might have given instructions to retaliate against Moscow, Beijing or Pyongyang; the world incinerated on the instructions of a forty-nine-day Prime Minister no longer in office.

In the early evening, she went back to the Cabinet Room for Fullbrook's carefully choreographed plan of appointing new ministers. 'It worked like clockwork,' said a member of her team. 'They would go in to see her one by one, then out they would come, meet their new principal private secretary from their department then their close protection team, have a session with Propriety and Ethics to talk through the hazards of their jobs, and forty-five minutes later, off they would go as secretaries of state.' Phone calls also took place at 7.30 and 8.30 p.m. with President Zelenskyy of Ukraine and President Biden. The order was deliberate and noted in the White House and beyond.

Her team worked late into the night. Catsaras had wanted them to be given individual 'London Bridge briefings' (the name for the funeral plan for the Queen, first devised in the 1960s with many changes since), though most assumed this was just a formality for incomers and had no apprehension of the urgency. Case caught Clare Evans and asked her to check that Truss had some black clothes in the building. She went up to the PM's flat at the top of Downing Street and worked her way through the two suitcases that had already been taken upstairs. When she told Case she could find nothing suitable, he suggested that she go in his car back to the Truss home in Greenwich and come back with all the black dresses she could lay her hands on, plus a black tie for Hugh. With the Downing Street flat still a mess and lacking the family's furniture, the decision was taken that the family would be more comfortable spending the night together back in Admiralty House. Few arriving at No. 10 as Prime Minister fully grasp the extent to which their spouse and children are swept up into the experience, whether they want to be or not. Truss and her family were about to learn how radically their lives were to change.

Wednesday 7 September, her second day in office, was the crunch day; decisions piled in on Truss, not least last-minute appointments.

Even her most senior colleagues found it hard to obtain an audience with her. She managed a cool head nevertheless for her first Cabinet meeting as PM at 8.30 a.m., and then she went straight into her Prime Minister's Questions briefing, before being driven to the House of Commons for her first PMQs at midday, a baptism of fire for any incoming leader. First impressions count.

Given her concerns about the loyalty of her MPs, she was relieved when she heard them applauding her loudly as she said, 'I am honoured to take my place as Prime Minister in this House and to take on responsibility at a vital time for our country.' Her briefing was on the spot, and she was more than ready for Leader of the Opposition Keir Starmer's questions about why she wasn't going for a windfall tax on high-earning energy companies to pay for the energy support package due to be announced the following day. 'I believe it is the wrong thing to be putting companies off investing in the United Kingdom, just when we need to be growing the economy,' she replied, while praising Starmer for his 'strong support… in opposing Vladimir Putin's appalling war in Ukraine… which has led to the energy crisis'.

'But the money has got to come from somewhere,' Starmer responded. 'The Prime Minister knows that every single pound in excess profits that she chooses not to tax is an extra pound on borrowing that working people will be forced to pay back for decades to come.' Truss shot back with her prepared reply: 'The reality is that this country will not be able to tax its way to growth.'

Starmer was well aware that eyes were on him too as he levelled up to his second PMQ adversary, and a much more assiduous one than the first. 'The Prime Minister claims to be breaking orthodoxy, but the reality is that she's… protecting oil and gas profits, and forcing working people to pay the bill.'

Relief came from an unlikely place, Truss's former boss Theresa May, who, still joyful at having seen the end of Johnson's premiership, welcomed her as 'the third female Prime Minister of the United Kingdom', asking, 'Why does she think it is that all three female Prime Ministers have been Conservatives?' Truss, thanking her for her 'fantastic question', responded that it was indeed extraordinary that Labour was unable to find a female leader, 'or a leader who does not come from North London'. It was as if she knew May's question was coming.[12]

She emerged as the clear winner in the eyes of most observers. 'Liz Truss sailed through her first PMQs which will probably be her easiest. It may turn out to have been her best,' wrote Lloyd Evans in the *Spectator* with prescience.[13] 'Tory MPs will feel relieved… She does have skill, and she showed it. She has the immense advantage of knowing what she thinks, and briefing herself properly, advantages Johnson did not always possess,' Daniel Finkelstein wrote in *The Times*.[14] Tory MPs liked her advocacy of lower taxes and no windfall tax, the upbeat mood continuing that afternoon when she addressed the 1922 Committee at 4 p.m. 'Teamwork', she told her backbenchers, would be central to her government, announcing with pride that she was going to be moving the whips' office back into the heart of Downing Street thereby ensuring close liaison with the parliamentary party. She knew how frustrated many MPs had been with the figurative distance between No. 10 and the parliamentary party in recent years. 'She was very good at understanding some of the real concerns of backbenchers… in terms of some of the changes at No. 10,' said prominent Brexit and ERG member Mark Francois after the meeting.[15] But, despite the generally good-tempered reception, the MPs at large were still deeply suspicious of their new Prime Minister.

She was back at work early on the morning of Thursday 8 September finalizing the details of the Energy Price Guarantee. Energy Secretary Rees-Mogg suggested that she announce it not as a separate statement, but as part of the debate, which her officials thought a mistake because it meant 'that she was regularly interrupted, and couldn't deliver it in one piece'. Choosing to announce the measures herself, she rose to her feet at 11.40 a.m. to say energy bills would be frozen at an average of £2,500 a year for two years as part of a package of support for homes and businesses, the money to be funded through increased borrowing. Her plan included a review of Net Zero, suspension of green levies, ending the moratorium on extracting shale gas, and 'a Great British Nuclear' project to be launched with the aim of delivering a quarter of electricity generation by nuclear power by 2050. The figure of £150 billion in transfer of taxpayer funds to energy suppliers was being widely talked about, though she did not give any indication of the cost in her speech, saying only that the Chancellor would provide figures later in the month.[16] Her speech received a scathing response from Starmer, criticizing the reliance on borrowing, the strong focus on oil and gas, the lack of encouragement for home insulation and the failure to place windfall taxes on the profit-rich suppliers.[17]

That judgement was harsh. Truss showed decisiveness in pushing ahead in response to the significant inherited crisis with her Energy Price Guarantee, which ended up costing a fraction of the £150 billion predicted – £27 billion overall.[18] It did bring comfort and stability to both homes and businesses over the period of 2022–24.

What few predicted, though, was that the markets would not be as accepting of the scale of the intervention as they had been over furlough during the pandemic, especially when that was coupled with the ambitions of the Mini-Budget, and an absence of fiscal prudence.

The Death of the Queen: 8–19 September

Since the office came into existence in 1721, only nine previous Prime Ministers had witnessed the death of a reigning monarch and the coronation of their successor. Yet ten monarchs have witnessed the transition of fifty-six Prime Ministers.

Queen Elizabeth II presided over fourteen Prime Ministers in what became the longest-serving monarchy in British history at seventy years and 214 days. Truss, her final PM, was born (in July 1975) over a hundred years after her first, Churchill (born November 1874). Some of Truss's team speculated at the pride the Queen must have felt that her final Prime Minister was a woman bearing her own name to usher in a new Elizabethan Age. Confirmation of this claim from the Palace was not forthcoming.

Truss was on alert following her tipoff from Edward Young at Balmoral, and, when securely back in Downing Street, was shown the London Bridge plans, many years in the making, to be activated on the Queen's death. These described in minute detail what the Prime Minister and other key people should do. On the evening of Wednesday 7 September, a virtual Privy Council meeting was due to be convened at the secure COBRA conference room beneath Downing Street to allow Truss to swear her oath as First Lord of the Treasury and for Cabinet ministers to be sworn in.

The Queen was to join remotely, conducting the meeting from her bedroom at Balmoral. Thirty minutes before the meeting was due to start, the message came from Balmoral that the Queen would be communicating by conference call, and would not be visible. Then just five minutes before the start, Young telephoned Case to say that the Queen was too unwell even to talk over the phone, leaving Case to announce the news to curious attenders. Shortly after, an official bulletin from the Palace said: 'After a full day yesterday, Her Majesty has this afternoon accepted doctors' advice to rest.'[19] Case and Young had been communicating for several months about the Queen's health, but even so, neither fully anticipated this precipitous deterioration.

Early on Thursday morning, 8 September, Truss was in Parliament to announce her energy support package. Young called Case's mobile: 'I think it might just be hours,' he announced solemnly. Nadhim Zahawi was in the Cabinet Office when 'I had a call to say that she was deteriorating rapidly, and that the Palace would be putting out a bulletin about her health at 11.15,' he recalled.[20] As Chancellor of the Duchy of Lancaster, having been Chancellor of the Exchequer just forty-eight hours before, he suddenly had to absorb the fact that he was now the national lead on Operation London Bridge. He quickly sized up the position. 'Where is the Prime Minister?' he asked.

'In the House of Commons speaking,' his staff told him. 'We can't have her in the Chamber when the Palace makes the announcement because she won't have been briefed,' he said. He urgently needed to speak to the country's most senior official: 'Where is Simon Case?' he demanded. 'Already in the Prime Minister's office in the House of Commons waiting for her,' came the reply. While travelling the short distance to Parliament, Zahawi spoke to Case, who had penned some words for the PM to say from the despatch box, and had them cleared with the Palace. With events moving very rapidly, the Palace then said they needed more time before anything was said.

Zahawi arrived in Parliament and made his way to Truss in the Chamber to hand her Case's notes and brief her on the fast-developing situation. Once extracted from the Chamber, he told her that they needed to proceed urgently to her room where he and Case were about to chair a meeting with London Bridge top brass, including Sarah Healey, permanent secretary at the Department for Culture, Media and Sport, who now assumed a new responsibility leading the team in the Cabinet Office coordinating all the arrangements across government and partners. 'The mood was very odd. Some were thinking she had already died. Others were just aware that something momentous was unfolding. We all felt for the London Bridge team, which was on the cusp of being activated,' said an aide. One old hand reflected, 'It was as if the 2012 Olympics was suddenly roaring to life with less than twelve hours' notice.'

Truss herself remained very quiet, her head reeling after her energy announcement and trying to absorb the news about what the Queen's death would mean for her and her premiership. She intervened with a couple of practical questions about timing, but was content that others were leading the way. At 12.30 p.m., the meeting was over. The Palace publicly announced: 'The Queen's doctors are concerned for Her Majesty's health and have recommended she remain under medical supervision.' A few moments later, the short statement that Zahawi and Case had cobbled together on the Queen's health was read to the Chamber by the Speaker.

Zahawi had arranged for a message written by Case to be passed to Starmer and Labour's deputy leader Angela Rayner asking them to leave the Chamber and to meet him and Case in a small room behind the Speaker's chair. Then Case called Scottish First Minister Nicola Sturgeon to break the news to her in Scotland.[21]

Truss's team had been agonizing over whether she should cancel an evening call with French President Emmanuel Macron. 'The pressure was on to postpone it, but we wanted to keep everything in the diary so that our allies wouldn't assume that the monarch had already died,' said an official. The key decisions on such occasions were being taken by Britain's three top officials: Simon Case, Nick Catsaras and Edward Young at the Palace. The similar-ranked permanent secretary at the Treasury would have been checking in with financial updates, had there been one. This was, perhaps, the 'deep state' in action, but even Truss on this occasion did not think they were acting with any sinister motive.

She was driven back to No. 10 where the decision was taken for her to proceed with another scheduled call with allied leaders including President Biden, President Macron and German Chancellor Olaf Scholz, to discuss Ukraine.[22] While it was in full flow, she received a message that the Queen was deteriorating rapidly. 'I will have to leave,' she told her fellow leaders. President Biden made a point of sending his best wishes.

Truss needed to be somewhere more secure and quiet than her office in the Cabinet Room, so she asked a small group to convene in the still largely empty flat at the top of Downing Street. Her most trusted team had gathered round her on sofas and boxes when Case's phone vibrated. 'It is Sir Edward calling,' Case said to the assembled group. London Bridge decreed that the Queen's

Private Secretary (rather than a member of the family or a medic; this was, after all, still an official duty) would convey the news of her death via a secure telephone line to the PM direct, or to their most senior official, who would then pass on the news that 'London Bridge is down'.

Case tried to find a quiet space by the window a little distance away from everyone but they could hear his every word. 'Good afternoon, Sir Edward,' he began. The group could only hear one side of the call but it rapidly became clear that Young was telling him that the Queen had died, at 3.10 p.m. When Case said, 'Please pass on my condolences to His Majesty the King', there was an audible gasp in the room. Conversation between the two then focused on the timing of the official announcement once the family had been told. 'There was an electric response when we all heard for the first time the words "the King",' said one. Everyone sat in total silence till Case concluded his conversation with 'God save the King'.

Accounts differ about how the company reacted, but it is clear that the silence lasted some five to ten minutes, and that Truss herself, as most present, shed a tear and more at the news. The stillness was only punctured when Case and Catsaras announced, 'It's time for us to get back to work', as the housekeeper arrived with cups of tea. 'It was all very British,' one present recalled. The housekeeper then had to be asked politely if she would mind waiting with them in the flat till the news was generally known, as it was so obvious to her what had happened.

Truss had already wanted to make it clear via Catsaras that there would be no interference whatsoever from Downing Street in Operation London Bridge. 'The last thing anyone needed was No. 10 meddling,' said an official, scarred by memories of No. 10 interventions in royal matters dating back to the death of Princess Diana in 1997. The bond between Downing Street and the Palace, which had several low points during the Queen's reign, was significantly aided by Case having worked as Prince William's private secretary as well as principal private secretary to the Prime Minister before becoming Cabinet secretary. 'Simon was indispensable throughout,' said one of the team. 'Calm, assured and strong, and she trusted him completely.' On Case's side, he was struck by how Truss, not renowned for her ability to listen to advice, least of all from officials, went out of her way to follow London Bridge advice to the very last letter.

Eyes dried, preparing Truss's statement was now the priority for the team in the flat. She read the long-prepared draft that came from long-standing and respected Downing Street speechwriter Tim Kiddell. But she decided there and then to discard the official text, and wrote her own with some assistance from Jones and Kiddell.[23]

Shortly after the news was broadcast on the BBC and across all outlets at 6.30 p.m. she went downstairs to deliver her speech. Churchillian it was not: 'The death of Her Majesty the Queen is a huge shock to the nation and to the world. Queen Elizabeth II was the rock on which modern Britain was built... Through thick and thin, Queen Elizabeth II provided us with the stability and the strength that we needed.' Her speech was the first official confirmation of the 'regnal name' (to give it its official title) of King Charles III. This put to rest years of speculation, given the unhappy stories of the two earlier Charles, that he would call himself 'George VII' or some other name. She finished by declaiming, 'God save the King.'[24] It was an effective and heartfelt tribute, if not memorable. When Truss came back into the building, she sought affirmation from her team, but no one was in the mood to give it.

Afterwards, she was rushed down to the COBRA room for the first daily meeting of the committee that would oversee the entire operation. She spoke briefly at the start to say that she would be handing over the chair to Zahawi, wished them luck and crisply departed. Later that evening, utterly drained, she retreated to the Downing Street flat with Hugh and their daughters.

Downstairs, in the bowels of Downing Street, the Private Office team battled to rearrange her diary, weeks in the preparation, and to work out how they could secure sufficient black clothes for her to cover the entire ten days of official mourning.

Truss found the sudden loss of ten days challenging. One of her advisers said that she seemed to be 'the deputy monarch', operating under instructions from others, and the attention of the national and world media was no longer on her but on the Royal Family. She rued the total lack of publicity for her bold energy support package, utterly swallowed up by wave after wave of royal stories as if the announcement had never happened. Yet it seemed she never resented the intrusion on her space; she understood that this was a pivotal event in the history of the nation.

Attempts to make a storm over a video of anti-monarchy comments she had made aged nineteen in 1994 came to nothing (when she told the Lib Dem conference that she was against the 'born to rule' royals and favoured the abolition of the monarchy).[25] Whatever she may have believed as a young woman, by 2022 she was solidly, if never exuberantly, a monarchist. 'For all her dislike of the status quo and the "blob", she felt nothing but dutiful honour to be the Prime Minister at such a momentous point in British history,' said an aide. 'She was reverential to the institution and the incumbent,' said another. Nor did stories damage her that circulated just after the Queen's death that she planned to tour the UK with the King on walkabouts. No. 10 quickly moved to pour cold water on the idea, pointing out that she would be attending services in Scotland, Northern Ireland and Wales, but nothing more.[26]

Truss was not involved in day-to-day operations after her brief initial appearance at COBRA as London prepared for the biggest gathering of foreign leaders in British history, including one hundred presidents and heads of government. Keeping them safe and their schedules working on time when flights over Windsor Castle (directly under Heathrow's flight path) were often impossible, and when many had to leave straight away after the funeral to go on to the annual United Nations General Assembly in New York, was a challenge. So too was keeping a close eye on the '700 obsessives' whom the intelligence agencies had identified as potential risks while also ensuring maximum freedom of movement for the 250,000 who filed past the Queen's coffin in Westminster Hall during the four days of lying in state. 'Let me know anything I can do to help, or any blockages I can remove,' she said very early on to Zahawi. But he never called on her help, not once.

Working on her tribute for the formal ceremony in Parliament took her attention from early the following day. Cabinet, the second she chaired, met at 9.30 a.m. She opened the meeting by saying the whole country was in shock, and it was 'especially poignant' that they were sitting around the table as the last Cabinet members ever to serve under Elizabeth II. They also had the honour, she said, of being the first Cabinet of King Charles III: 'We will serve our new sovereign with the same loyalty and devotion.' She continued by talking about the 'great responsibility' they all had to lead the country through this time, 'a huge logistical undertaking', with 'the eyes of the world… on us. And we've got to get this right.' She then turned to Sarah Healey to provide an overview of the arrangements for the following ten days, before asking for tributes from each Cabinet minister in order of seniority. She concluded by saying, 'Thank you for your tributes. In the coming days, we will have the opportunity to mourn with the nation and the world… And to do whatever is necessary to support a smooth transition to the new reign.'

The meeting finished at 10.30 a.m., allowing her an hour to prepare for tributes in the House of Commons, which opened at noon. Truss had forged what she regarded as a personal relationship with the Queen over the years. 'She remained determined to carry out her duties, even at the age of ninety-six. It was just three days ago, at Balmoral, that she invited me to form the Government and become her fifteenth Prime Minister… She generously shared with me her deep experience of government, even in those last days,' she concluded. The speech was sincere, and acknowledged as such, even if overshadowed by Johnson, who spoke about 'her humility – her single-bar electric-fire, Tupperware-using refusal to be grand. I can tell the House… she drove herself in her own car, with no detectives and no bodyguard, bouncing at alarming speed over the Scottish landscape'. Theresa May then delivered one of her best speeches, moving and witty, as when she described the weekly audience as 'the one meeting I went to that I knew would not be briefed out to the media', or when she dropped some cheese on the ground at a picnic during the annual PM visit to Balmoral, and when she furtively placed it back on the table, she saw the Queen smiling at her.[27] Truss could not compete with either of them, 'but it didn't seem to trouble her: she just accepted it', said an aide.

That evening, Truss went to Buckingham Palace for her first audience with the King. She knew him far less well than the Queen, and his passions, not least the environment and scepticism about unbridled growth, were not hers. But, according to an aide, 'they hit it off at once'. Not naturally one to let others set the agenda, she opened up her first audience with the new monarch by gaily opining on planning policy and restrictions, which, according to her, proved 'a topic in which they were both interested'. That evening at 6 p.m., a service of prayers and mourning was held at St Paul's Cathedral.

Saturday 10 September saw the formal Accession Council at 10 a.m. at St James's Palace, where again Truss played second fiddle, this time to the woman who all but wrested the leadership from her, Lord President of the Council Penny Mordaunt. It was she who invited the Clerk to the Privy Council to read the Accession Proclamation that pledges loyalty and announced the King's regnal name, Charles III. The document was then signed by the King, Queen Camilla, the Archbishop of Canterbury and then the Prime Minister.[28] Mordaunt later spoke of her private apprehensions that 'it was not a foregone conclusion that the new monarch would be accepted. I felt a huge responsibility through the accession council.' Her particular worry was that the traditional three cheers might be half hearted. 'It was afterwards, when I went outside to hear the proclamation being delivered from the balcony and hear the crowds cheering their new king that I knew all would be well. And of course it was, an outpouring of love for both the late Queen and the whole royal family.'[29] In Mordaunt's own tribute, this time to Truss during her final Cabinet, she reflected back on these momentous days. She reminded fellow ministers that the work around the assessment of Britain's strategic position, the Integrated Review, published in

2021, had identified the passing of the Queen as a moment of peril for the nation; Truss had served the nation well in that respect 'by being at the helm when the transition happened and helping the nation grieve'.[30]

Truss was assiduous over the days following the Accession. She attended events across the kingdom, notably services in Edinburgh, Belfast and Cardiff. At the State Funeral in Westminster Abbey on Monday 19 September, she read the lesson from John chapter 14; 'What I worried about was not the reading itself, but "Will I trip up on the step?" Or "Which verger am I supposed to follow?"' she later said.[31] A Prime Minister with more sense of history and personal gravitas might have expressed different sentiments.

The death of the Queen can be seen as a considerable hit to Truss's premiership. The loss of such a commanding and iconic figure as Elizabeth II had an impact, even if imperceptible, in creating uncertainty and unsettling people. The loss of ten working days just three days into her premiership meant Truss was unable to build momentum after her signature energy initiative. The initiative missed out on media commentary, much of which would have been positive. This might have been mitigated if she had listened to advice from Party Chair Jake Berry and Chief of Staff Mark Fullbrook to relaunch the package once the period of mourning was over. The almost total dearth of commentary and reaction meant she was unable to learn from the inevitable backlash to her largesse. Officials felt that mourning thus denied her a reality check. 'She needed a warning shot across her bows, a dose of financial reality,' said one. 'Do you think I'm going far enough?' she asked an official the night before the Mini-Budget, who worried that she was losing touch with reality.

Cabinet did not meet again after 9 September until the official mourning period was over. 'We lost any sense of Cabinet collectivity at that time,' said Simon Clarke. Lost too were opportunities, badly needed, for her to bond with her MPs. Meanwhile, with nothing political to do, Truss focused on the Mini-Budget. 'Liz was on fire, full of pent-up energy. She was frantically pushing supply-side reforms; the plans were not radical enough, they had to go further: why not more "investment zones", why not more road projects, why can't we go further? she kept asking. The sense was that Liz was moving ahead of the entire field,' said a supportive Cabinet minister. Did ten days of enforced passivity, playing second fiddle to the Royal Family, members of her own Cabinet and officials get to her, making her even more assertive and strong willed? Quite possibly, given her character.

The suspension of normal life damaged the formation of new relationships and working patterns too in No. 10, an office like no other. Without normal job descriptions and chains of command, trust and personal contacts are all important. 'No patterns of meetings were laid down and consolidated during this period,' said a senior official, 'and they never became embedded, till the final week, when it was too late.' 'The Queen's death created an unnerving atmosphere: it made us more detached and cut off,' said a senior Cabinet minister. For Truss, given to quirky working habits, the hiatus was particularly unfortunate: 'Liz appeared much more keen on where everybody should be located than on the rhythm of regular meetings in No. 10,' said an aide.

More damaging still was the lack of consultations that normally would have been held before an event as wide-ranging as the Mini-Budget. Friday 23 September was pencilled in for it, but for all the preceding week, Truss was preoccupied with ceremonial activities. On Friday 16 September, her entire day was devoted to attending a service at Llandaff Cathedral in Cardiff, before returning late to a rushed 'economy meeting' in the Cabinet Room. Lackadaisical debates took place about whether the fiscal event should be shifted earlier to capitalize on the muted afterglow of the energy support package, or delayed until October after the annual party conference. But Truss would hear none of it. 'We've had ten years of stagnation and no Conservative policies. We need shock and awe: we are not going to wait,' she said.

The political pause also provided the opportunity, Truss realized too late, for supporters of Sunak to regroup. 'Rishi had five former Chief Whips on his team working for him. It was all about power. They had seen their power base ripped away from them, and they were going to get it back,' said a Truss whip.

Tensions flared up over invitations to the Queen's funeral. Some senior Conservatives were angry not to have been included in the 'more inclusive' seat allocation, few more so than Gavin Williamson, who, as later quoted in the Independent Expert Panel report, messaged Chief Whip Wendy Morton to say 'don't forget I know how this works so don't puss me about', and 'you are showing f**k all interest in pulling things together. Don't bother asking anything from me', and 'let's see how many more times you f**k us all over. There is a price for everything.' Morton received the texts early in the mornings and, feeling intimidated by them, put in a complaint to CCHQ. When the messages were leaked in November, Williamson was forced to resign as a minister. The Independent Panel in September 2023 said he set out to make Morton's position difficult and frustrate her as she adjusted to her new job in revenge for his perception that he and others had been denied seats because they were not supporters of the new Prime Minister.[32] These exchanges indicate what was to follow before the premiership was over.

By the day of the Queen's funeral, 19 September, Truss had just thirty-one days left before she terminated her own leadership.

The Verdict: Command the Big Events?

From her handling of the twin shocks she faced, Truss emerged as a plausible if not fully convincing figure. She was strong and decisive in her reaction to the energy crisis, where a more cautious approach could have caused widespread hardship, economic turbulence and likely U-turns. The markets, as expected, accepted the logic; the mistake came in their imagining they could expect the same reaction with the Mini-Budget fifteen days later.

Truss met the Queen's death with a lacklustre response that avoided glaring errors. She may have been the tenth Prime Minister to oversee the death of a monarch, but none previously had to manage it anything like as early in their premiership. Most had six years and more, including Walpole when George I died in 1727, and Lord Liverpool when George III died in 1820; while the most inexperienced were Wellington in 1830 when George IV died, and Asquith in 1910 with Edward VII.

But there was no seizing of the agenda as there had been with Asquith in 1910, no commanding of the national story like Baldwin in 1936, nor silken words to soothe a nation like Churchill in 1952. Indeed, it seemed almost that the office of Prime Minister had shrunk over the years, rather than becoming presidential as politics students are often told.

Truss acquitted herself well enough for the nation and her party to continue to suspend their judgement on her premiership. But she needed to prove that she could step up to the challenges of office. These first two shocks were beyond her control: it was her response to the third shock, which she herself engineered, that was to prove fatal to her premiership.

Rule Number Five: Prime Ministers need to be credible figures on the world stage. Truss never won the respect of world leaders, notably President Biden. At the UN General Assembly on 21 September

5

BE CREDIBLE AND HIGHLY REGARDED ABROAD
19–22 September 2022

Many of Britain's top Prime Ministers – Pitt the Younger, Palmerston, Disraeli, Lloyd George, Churchill, Thatcher included – were giants abroad as well as being formidable presences in Britain. Applause on one stage boosted the PM's standing on the other. Equally, it's difficult for a Prime Minister who is failing at home to have much credibility with their peers abroad. International top dogs are proud of belonging to their exclusive club and much prefer stars, not losers, at their table.

For that reason, foreign policy matters to prime ministerial standing more than we might think. We cannot understand a premiership, Truss's or any other, without reckoning on their mark in foreign lands.

Truss: a Foreign Policy PM?

Truss came into No. 10 better prepared for the foreign stage than most of her predecessors. Since 1964 and the era of jet diplomacy, many incoming PMs were low on foreign experience, including Wilson, Thatcher, Blair, Cameron and May. On arrival in Downing Street, they were not known on the world stage and lacked a background in foreign affairs. Few remedied the deficiency quicker than Blair: his first major international meeting, an EU summit in Amsterdam in his second month as PM, saw him wow other leaders both within the conference hall and outside.

Truss was one of four Prime Ministers since 1964 to have been Foreign Secretary before assuming the highest office, alongside Callaghan, Major and Johnson. She was delighted when Johnson, in the wake of the withdrawal from Afghanistan fiasco in the summer of 2021, made her Dominic Raab's successor as Foreign Secretary, not least because of the prominence the job gave her on the international stage. She hoped this would allow her to outshine her competitors as Johnson's successor. Her views were inspired more by gut instinct than deep intellectual thought. As Adam Jones has noted, she saw the world in Manichean terms, the good guys against the bad. China and Russia were most certainly the latter, while the former was exemplified by the United States, perhaps best typified by the bond between Thatcher and Reagan at the time when Truss had come of political age. She was definitely not Trumpian: Reagan was the US President she most admired and sought to emulate. She was attracted to countries for their values. Democracies under threat from autocratic regimes, whether Israel, Taiwan or Ukraine, merited her ardent support and admiration.

Truss believed that Britain had a once in a generation opportunity post-Brexit. She imagined a new Britain on the world stage, just as she was to imagine a new Britain at home galvanized by her growth plan. As Foreign Secretary, she saw herself leading British attempts to play a pivotal role in supporting the liberal order. The AUKUS trilateral security agreement with the USA and Australia, happily announced on the day she became Foreign Secretary, was a totem of this. Underpinning her whole outlook was free trade, with like-minded countries clubbing together to protect their economic interests. 'Aid for trade' was her cause; she supported the cut in development spending to 0.5 per cent of national income in 2020 (from Cameron's 2013 commitment to 0.7 per cent).[1] Any human damage caused by these cuts was of no apparent concern to her.

Leading on Ukraine

The event that energized Truss the most during her political career was the Russian aggression against Ukraine. It involved the two countries she despised most: Russia and, eventually, China.

Ukraine, she sensed, was her Churchill, her Thatcher moment. The massive build-up of Russian troops on the Ukraine border in March and April 2021 while she had been Trade Secretary had excited her interest. By the time she became Foreign Secretary three months later, tensions had risen much higher, catalysed by Putin's open 'essay' in July 2021 claiming that Ukraine was historically part of Russia. That autumn she followed developments intensely, while focusing on completing her round of free-trade agreements. 'Liz always felt deep down that Putin intended to invade,' recalled an aide who remembers Truss being asked by an official in mid-February 2022 what she thought would happen: 'Putin has made up his mind to do it. It's not a case of if, but when,' she said decisively. Her battle was to convince foreign ministers across the EU who continued almost unanimously to believe that Putin was merely playing games in amassing troops on the border, trying to extract concessions.

As Foreign Secretary, she had been fighting a war not just against the Kremlin and the EU, but also, as we have seen, against Boris

Johnson at No. 10 and Ben Wallace at the Ministry of Defence about who could appear the most hawkish. Johnson clung to the crisis as a life raft, leveraging the benefit the PM has in a crisis of becoming de facto Foreign Secretary themselves. In January 2022, Wallace, then the man best placed to succeed Johnson, had been responsible for sending light anti-tank missiles to Ukraine. That month, not to be outdone, Truss, as the minister overseeing MI6 and GCHQ, and in consultation with the US, released secret intelligence to show that Russia was intent on invading Ukraine. 'This was vital in waking up the EU to Putin's true intentions,' said a senior official. She had visited Moscow in early February for uncompromising talks with Russian Foreign Affairs Minister Sergey Lavrov, challenging his argument that Russia felt threatened. On 17 February, the day after Johnson himself ordered the release of intelligence to show Russian troop numbers were increasing on the borders, she visited Kyiv where she demanded Russia withdraw its forces from Ukraine's borders: 'Russian aggression… menaces our friends in Ukraine, and threatens security and stability for us all.'[2] The visits gave her opportunities for grandstanding. Photographs of her in Moscow's Red Square in a black fur hat, and another on a tank in Estonia, were shared widely: one paper noted that there had been 700 Truss photographs released during her five months as Foreign Secretary, averaging four and a half a day.[3] 'One hundred per cent calculated decisions,' said an aide. 'The position of Boris was getting a lot weaker all the time. Of course we were alert to it.'

Shortly before 5 a.m. Kyiv time on 24 February, Putin announced a 'Special Military Operation' to 'defend' the Russian-controlled breakaway republics in Eastern Ukraine. He said that Ukraine would be 'demilitarized' and 'denazified'. Within moments Russian missiles poured down on the country, and Russian forces attacked from the east, south and north. Truss was woken to be told the news, and immediately key staff were called in for a meeting in the Foreign Office. 'I will remember it to my old age,' said one. 'It was about 4 a.m. I had been expecting the call, so wasn't really asleep. This is the call neither of us wanted to be having: "There are cruise missiles over Kyiv. The Foreign Secretary has been told. She has asked that you come in at once."' Once in the office the team were briefed on possible responses, including sanctions and the confiscation of assets. The official predictions were bleak – that Ukraine would be rapidly defeated by the Russian juggernaut.[4]

What followed surprised everybody. Ukraine's armed forces were much better prepared than the Russians expected. Within days, the Russian advance on Kyiv had been halted, and then Putin's lightning strike against Ukraine's capital degenerated into military catastrophe. President Volodymyr Zelenskyy inspired the world with his defiance of Russia. Defeated, the Russian army withdrew from the outskirts of Kyiv and Ukraine's north, and concentrated on less ambitious and more easily supported objectives in Ukraine's south and east. Ukraine had endured the first round.

The invasion, close observers of Truss believe, produced a metamorphosis in her outlook. 'That was when we started noticing a different side to Liz. We saw papers in her boxes coming back with fewer comments. She became less involved in the process of government, and more focused on the big picture. Suddenly, she was a figure of global importance,' said an aide. '"I know what I'm doing and I'm going to do it" became her default stance. She began not listening in the same way. By Easter 2022, it was clear we had a very different Liz.'

The speech she gave on 28 April at Mansion House calling for Russia to retreat to the pre-2014 borders, i.e. to relinquish Crimea which it had annexed that year, caused consternation in the White House. It briefed that it was irritated by her, and her hectoring request that the US increase its support for Ukraine (while not acknowledging that this was already many times what Britain contributed).[5] A more measured leader would not have provoked Washington in this way.

As if Russia was not enemy enough for her, she opened up a second front on China. This played well in sections of the party she needed to win round, not least Iain Duncan Smith. Here was a subject too on which she could 'out-Boris Boris': as one of her team said, 'there was always a sense that Boris hadn't felt the anti-China thing in his bones like she did', not least when he'd cosied up to Beijing as London Mayor. It provided the opportunity to put deep blue water between her and Sunak in the leadership election. At the end of August, with the last week of the campaign approaching, she let it be known that under her premiership, policy would be 'reshaped' and China would be designated as 'a threat' to national security of a similar status to Russia.[6] The foreign policy establishment pooh-poohed the notion when they heard it. 'It sounded very TV [worthy]. It didn't really mean anything,' said one. They waited to see whether it would amount to anything more than attention-seeking.

Of course, Truss was not alone in her views. Hardening attitudes to China were a feature of Western politics during the late 2010s. The election of Donald Trump in 2016 in the US had both demonstrated and sped up this trend, as did the Covid pandemic, for which some – not without reason – held Beijing responsible. It made sense – from a values-based perspective on foreign policy – to support democracy in Taiwan against autocracy in Beijing. But the darkening diplomatic climate saw China move closer to Russia and provide Moscow with much-needed equipment and technology in its war on Ukraine. 'China is the biggest enemy,' she said later. 'If Ukraine falls, it will give China a huge boost, which is right behind the war.'[7] After she stood down as Prime Minister, she developed this thesis in her book *Ten Years to Save the West*.

Northern Ireland

It wasn't just the brightest lights of great power politics that caught Truss's interest. Northern Ireland was another matter on which she was keen to gain support. This time it was the 'no-surrender' ERG MPs she had in her sights.

The issue had been a sore in the party since long before the compromise solution of the Northern Ireland Protocol, stuck together by Johnson in 2019 to replace May's 'backstop' to ensure Northern Ireland would remain aligned with the rest of the UK post-Brexit. For two years, inertia had reigned while hardline Brexit minister David Frost had been overseeing it. But possibilities for progress were suddenly opened up when he resigned from Johnson's government the weekend before Christmas in 2021. Insiders saw this as a way of launching his own political career.[8]

Johnson alighted on the Foreign Secretary as the ideal figure to take on the matter. Truss had no delusions that the master schemer was offering it to her knowing it would be 'a poisoned chalice', a clever wheeze his team had concocted to trip up a rival whose star continued in the ascendant. Thoughts of finding the most skilled minister to clean up a dangerous mess partly of his own making never entered his head. Her team fully intended it would rebound against No. 10. Their rivalry reached a high point in March when a paper she had placed in his PM box was leaked to the *Sunday Telegraph*. The press report, which painted her as trying to stop Johnson from invoking Article 16 of the Northern Ireland Protocol, provoked fury against her among Brexiteers.[9] 'It was not true, and they knew it. It was No. 10 making mischief so Johnson could be seen to be tougher on Northern Ireland than Liz, and good in the eyes of the right wing,' said an aide. Truss was furious; 'We're not going to submit anything on paper to No. 10 ever again,' she fumed. She stormed into No. 10 to see Johnson on Monday 28 March, the day after the article appeared. 'Right, we're going to legislate on this, no compromises,' she told the PM, one aide recalled. They agreed that any hope of support from the EU was forlorn, and from their deliberations emerged the hardline Northern Ireland Protocol Bill, which ground through the system until Johnson resigned in July, for her to pick up when she became PM.

Realizing the Brexit Vision

Truss despaired too of Johnson's half-hearted approach to optimizing the freedoms of deregulation Brexit promised. She saw 'investment zones' as her way to get to Brexit nirvana. While planning at Chevening during the leadership campaign, the Treasury told her repeatedly that these zones wouldn't generate any new investment, but merely suck investment away from neighbouring areas. 'But she didn't care if that was true or not. Her ambition was to create an overall appetite for low taxation and high investment to show that, once outside the EU, Britain can seize the advantages of deregulation,' said an official.

Johnson, who had been one of the most visible figures among the Vote Leave movement in the 2016 referendum, had done little as Prime Minister to capitalize on the opportunities of Brexit. Truss, who had voted for Remain but now believed in Brexit, also did little to optimize the possibilities, though that was rather forced by circumstance and the brevity of her tenure.

Truss: the Foreign Secretary Prime Minister

Most PMs sooner or later become captivated by foreign policy. For Truss, this came sooner. The opportunities for grandstanding on the world stage; the pampering on flights; grand British embassies and international conferences; meetings at the White House or the Élysée Palace; the elixir of making important decisions, unshackled from the grungy reality and constraints of domestic politics all propel the Prime Minister upwards from Heathrow or RAF Northolt. It can seem much easier to achieve things abroad than at home.

Some Prime Ministers appoint themselves Foreign Secretary, as did Salisbury and MacDonald. Others like Macmillan, Thatcher and Blair dwarfed their Foreign Secretaries. For Truss, she knew she would have a Foreign Secretary in James Cleverly who would do what she wanted. In the letter she presented to him on 6 September, she gave him seven priorities and nil surprises. Supporting Ukraine against Russia was first. Then came a renewed focus on the Indo-Pacific, meaning responding to China, with the instructions to 'increase support to Taiwan' perhaps the most striking, while taking on China's Belt and Road initiative by cranking up British investment partnerships was another exhortation within that focus. Then came Northern Ireland, preventing illegal migration and supporting international development. As Foreign Secretary, she had morphed the Commonwealth Development Corporation into British International Investment to drive British investment in South Asia and Africa.[10] The last two priorities were responding to international threats and boosting security partnerships. In these areas, Truss wanted Britain to be the primary European ally in NATO, to lead the international response to state threats and cyber security, to refresh the Integrated Review, strengthen long-term energy security and build a quantum computing partnership with the United States. In detail it certainly trumped Blair's terse instruction to the incoming British ambassador to Washington Christopher Meyer back in 2001 to 'get up the arse of the White House and stay there'.[11]

'Up the Arse of the White House'

Truss herself fulfilled Blair's instruction, if not quite in the way he intended. She had seen several world leaders when they were in London for the Queen's funeral and she was impatient to get to work on foreign issues. The annual UN General Assembly debate was to begin the next day. She was given the advice, not least by Catsaras, not to go herself, given that the Mini-Budget, the keystone of her premiership, was due three days later and her presence was needed to finalize details (in her absence, she deputed Coffey to chair discussions).

The Prime Minister did not always attend the UN General Assembly: Cameron had missed it in 2010 and 2013. Folk memories in Whitehall of Chancellor George Osborne being in the US just before his botched March 2012 Budget were still in circulation. But Truss's political team said she should go, and she herself was anxious to have her planned bilateral with EU Commission President Ursula von der Leyen on the Northern Ireland Bill. Approval was obtained from Buckingham Palace for her to leave straight after the funeral on Monday, still officially the mourning period; she departed still wearing black. She ended up seeing von der Leyen twice and she proved key to unblocking the impasse. Their meeting secured agreement for back channels to open up, and for ideas to be explored and tested. After the Mini-Budget momentum was lost, and it was left for Sunak to pick up the pieces. The result was the Windsor Framework of February 2023, a legal agreement between the UK and the EU to adjust the Northern Ireland Protocol, bearing more than a passing reference to the ideas that Truss had promoted the year before.[12]

Meeting President Biden was to be the other highlight of her two days in New York. He had first been elected to the US Senate in November 1972, over two years before she was born. Fiercely proud of his Irish roots, he was critical of her Brexit and Northern Ireland machinations: 'We can't allow the Good Friday Agreement that brought peace to Northern Ireland to become a casualty of Brexit,' he had tweeted in September 2020.[13] Indeed, he and his administration regarded Brexit as a huge mistake. He viewed Truss sceptically as a know-nothing upstart. As Foreign Secretary, she had displayed little interest, for all her admiration of Reagan, in contemporary American politics or wanting to build relationships with US politicians. She further irritated the White House when, at the NATO summit in Madrid in June 2022, she had met a congressional delegation and was heard to be critical while venting her frustrations on US policy on Ukraine. Inevitably, it got back to Secretary of State Antony Blinken. 'The Democratic Administration was very, very conscious of foreigners stirring things up on domestic politics and it went down badly,' admitted a British official. Her frustrations with the Biden administration were no secret: she regularly complained that 'We have worse trade terms with the US than with any other country.'

So all eyes had been on that all-important first conversation on 6 September between the new Prime Minister and Biden. It didn't start well. Truss's political team complained that the President kept her waiting for twenty-three minutes. After holding on for quarter of an hour, they started joking, 'Perhaps he can't find the Oval Office', 'Perhaps he doesn't want to find the Oval Office', and 'He's overslept'. 'We were pretty cynical. We thought his lateness was power play,' said one. 'Not at all,' said an old diplomatic hand later. 'Frankly, the Americans are always late – so are the French. She might have taken it personally, but it happens all the time.' When the President eventually came on the line, he congratulated her politely, but made it clear Northern Ireland was all he wanted to talk about. 'He didn't want to discuss free trade,' said one of the team. Their initial call must have ranked at the bottom of all the congratulatory calls from US Presidents to new Prime Ministers since the special relationship kicked off in earnest in 1941. At the Queen's funeral, protocol prioritizing the abundant number of Commonwealth guests resulted in Biden being placed in the fourteenth row, a fact eagerly leaped on by Trump, who wrote, 'this is what happens to America in just two short years… No respect!… If I were president, they wouldn't have sat me back there.'[14] It wasn't an auspicious start.

They met in person on 21 September, before Truss's UN speech. The day before, he had tweeted, 'I'm sick and tired of trickle-down economics. It has never worked. We're building an economy from the bottom up and middle out.'[15] This was seen in London as a direct criticism of Truss and her policies, all the harsher for coming the day after the funeral. They met in one of the bland UN bilateral rooms and flicked through the major points in an almost perfunctory way – there was no warmth or meeting of minds as they discussed Russia and Ukraine, China, and Iran. The Northern Ireland Protocol wasn't discussed in any detail, and Truss continued to think the US was unhelpful, but she did say that British defence spending would rise to 3 per cent of national income – a pledge she was ultimately unable to fulfil.[16] Biden's final intervention on 16 October came nine days before she quit when, while insouciantly waiting for an ice cream in Oregon, he suggested to reporters he wasn't the only world leader to think her economic measures had been 'a mistake'.[17] 'The President would never have uttered such words about a fellow leader if he had not thought that she was not long for this world,' said Kim Darroch, former British ambassador to the US.[18] 'Biden's intervention was devastating and calculated,' said an insider. 'Outrageous', was Truss's verdict on his comment. 'He was very unhelpful frankly from the start, in favour of a high-tax Europe and high government spending.'[19] There was, most unusually with a departing PM, no farewell call with the President after her resignation.

Her only other overseas trip as PM came on 6 October, when she flew to Prague for the inaugural meeting of the European Political Community (EPC), a forum that had been proposed by Macron earlier in the year to provide a platform for all forty-seven European political leaders (both EU and non-EU) to discuss common concerns. She requested that the name 'EPC' be changed so it was not reminiscent of the EEC, forerunner of the EU; she also called for a roundtable discussion on immigration, and asked if London could host the second meeting. As evidence of her poor international authority, she was successful on none of these.[20]

Her last real intervention in foreign affairs came on a G7 video conference call on 11 October focusing on Ukraine. President Zelenskyy was also on the call. It was not his, but her, premiership that was crashing. She spoke about an 'increasingly desperate Putin' and said 'he is losing', comments that, though aligned with conventional analysis at the time, now seem both complacent and sadly optimistic. She said that she wanted the G20 meeting the following month to mobilize support from key G20 players, including India, Brazil and South Africa, to make it clear that they would not support any further escalation, and that any use of nuclear weapons by Putin would 'lead to severe consequences for Russia'. She was listened to carefully, if not with obvious respect.[21]

A final late flaring of her flame before it was extinguished came after the appointment of Jeremy Hunt as Chancellor. Hunt effectively became, on appointment, the domestic Prime Minister for as long as she remained. 'She liked the idea that she would run foreign policy like Blair, leaving domestic policy to Hunt like Brown. For a few hours, at least, it seemed credible,' said an official. The idea wasn't entirely mad. She had laid out her store on foreign policy with admirable clarity, not least at her speech to the United Nations when she spoke of Britain's post-Brexit mission 'to champion freedom, sovereignty and democracy'. Not entirely mad, but certainly for the birds.

On the morning she returned to Britain from the UN, Thursday 22 September, she had just twenty-eight days till her resignation announcement.

The Verdict: Be Credible and Highly Regarded Abroad?

Truss's aspiration to be Britain's de facto Foreign Secretary (alongside de facto Chancellor) came to little. Ukraine was to be her flagship foreign policy; she wanted to be seen as 'continuity Boris', and even 'turbo Boris' in Kyiv and beyond. But even on her call with Zelenskyy on her first day in No. 10, it was clear that the chemistry wasn't there, and that the Ukrainian leader was still uncomprehending about why she had taken the place of his beloved Boris. ('You're a hero,' Johnson had said to Zelenskyy on their final emotional call. 'No, *you're* a hero,' the Ukrainian leader said back to him.)[22] She planned to visit Kyiv shortly after the Mini-Budget, but the subsequent nosedive meant 'everything was off the table with the trip', as an aide said. By that point, the ongoing political crisis meant that she could not be away from London and out of communication long enough to facilitate a secret journey of that kind. She was therefore unable to share in the glory of the major Ukrainian breakthrough and victory near Kharkiv that began on her first day in power. She rued that so little credit fell on her.

Truss had several of the qualities needed by a Prime Minister on the foreign stage. Unlike some PMs, she was good on intelligence and reading reports, which her team brought to her by hand rather than putting in her box. She dealt well with a couple of alerts where RAF planes were scrambled to intercept unidentified or unresponsive aircraft in British airspace. She had a clear agenda on Ukraine, Northern Ireland and China, and wanted to bring to fruition her long-term gas plan with Norway. She was working with Macron, despite her campaign gaffe of saying 'the jury is out' on whether he was a 'friend or foe'. Ultimately, she developed a generally positive relationship with him, including plans for Anglo–French cooperation on nuclear power stations.[23] She had plans for building on her relationship with Australia (her strongest overseas relationship, albeit one damaged when the Liberal–National Coalition lost power). In addition to her visit to Kyiv, she had a trip to India slated for 7–9 November, and a British–Irish Council meeting in Blackpool on 10–11 November. The following week, she was due to return to Bali for the G20 where her premiership had first become a possibility. On her return she was due to visit South Africa for three days, before going to Montréal for COP15 in December.

None of this was to transpire. Rather than being seen as a heroic leader on the world stage, she was seen as a curiosity, an aberration who led a country desperate to find, but ultimately failing to achieve, a respected independent voice, post-Brexit. Worse, the reaction to the Mini-Budget damaged the perception of Britain as a stable, predictable and dependable country in foreign capitals, though it seems fair to say that the brevity of Truss's tenure limited that damage. The relationship with the US President had sunk to the lowest level since Eden in 1956, and hard work was needed after her departure to restore trust, as it was to re-establish confidence in Britain in other overseas capitals. One senior Foreign Office figure felt that perceptions of the UK had returned to 'normal' within a few months.

It's hard to reach any conclusion other than she failed to meet the fifth test of premiership: to be a credible leader of Britain abroad.

Rule Number Six: The Prime Minister needs the right character and a willingness to learn on the job. Truss was unwilling to learn or to accept she had anything to learn. Here in the Commons on 23 September

6

LEARN HOW TO BE PRIME MINISTER

The story so far is not without cause for concern – the shallowness of Truss's support and her provocative Cabinet selection prominent among them – but the positives perhaps outweighed these: a decisive response to the energy price crisis, unobtrusive leadership following the death of the Queen, and a competent start on the world stage. We have seen little to suggest, on the surface at least, that within just twenty-seven days she would have thrown in the towel. Can clues be found in her character?

'Prime Ministers need three qualities,' an adviser remembered her saying. 'Charisma, vision and implementation. Boris had the first, I have the second and Rishi had the third.' There is an element of truth in that, as well as self-knowledge. But we need to probe deeper. Because character matters. The qualities that are needed to get the incumbent into Downing Street – charisma, appearance and communication skills – are not necessarily the same as those required to make a success of the job once inside. Sometimes, the very qualities that take a politician to the top, including political pugnacity, tribalism, populism, egotism and economy with the truth, undermine them once in Downing Street.

Truss had breezed her way up through the ministerial ranks. The question was, how would this highly impulsive politician cope when she no longer had anyone above her to push back?

Truss's Positive Character Traits

To dismiss Liz Truss as always destined to fail at No. 10 is too simplistic and does not help us understand the task of the modern Prime Minister, or specifically what went wrong in her premiership. She had some of the qualities successful Prime Ministers need. They are not always the qualities that we might presume. We cannot understand her premiership in isolation but only through the lens of the experience of other Prime Ministers, successful and otherwise. It takes time for PMs to display their full abilities. True, she had just forty-nine days in office. But there is no evidence that she was willing to learn from history or from advice. She knew best.

Those Prime Ministers who have succeeded in the modern era, like leaders in all fields, have needed to be *optimists*. Truss most certainly was. She spoke repeatedly in public and private about how she was going to be the leader to reverse ten years and more of national decline, possessing an almost messianic belief in her ability to achieve it where others had fallen short. She exuded positivity from every pore. Her irrepressible optimism was perhaps her most winning trait. But to bring about national transformation required more than self-belief and drive from the top. Prime Ministers need to temper optimism with realism. Churchill, while never communicating his doubts about ultimate victory in the Second World War, never ceased to remind the country about the toll it would take. Blair and Cameron were, in contrast, overly optimistic about the extent of the change they could deliver at home and abroad. They might well have achieved more with realism and graft. Johnson's boosterist optimism and habit of playing to the gallery were substitutes for putting in the hard yards and carrying his Cabinet with him.

'Liz was prone to taking up positions and championing them without thinking through the consequences,' one former Cabinet minister noted. She repeated the same mistake in No. 10, not thinking through the risks and consequences of her growth plan. Optimism is a necessary but not a sufficient condition for a successful Prime Minister. Truss ultimately failed because she never managed to enthuse her MPs with her optimistic vision nor exercised sufficient caution. Some just thought her manner and plans plain bonkers. Rather admirably, if a little eccentric, she retained her optimism right to the very end. Seldom has a Prime Minister been happier after they knew the game was up. 'She radiated positivity in her final days, as if she was almost happy it was over,' said an aide.

No job in Britain bears more responsibility or is more relentlessly demanding than that of Prime Minister. Without boundless *energy*, and a strong physical constitution, Prime Ministers underachieve. They will be woken during the night when their ever-watchful Private Office deems a crisis in Britain or globally merits it. They need to be awake before 6 a.m. to spend an hour or more going through papers in their overnight box, and they are often at work at their desk by 7 a.m. Living above the job, as the No. 10 flat allows, can be a boon. They may have flown home overnight, as Truss did from New York on the morning of Thursday 22 September after the UN General Assembly, to be whisked by police outriders into Downing Street, but they're straight back into work, with meetings, briefings and public appearances throughout the day. No chance for a catnap. Prime Ministers have too little time set aside for exercise, resting and reading, and evening engagements spent schmoozing will mean they're rarely back up in the flat before 10 p.m., with papers having accumulated for them to read through.

Ultimately, Johnson's lack of effort undermined confidence in him, but no one had such concerns about Truss's energy, even after eight punishing weeks on the campaign trail. Officials described how 'she would take great trouble with her boxes, would read the papers, was very iterative, quite geeky with a pronounced policy mindset'. After three years of her shambolic predecessor, they were delighted to have someone who promised to be more businesslike back on the bridge. She put more thought into how to structure No. 10 than many others. Her promise, made in her leadership acceptance speech, that 'we will deliver, we will deliver and we will deliver' was not idle: she put great effort into planning the first thirty days, the first hundred days and beyond. Her many critics in the party might not have liked her personally, or her policies, but few felt she was lacking the serious intent required for the job.

At forty-seven, Truss was arguably the right age: she'd gained plenty of experience but was young enough for her energy levels and health to be undiminished. Aged forty-two, Sunak was certainly too young, as were Blair and Cameron at forty-three: all would have been better Prime Ministers if they had more life experience. Gladstone, conversely, was clearly too old when he came back at eighty-two in 1892 for his final period in office. More recently, Jim Callaghan was sixty-four when he became PM in April 1976: no longer the firebrand he once was, he paced himself well, never having late meetings and calling out to his Private Office 'I'm going up now' at sensible times in the evening. He told one aide that he had a duty to keep fit, 'just as an athlete keeps himself fit'.[1]

Illness dogged many PMs impeding their energy and effectiveness, including three in a row in Churchill, Eden and Macmillan. Woe betide any Prime Minister who looks tired or is unwell: nothing starts tongues wagging like an ailing or fatigued premier.

Truss was almost preternaturally healthy, ate sensibly and was rarely unwell. She liked her white wine for sure. Witnesses testified, though, that she was often 'high' on caffeine from her beloved double espressos. But there is no evidence, as there was with other PMs like Rosebery (morphine) and Eden (Drinamyl), that her judgement was impaired by stimulants and drugs. In her memoir, she wrote that she had, in an echo of Rosebery, suffered insomnia, lying awake counting quarter-hours as they chimed on the nearby Horse Guards clock.[2]

Did the extreme stress of the final days in No. 10 cause a breakdown of sorts? Certainly her mood was extremely volatile. She later described the press conference announcing Kwarteng's sacking as like 'officiating at my own funeral' and listening to Hunt's statement in the Commons as an 'out of body experience [and] uniquely painful'.[3] One of her advisers said that 'she knew that she had f***ed up, and that made it so hard on a human level, to watch someone go through that'. They commented that in those last few days she became 'unhinged', stubborn and angry. She was certainly swamped and politically overwhelmed. But there is no evidence of an incapacitating breakdown. She responded calmly to a security incident on 12 October when a commercial aircraft was causing concern and an alert was issued (the incident was resolved without action). She also came to accept her own political mortality rather quicker than some other PMs.

Neither her colleagues nor her team could cavil at her ability to *work hard* and keep ahead of the job. Word soon spreads if the

Prime Minister is not on top of their paperwork, properly briefed for meetings, or appears at a loss in public. The Private Office and team around them in Downing Street are vital to ensure that the PM's time is optimally used each day. Any Prime Minister is only ever as good as their official team, which is why they need to have the very best principal private secretary available, as Truss had in Nick Catsaras (albeit one lacking Treasury experience, and whose advice to appoint a No. 10 permanent secretary who did have it she shunned). The PM's margins are so tight, their time so pressured and the damage from mistakes so unforgiving that without the very best team, they fall down. While not matching the boundless work levels of Thatcher, Truss met the standards for shouldering the Prime Minister's burden of red boxes and exhaustive paperwork. Hard work was not the issue, though typically she was very selective in where she focused her attention.

Nor was there a want of *high intelligence*. While not an intellectual, nor possessing the first-class academic mind of a Clement Attlee (a former lecturer at LSE), Harold Wilson (an academic at Oxford) or Gordon Brown (a PhD, lecturer and author), she was more than bright and sharp enough for the job. 'Analytical, quick and intelligent, if not profound', was the verdict of Hammond who had worked with her closely at the Treasury.[4] One of many unwelcome surprises for incoming Prime Ministers is the almost limitless range of topics that they need to master, and the speed at which they have to do so.

Prime Minister's Questions is merely the most visible way in which they are challenged and probed under the merciless eye of television cameras and fellow MPs. She passed her first PMQ test comfortably, but she lacked the fleet of foot of a figure like Blair or Cameron, and her final PMQs on Wednesday 19 October was a fiasco. Searching questions by journalists would often catch her out, not so much because she didn't understand the question but more that she was trying too hard to calculate the response. Her reading was broad rather than deep and was in narrow and self-confirmatory waters. She lacked the intellectual confidence to have her ideas challenged, and would seek out affirmation rather than challenge or contradiction. In her defence one might say predecessors who saw too much of the other side of an argument, such as the intellectual Lord Rosebery and Arthur Balfour, didn't always make decisive Prime Ministers. But her single-mindedness was obtuse and became progressively so in No. 10: insiders noted how impatient she became with any questioning, how she would increasingly swear, with her language scattered with the F-word.

The flip side of this was that the Prime Minister needs to be *decisive*, and Liz Truss most certainly could be. She displayed that quality in defining her agenda, choosing her Cabinet, and then changing the direction and her Chancellor when under intense fire. It may have been wrong to have done so, but no one could say she was incapable of taking tough decisions. May and Sunak in contrast struggled at times to say 'enough: this is what we will do'. Brown did too, as in the decision in the autumn of 2007 on whether to call an early general election. Johnson in his most effective period as Prime Minister, his first six months stewarded by Dominic Cummings from July to December 2019, was decisive on many occasions, including prorogation and the decree in September 2019 to expel twenty-one moderate Conservative MPs for voting against a 'no deal Brexit'. But after his election victory in December 2019, and especially after Cummings left, Johnson's decisiveness collapsed disastrously until he found a cause in Ukraine.

All leadership is lonely, but none more so than heading up a country. 'You want a friend in Washington?' President Truman asked on the election trail in 1948. 'Then get a dog.' Truss didn't have a dog. But she had what all the top tier Prime Ministers have benefited from in Downing Street: a *strong family base*. She had an unfailingly loyal and supportive spouse in Hugh O'Leary, an accountant, who, as with Denis Thatcher and Philip May with their respective wives, judged his own all but impossible job to perfection, supporting but not intruding. Unsubstantiated stories circulated in high places and low, sometimes egged on by her political opponents, of her personal life. During the leadership campaign, she was grilled intensely until her staff were satisfied that there was no substance to the allegations. Suspicions of her phone being hacked by Russia's intelligence agency, the FSB, led to two changes of device. During an inquisition she was asked whether there was anything on the phone she should be worried about; but there was nothing untoward bar some periodic playful if harmless messages, as was her style. What is known to be true is her affair with fellow MP Mark Field, which became public knowledge fifteen years before she became Prime Minister.[5] But it did not stop her resumption of a happy and close marriage. In moments of high pressure in No. 10, she would often say 'I'm just going upstairs to talk to Hugh', without doubt her closest confidant. Little commented upon, she managed to also be a loving and devoted mother to her two daughters, a huge challenge for any top level politician.

Truss could be *politically savvy*. Prime Ministers who are not, like Eden, Heath and Sunak, can stumble. They need to be able to read the political room better than others, or at least to listen to those who have a better political nose than them where they don't. 'Liz had tremendous political skills and saw quicker than any other in the team who was stuffed and who would make it,' said Stein.[6] She calculated that it would be better to stick with Johnson during the July 2022 crisis, rather than join her colleagues in resigning, which enabled her to become his heir. She had negotiated the turbulent waters of Brexit, shaking off her Remainer credentials, to become the standard bearer for Brexit. Her political antennae on her journey upwards could be peerless. Only once entombed in the catacomb of No. 10 did she fully lose her touch. Ultimately, the savviness was micro and self-centred when it needed to be macro and inclusive: she never really understood either the job or the country she now led. A savvier Prime Minister, like Blair after the death of Princess Diana, would have sensed the opportunity after the death of the Queen to reach out to the whole nation.

Being willing to *take advice* is another necessary prime ministerial quality, and knowing *who to trust*. Surprisingly, perhaps, given she was such a strong personality and working in a Whitehall rife with abrasive special advisers, the people she chose tended to be courteous and mild-mannered. Thérèse Coffey as her DPM and Wendy Morton as her Chief Whip could indeed be criticized for being insufficiently daunting or tough. Her special adviser team was populated by people who were bright, smart and loyal. She didn't repeat Johnson's mistake of ditching those who had served her before Downing Street and substituting them with hard-nosed bruisers. The reason it happened with Johnson is instructive: he was known to be so weak and ineffectual he needed strong minders to keep him on track. Truss was not like that.

With the exception of the sacking of Tom Scholar, and despite her well-known criticisms of the civil service establishment, she trusted her officials, including, initially at least, figures such as Simon Case who were relatively new to her. She readily accepted advice on the Queen's funeral arrangements, as she did on how to change direction after the Mini-Budget meltdown. She found, though, in common with all other Prime Ministers, that the speed of operation of No. 10 made it difficult to know whose advice to trust, and she very quickly found herself caught up in a bubble, without the time to reason matters through with her trusted team.

No relationship has caused Prime Ministers more anguish than that with their Chancellors. The PM needs to be able to *work harmoniously* with them and all their senior ministers, and this Truss mostly did. The departmental objectives she presented each Cabinet minister with came with the instruction that she did not want to interfere unduly. Most post-war PMs had difficulty at some time with their Chancellors, Churchill with R.A. Butler (1951–55) and Cameron with Osborne (2010–16) being among the exceptions. Truss managed to demote her inherited Chancellor, Zahawi, and park him contentedly into his new berth, while working relatively well with his two successors, Kwarteng and then Hunt. She enjoyed good relationships with some others including Foreign Secretary Cleverly, though relations with her DPM Coffey became fraught, as they were from day one with her leadership rivals Braverman, Mordaunt and Badenoch. There was of course little time for relationships to sour, as inevitably they do around the Cabinet table, but she showed some promise at handling relationships in the brief period she was there.

The Prime Minister needs to display *moral seriousness* and a sense of mission, which Truss most certainly did. There can be no doubting her sincerity or determination to do what that she thought was right for the country. Prime Ministers who lack these attributes learn that their indecision soon characterizes their whole government.

To the surprise of many contemporaries, Truss showed some promise too on a final character quality required for the office, *acting with dignity*, although her rudeness in gracelessly not acknowledging Sunak when the results of the leadership election were declared on Monday 5 September was a worrying start. Aware that she had a reputation as a leaker, she made moves to ensure that she herself would lead a confidential and collegiate government that revivified the doctrine of collective responsibility. Too many Prime Ministers have been obsessed by the demands of the media cycle. 'She wanted her premiership to be strategic, not tactical and day-to-day,' said an official. 'She took it to the other extreme, and refused to let it impinge on her premiership,' said Fullbrook: one day, she even announced, 'We're not having newspapers in the office any more.'[7] During the Queen's mourning and funeral period she made no attempt to upstage the Royal Family, and she was never more statesmanlike than in the manner of her departure and the arrangements she made for the succession. She performed often well and appropriately in public, if never spectacularly, all the way through to her final speech on 25 October at the conclusion of her premiership. At times, towards the end, she appeared to find almost superhuman self-belief and gall in putting on a positive face when her premiership was crashing to the ground.

Subsequently, though, with her triumphalism and refusal to acknowledge mistakes after she ceased to be PM, she reverted to type.

Truss's Character Shortfalls

None of the fifty-eight incumbents, not even the most successful, have had a complete set of prime ministerial skills. Some of the most adept, like Palmerston and Lloyd George, have also been the most flawed. So we should not expect Liz Truss to display all the character virtues required, let alone in her very brief premiership. Many of the best have been highly idiosyncratic too, including Walpole, Gladstone, Salisbury and Churchill. Her flaws in character and skills nevertheless take us a long way to understanding the premature and cataclysmic end of her premiership.

First up, the Prime Minister must be able to set out and communicate their stall. That is the whole point of the job. But *public speaking* was never a strength. While some of the top tier Prime Ministers such as Disraeli, Gladstone, Lloyd George and Churchill were exceptional orators, many, including Attlee and Thatcher, could be quite wooden. Given her thin support among MPs Truss badly needed to be able to talk in public in a way that won their sympathy and support. But her appearances before the 1922 Committee, in Parliament and at the annual party conference failed to connect with or inspire her audience. Disenchantment with her rapidly grew as a result.

All successful Prime Ministers need to be, even when not natural speakers, *good storytellers*. They need to be good teachers or explainers to the nation at large about the challenges they face, and what they're trying to do. Gladstone, Attlee and Thatcher all communicated a narrative that threaded their policies together and illustrated what their leadership could bring. One of the best was Stanley Baldwin, who mastered the radio as a tool of communication, and used it to communicate his vision of a reassuring stability during the uncertainty of the 1920s and 1930s.

Truss found it hard to manage that and difficult to persuade those beyond her immediate constituency of her cause. She lacked charm and had none of Blair's persuasive appetite to sway sceptics, as he did before and after the invasion of Iraq in 2003. She did not convince others that she was the heir to Thatcher, least of all when Sunak and every other candidate was claiming the same mantle. She was better at persuading people to join in common cause against others, expressly the 'unity candidate' against Sunak, than she was at gaining genuine converts to her own platform. So, when the common enemy evaporated, to the extent he ever did, she was exposed.

The Prime Minister needs a *steady temperament*. This cannot suddenly be acquired in Downing Street, which soon exposes every last character flaw of the incomer. Impulse control and maturity, especially in the face of people advocating risky actions, is a quality they must possess. Baldwin, Attlee and Macmillan were the ultimate 'steady hands' at the tiller in the mid-twentieth century, while in their different ways, Major, Blair and Cameron exemplified the quality more recently. At the heart of this attribute is that the greater the pressure becomes in a crisis, the more focused, not more panicky, they become. Their coolness fortifies the Cabinet and the wider government. Psychological security and maturity is vital because the Prime Minister has to be the most grown-up person in the room. Too often in those final thirty-two days, Liz Truss was not. 'Liz became very irritable, paranoid and even unhinged: she knew that she had f**ked up, which made it worse for her,' said an aide. After the Mini-Budget backfired, she would be angry with her staff. 'She's shouting at everyone – at aides and officials – that "we've got to somehow find the money"', said one witness. 'When we tell her "it can't be done", she shouts back, "It's not true. You've got to find it."' 'Some Prime Ministers were brittle, like Eden and Brown. But Liz took it to a whole new level. She simply wasn't suited to the job,' concluded Kwarteng.[8]

The Prime Minister must be *generous* and *inclusive*. She fell down more completely on this than in any other single area. Her decision that there were to be only 'true-believers' (true-believers in what?) fatally undermined her government. Divide and rule was her philosophy. It may have worked before Downing Street, but it certainly didn't once in the building.

Prime Ministers must have *iron self-control*. But Truss never mastered her inner demons. The two months of the leadership election 'was like a hot house', recalled one of her team. 'It took a massive toll on everybody physically and emotionally.' Once in No. 10 she drove herself and her team to almost absurd limits of endurance. 'She took an almost perverse pleasure in denying herself sleep and her team sleep,' lamented one.

Prime Ministers need to build close, high-performing and loyal teams in No. 10, as Blair and Cameron did so conspicuously. Her team-building skill was totally absent. Even senior Cabinet ministers like Kwarteng, Philp and Clark could be treated with contempt and humiliated in public. She regularly told her personal staff to 'shut up' or simply blanked them. She had little awareness of social space, and she could be unpleasantly caustic in her sense of humour. Her team would regularly feel that she was talking behind their backs and playing one off against the other. 'Divide and rule was the method, she never said sorry, and hardly ever said thank you,' recalled an aide. 'While Dominic Raab was unpleasant to everyone when he was

Foreign Secretary, Liz would pick out individuals,' said an observer.

All Prime Ministers have had outlier personalities – you have to be a bit unusual to want the role – but hers was one of the oddest. 'She's hard work to be with. You can't sit and have a conversation with her. She doesn't emote,' said one of her close Cabinet ministers. 'Liz never understood Cabinet, or that collective responsibility is a two-way street,' said Mordaunt. 'Politics is a team sport, and she never understood that.'⁹ On an individual level, she was not skilful at building personal relationships with MPs and key stakeholders, as Prime Ministers need to do. Outside her immediate family, friends were almost totally lacking; Coffey, Morton and Chloe Smith (whom she appointed as Coffey's successor at Work and Pensions) were rare exceptions. 'No one used the word "autism",' said one of her ministerial colleagues. 'But it's what we were thinking – her reluctance to engage with people, her fixation on precise numbers, and her unpredictability when the s**t hits the fan.' Before No. 10, she outsourced her emotional intelligence in particular to Jarvis and Porter, but the filter fell away when she became PM.

'She's totally, totally full of self-belief,' said one observer. 'A symptom of her processing difficulties was that she didn't see the world as others saw it, and had difficulty understanding why her views and proposals were not immediately taken up,' said another. 'Years of frustration, as she saw it, of being talked down to and dismissed as a female politician and as a minister gnawed away deep inside her. She hated people not taking her and her ideas seriously. I suspect that over the years, there was a great swelling of anger and resentment, building up in her mind against people mocking her. So when she had the opportunity of ultimate power, it was payback,' said a senior Cabinet minister. Payback came in her speech at the party conference on 5 October. 'I know how it feels to have your potential dismissed by those who think they know better', was a line proposed by a speechwriter that made the final cut. 'I love it! – It's a massive f**k you. It's great. It's kind of deeply true,' she told her team, adding, 'It's a bit too honest.' By now, she was venting her full feelings. 'It's basically a class-related issue as well. That's the other reason people call me "stupid", "mad". Public schoolboys!' Then a pause and a rare moment of self-reflection: her staff came largely from these schools. 'Forgive me… I don't dislike *all* public schoolboys.'

The most essential quality that every Prime Minister must possess is *judgement*. She had the self-awareness to know that she might not be ready for the job; indeed, that she might never be ready for it. But she never appreciated that she lacked the elusive quality of judgement, i.e. of people, of timing, and how decisions would be received. As Prime Minister, without even understanding or acknowledging the need for judgement, she was reckless. 'Earlier in her career, she always had a boss above her. In No. 10, there was no one to rein her in, and she couldn't cope with it,' said an official. Only when it became impossible for her to continue with the Mini-Budget decisions did she listen to advice; by then, her premiership was effectively over.

Prime Ministers need to understand the limitations of the job; they need to *delegate* and trust those they have appointed. Truss's instincts were right before she came into No. 10: she wanted her team to be small, like she remembered Cameron's as being; she wanted to be the chair rather than the chief executive; she wanted to rely on her Deputy Prime Minister to oversee the details; and she wanted to trust her departmental ministers to execute the plans she had given them. These good intentions quickly crumpled in the frenzy of ultimate power. 'Fundamentally, Liz misunderstood the job of Prime Minister. It's not to be the policy chief or driver, but instead to set the direction and support others doing the work,' said one aide. The moment she came in, she asked her staff to 'clear her diary' as she had done at the Foreign Office. 'I'm not going to do this. I'm not going to do that,' she would say. Officials were soon tearing their hair out telling her, 'But Prime Ministers have to do ABC or see XY and Z.' 'Why? I'm not going to do it,' she replied flatly. So meetings were missed with key people at home and abroad. Her team recalled her spending days after the Mini-Budget sitting in the Cabinet Room trying to drive everything herself. 'Action this day,' she said like Churchill during the Second World War. 'I want everything now, five minutes ago,' she would demand. But it left no time for the necessary political, administrative and legal checks. 'We've got to do this *now*. The general election is only two years away. We need to deliver now,' she repeatedly said.

'Liz was not good enough to manage No. 10 and be CEO. No one could tell her. She always felt she knew the answer. She would arrive at meetings telling people what she wanted. We were the executors and she was giving us instructions,' said an aide. This trait was fortified by her partial reading of Thatcher's premiership, as we have already seen. 'She liked the fact that Thatcher would say what she thought at the beginning of the meeting,' said Hammond. 'Liz would say, "I think we should do this," and then she wouldn't listen to what others said. But Thatcher did listen, and had the confidence to absorb contrary viewpoints,' he concluded.[10]

She failed in two final ways. Prime Ministers have to be able to *understand nuance* and to see shades of grey. But her world view was totally black and white. 'Reagan and free markets good; most other politicians and most other things bad,' said an official. Finally, they must have a sense of *tempered egoism*. Most PMs are relentlessly egotistical, and sacrifice family, colleagues and friends for power. But her vanity, neediness and willingness to trample over others was of Johnsonian proportions.

The Verdict: Learn How to Be Prime Minister?

Truss's very considerable character flaws swamped her qualities, above all having a much clearer purpose than the other four Prime Ministers in the fourteen years of Tory rule. She did set the agenda. She did use her preparatory time before No. 10 to prime her ministers. But she didn't do her homework or alter course until it was too late. And then she was finished. Why? Because in the final analysis, she lacked the single most important quality a Prime Minister needs: *judgement*. Yet not even her greatest enemy expected it to implode within twenty-seven days. So what happened?

Rule Number Seven: Avoid major policy failures. Kwarteng delivering his budget speech on Friday 23 September

7

AVOID MAJOR POLICY FAILURES
23 September–2 October 2022

Policy failures and reversals *on the way up* do not stop an ambitious politician from becoming Prime Minister. After all, many Prime Ministers sat as a minister in a previous and, most likely, defeated government. But major errors *in office* are a totally different matter.

Gladstone's last ministry of 1892–94 was unable to pass Home Rule for Ireland, and once the Lords had rejected the measure, his eventual departure was inevitable. Thatcher never recovered from her unpopular poll tax policy in 1989 and was out of office the following year, nor did Major restore his authority fully after Britain's ejection from the European Exchange Rate Mechanism in September 1992 on Black Wednesday. Blair's position was never the same after the widely criticized invasion of Iraq in 2003. Cameron chose to jump before his position became untenable following the defeat of his Remain side in the Brexit referendum in June 2016. After May's Brexit deal was defeated in early 2019, her authority steadily diminished to nothing before the axe fell.

Truss's Bold Economic Vision

Not since Thatcher had a Conservative Prime Minister believed so deeply in a small state, economic growth, cuts in government spending, lower taxes, supply-side reform and deregulation. After Thatcher fell in November 1990, Major had not been able to achieve these goals, neither had Cameron, May or Johnson. Indeed, to the disillusion of many Tory voters and MPs, and not just on the right of the party, they had not even seriously tried.

Few Tories could question her conviction. Again and again on the campaign trail, she articulated that vision. No one could have been in any doubt about what she planned to do, or how she planned to do it. It was her vision, her insights, her passion and her method. Others encouraged and emboldened her, none more so than her old friend Mark Littlewood, but no one gave her these thoughts.

All her ambitions for the economy were brought together in the 'Departmental Priorities Letter' she presented to Kwarteng once in office. The mission was unambiguous: 'Driving up trend GDP growth to 2.5 per cent a year' was her first instruction. 'You should be radical and establish an immediate two-year plan, supported by a medium-term plan, to boost UK productivity and ...increase trend growth,' she said. To assist this, the Bank of England mandate 'should be reviewed'. Next, he should 'reform the supply side to increase business investment, innovation, and growth', noting that the largest barriers to achieving this are 'excessive state regulation and insufficient investment'. The policy of new 'investment zones' with bold tax breaks was said to be fundamental to increase growth locally.

She charged Kwarteng next with 'reducing the overall tax burden on businesses and households', which she described as 'the government's mission'. This would entail implementing her campaign pledges to reverse the National Insurance increase, cancel the scheduled rise in corporation tax and provide for a temporary moratorium on green levies. She said she would be writing to him subsequently for 'a review of [the] UK tax system' that he would oversee. Next, he was to 'turbocharge the City', which she said was hampered more by EU legislation than any other area of British life; it was in need of drastic deregulation, and stimulus to ensure that it retained its long-term status as 'the world's leading financial centre'. Prudence, she said, was going to be a watchword for them: 'I will lead a fiscally responsible government that scrutinizes every pound of spending for the taxpayer.' She exhorted him to work closely with Chief Secretary to the Treasury Simon Clarke in order to control public spending, while reviewing the Treasury's rules to ensure spending decisions really did stimulate investment across the UK. Finally, 'You should implement a review of the mortgage market with a focus on first time buyers.'

Had a Prime Minister ever given such precise and comprehensive orders to a Chancellor? Certainly not in modern times. There could be no doubt in this premiership who the Chancellor was really going to be.

Warnings Unheeded: 6–22 September 2022

From the moment she realized she would win the leadership, nothing was going to stop her. 'Liz was the driver. The economy was always going to be the focus of her premiership. It was all about "letting Liz be Liz",' said one adviser. Three deep forces were driving her on: a manic urgency about there being only two years to the general election, and everything needing to be done now; the populist and even reckless streak in her that actively relished the bravado and risk; and rage against the establishment, bordering on paranoia. The 'blob' was out to stop her and all she was trying to do; it was almost exclusively peopled by public school men who had patronized her and belittled her, and she was going to slay it. After she left No. 10, she implied that the 'blob' had not warned her of the risks in what she was doing.[1] The deep mistrust explains why she didn't try to prepare the markets, the financial community and the economic establishment at large for what was coming, nor to try to enlist their support and understanding. Why not? To her, they were associated with failure, and irredeemably beyond the pale. 'She felt that politicians were no longer in charge of running the UK, but [that instead it was] faceless people in the OBR, the Bank of England and the Treasury with completely different views to her on what was best for the country in terms of tax cuts and promoting growth,' said Mark Fullbrook.[2]

But why the urgency? The economic outlook in late 2022 was sluggish indeed. Growth had been slow in 2022, and had fallen during the second quarter (the last period for which figures were available before she became PM), while growth for 2023 was predicted as, at best, 0.2 per cent, with a recession more than likely, according to analysis by professional services firm PwC.[3] On top of that, the Russian invasion of Ukraine had put considerable pressure on energy supplies, raising energy prices and causing wider market discomfort. The cost of living created widespread apprehension, while inflation, nearing a staggering 10 per cent, was compounding the problems. Interest rates had risen to 1.75 per cent in August 2022, the sixth time that year, and were widely expected to rise again. This was a clear signal that the era of cheap money that had followed the 2008 global financial crisis was over.[4]

As she came closer to becoming Prime Minister, concerns mounted about her economic thesis, expressly what the promised fiscal event would entail. Among her top four economic ministers, Rees-Mogg and Clarke were telling her to stick to her guns, while Kwarteng had growing qualms, and Philp was the most agitated. The one person who could have stopped her in her tracks was Kwarteng. Unlike Truss, he has since publicly admitted that mistakes were made. He had put his reservations to her at the Team Truss strategy meetings at Chevening during the summer, and then later, in Downing Street, but he now recognizes that he should have been more forceful. His suggestions included delaying the Mini-Budget to either November or even the spring; clawing back some of the cost of the energy support package; and, critically, incorporating reductions in spending as part of the Mini-Budget package. Truss referred back to her experience as Chief Secretary to the Treasury and, thinking that discussing cuts would be politically painful, dismissed his suggestions. And, to his subsequent regret, he accepted it.[5] Chancellors have formidable power to change policy, and he threw it to the wind.

In contrast, Philp was more forceful. He argued internally that to support the plan for tax cuts some accompanying spending restraint was needed, by comparison to the baseline assumptions. He wrote to her about this on 30 August. He submitted another document on 20 September arguing that, unless the Mini-Budget clearly stated that the government was trying to balance the books, the reaction could be very destabilizing. Her response? 'Liz was manic and made it very clear this was not something she wanted to do,' said one of her advisers.

Teaming up with Kwarteng, Philp inserted a page into the Chancellor's draft Mini-Budget speech on spending restraint, and switching resources from the public to the private sector. 'Rebalancing from the state sector towards the private sector will produce downward pressure on inflation by increasing supply of goods and services that people want to buy. We also need to maintain the confidence of the bond markets in our fiscal plans.' But to their disgust, as a witness recalled, the document came back from No. 10 with the passages about spending restraint and cuts chopped. 'What on earth has happened?' Philp demanded to know of Kwarteng. 'I called No. 10 and they told me in no uncertain terms to take it out,' the Chancellor replied. It's hard to think of any Chancellor in decades who would have meekly done as he was told by No. 10, reversing what he knew to be right.

Truss's own political team also expressed their concerns about her feverishly adding to the Mini-Budget. They were content with the three major items she had campaigned on – reversing the rise in National Insurance, cancelling the planned corporation tax increase and pausing green levies – but they were alarmed at raising the pension age to seventy, a change that she was particularly keen on. After a fight, they made her realize it was impossible politically. But they were unsuccessful in resisting her other additions. She was just about to unleash the mother of all add-ons. The change to the 45 per cent income tax rate had been discussed at Chevening, and then dropped, but she wanted it back in.

Truss's mind had been racing during the prolonged mourning period. On the evening of Thursday 15 September, she summoned Kwarteng up to the Downing Street flat: 'I've been thinking,' she told him. 'I've decided to abolish the highest rate [45 per cent] of income tax.' He was wary about such a bold tax cut so early, but he noticed that the PM was very determined. 'Let's just do it,' she said.

As soon as he left, Kwarteng dictated a note to his special advisers' WhatsApp group: 'Liz is happy with the budget, but she wants to do the 45p change now.' His special adviser team groaned. They saw the dangers. 'If you're going to do that, you'll have to do something for everyone to balance it or all hell will break loose,' said Cameron Brown. To compensate, he suggested they bring forward the 1p cut in basic income tax for everyone from 2024. Not that this move did anything to reduce the subsequent fury of Tory MPs against a change that was widely seen as favouring the wealthy at a time of economic hardship. By the morning of Monday 19 September, the date of the Queen's funeral, it was already on the Treasury scorecard, but with an even more limited circulation list than usual.

Scrapping the bankers' bonus cap also caused concern among her team. '"If you scrap it before you decide what to do with benefits, it will look very bad politically," we told her. But she was not listening.' They, like Kwarteng, queried why the Mini-Budget had to be so soon. 'She kept repeating again and again "I've only got two years. I've got to make my mark early on." We were getting absolutely nowhere.'

Some of her more independent-minded economists were warning her too, as we have seen, notably Gerard Lyons and Julian Jessop. The Sunday papers on 4 September, the eve of her victory, speculated about possible tax cuts in the Mini-Budget. Lyons was worried. Kwarteng received a message from him saying, 'The markets are unlikely to settle until interest rates have risen much further. It's important that they are convinced that your fiscal plans are necessary, noninflationary and affordable.' He received a perfunctory reply.

Treasury officials, still in shock at the dismissal of Tom Scholar, were reluctant to voice their concerns. 'Even after Chevening, there was much less pushback from the Treasury than expected,' said an aide. 'The sense was they were working for Kwarteng to produce the proposals for him that he wanted to articulate.' Suddenly shorn of their leader and without a permanent successor, officials were in no man's land at a critical moment. There *were* warnings: 'They had very clear warnings that were both written and spoken in advance about the measures coming at a time of very volatile and unstable markets, if they did indeed take large unfunded fiscal measures against this backdrop,' said one senior Treasury official. However, they added that 'the tone was very different. Of course we said what it would cost and the pros and cons of different options, but following the departure of Tom, the advice was more cautious.'

The Office for Budget Responsibility felt under no such constraints. Set up as the financial watchdog by George Osborne in May 2010 to enhance fiscal stability, it was an official but also independent institution. After twelve years in operation, its twice-yearly reports had become regular parts of the fiscal establishment, assessing policy and producing forecasts for the economy and public finances free of party politics. Bring in the OBR? 'You must be joking,' said Truss. To her, it was full of 'spineless' people who consistently produced inaccurate and pessimistic forecasts that were damaging the economy. 'She kept banging on about forecasting being anti-growth. It was a complete fixation for her,' said one minister. Richard Hughes, OBR Chair since October 2020 and ex-Treasury, and not adverse to strong judgements, was viewed with particular suspicion. Hence her decision with Kwarteng very early on to dispense with the OBR's forecasts –

taken at the same time as the decision to sack Scholar – a decision they kept tightly to themselves.

The OBR was trying to imagine what the next PM and Chancellor might do. In the leadership campaign, it kept away from all potential candidates because legally it can only assess current government policy. It had published a forecast for the March 2022 Budget when Sunak was Chancellor, but became concerned by how rapidly the economic climate deteriorated, with inflation and interest rates rising. On that occasion, it was Sunak who thought the OBR had been too pessimistic. The March 2022 report had envisaged some £28 billion of financial 'headroom', i.e. money available to be spent, and Truss and Kwarteng had seized on this sum as providing the money to pay for their planned fiscal measure.[6] But since March, rising interest rates added some £25 billion to government debt, and higher repayments and inflation added an extra £12 billion. Suddenly, the £28 billion of headroom had become an estimated £20 billion shortfall.[7] The impact of these dramatic changes on their plans was not properly considered by Truss or Kwarteng.

Once the leadership campaign began in earnest in July, the OBR began preparing forecasts based on the policies of the two front runners, Truss and Sunak. When criticisms emerged from the former that they were too slow for the timetable in mind, the OBR redoubled its efforts. In a letter to Mel Stride, Chair of the Treasury Select Committee, OBR Chair Richard Hughes wrote that 'if asked by the new Chancellor to produce a forecast on 14 or 21 September, we would be able to do so to a standard which meets the legislative requirements of the Act and Charter'.[8]

The OBR was shocked when it learned that it wasn't being asked to produce a forecast at all, and that no other forecast was being prepared. The argument came back that this was only a 'mini-budget' (a term Truss and Kwarteng used to try to play down its significance), and that some fiscal events, such as the emergency responses after Covid (notably furlough), did not come with a commentary from the OBR. The response within the head office was scornful: the reason why the markets responded as placidly as they did was because furlough was known to be a temporary measure (as was the Energy Price Guarantee), it was designed to protect the economy and the tax base, and every country was coming up with similar schemes. None of this applied to the Mini-Budget, which was unique to Britain, permanent not temporary, and the likelihood that it would strengthen the economy was far from assured. As a result of the exclusion of the OBR, a critical part of normal Budget preparations was removed, said one Treasury representative; 'it was more difficult to evaluate without the OBR' and the process was left 'truncated'.

The Bank of England was the third part of the unholy 'blob' trinity, as malign as the Treasury and OBR in Truss's eyes. She had rated Mervyn King (Governor 2003–13), but less so his successors Mark Carney (2013–20), who she thought should have raised interest rates earlier, and Andrew Bailey (2020–). To her, Bailey was the economic 'blob' personified, a past CEO of another part of the financial establishment she disliked, the Financial Conduct Authority, and before that working with the Financial Services Authority. In particular she thought he had reacted far too slowly in not raising interest rates. Reluctant to remove him in addition to Scholar, in as far as she had that within her power, she did the next best thing in her eyes, by distancing the Bank from the Mini-Budget. 'So many aspects about the Mini-Budget were odd,' said a senior Bank official. 'Treasury officials were unable to tell us about it, which was very unusual because the proposed changes were so large; no OBR forecast was unusual; and it was very unusual to have a big fiscal event the day after a Monetary Policy Committee [MPC].' The Committee had been due to meet the week before, but that meeting had been postponed because of the official mourning.

The MPC's brief is to set the Bank of England's monetary policy to meet the government-set medium-term inflation target of 2 per cent in a way that helps sustain growth and employment. When it convened on 22 September, the day before the Mini-Budget, it voted to increase interest rates by 0.5 per cent to 2.25 per cent. The day before, the US Federal Reserve had tightened policy with an increase of 0.75 per cent, and there had been some expectation in the markets that the Bank of England would follow suit. So when it didn't, the markets thought the Bank had been hopefully cautious. 'The markets thought we had more to do, and they were anticipating the need to do more later,' said one of the Bank's leading figures. It created a difficult economic and financial background for the Mini-Budget, and made Kwarteng's task even more difficult. Admittedly, the situation's volatility ought not to be overstated; writing to the Treasury Select Committee on 5 October, Deputy Governor Jon Cunliffe noted that 'Sterling was broadly stable and long-term gilt yields rose by around 20 basis points that day.'[9]

Timing had been fraught as well. Parliament was due to go into recess for two weeks from the end of Friday 23 September for the party conferences, and would not return until Monday 10 October. Until the Queen's death, Truss and Kwarteng had toyed with going at the end of the second week (Friday 16 September), but that was immediately ruled out by official mourning. The question was then asked whether to hold the Mini-Budget after the annual party conference in mid-October or later. But Truss would hear nothing of it. Like a cracked record she repeated, 'We've had ten years of stagnation, we can't wait.' Even the choice of Friday was awkward: Budgets, traditionally, used to be on Tuesday, and then moved to Wednesday, which gave time before the end of the week for the response to work through the markets. Friday left only half a day and then the markets were in suspended animation until the response was seen the following Monday. This potentially left a vacuum that could be filled with a sense of uncertainty or pessimism, influencing the markets when they reopened. Of course, if the Budget had been considered sound, the timing would not necessarily have been a problem. Instead, it proved to be historic for all the wrong reasons.

The Mini-Budget and Immediate Reaction: 23–24 September 2022

Shortly after 9.30 a.m. on 23 September, with Truss to his right and Clarke to his left, Kwarteng rose to deliver a budget that he and Truss hoped would become as celebrated as Chancellor Geoffrey Howe's monetarist Budget of 1981 or Nigel Lawson's tax-cutting Budget of 1988. They certainly hoped that it would be seen as the dawn of a new era in economic policy. The mood from the Conservative benches during the speech was one of noisy affirmation and excitement. Apart from occasional shouts of disapproval from the opposition benches and gasps from the press gallery, there was little sense of how it would land in the wider world.

The speech closely followed the plan of action that Truss laid out for Kwarteng in his letter of appointment. The government's aim, he said, was for the economy to grow at 2.5 per cent in the medium term, enabled by cutting taxes to boost growth, reforming the supply side and maintaining a 'responsible approach' to public finance.[10] 'For too long in this country, we have indulged in a fight over distribution,' he said. 'Now, we need to focus on growth, not just on how we tax and spend.' The two big fiscal measures – National Insurance and corporation tax – had been long promised. Truss had spoken out strongly against the former in Johnson's Cabinet, when Chancellor Sunak had insisted on increasing it, because she thought it wrong to raise taxes on working people, though she didn't have the same deep feeling about the corporation tax increase.

Next were changes to stamp duty to help first-time buyers (an idea that had been met with broad support at Chevening), the VAT-free shopping scheme and the IR35 reforms to payroll working rules. Most eye-catching was Kwarteng's announcement of the abolition of the 45 per cent income tax rate on income over £150,000. This had been discussed at Chevening, where the consensus was to do it early when Truss had most political capital, but was only finalized at a private meeting between Truss and Kwarteng at the beginning of the week.

Particularly controversial was the fiscally neutral measure that even the Treasury didn't think made sense: the removal of the cap on bankers' bonuses, which Kwarteng argued only pushed up their basic salaries or drove financial activity elsewhere. Next came the idea that the Treasury strongly resisted: the establishment in England of 'investment zones' that would benefit from a range of tax incentives, liberal planning rules and no stamp duty. Kwarteng remained uneasy with the proposal, but Truss insisted on sticking with it. Buried in the Mini-Budget's documents was also the first estimate of the cost of the energy support package for 2022–23: a total spend of £60 billion for the domestic Energy Price Guarantee and the business Energy Bill Relief Scheme.[11]

It was heady stuff, which the Tory MPs enjoyed, but how would it all be funded? Kwarteng did not explain. No one imagined the economy was going to improve and provide vastly increased tax revenues in the short term. However, instead of fiscal prudence or spending cuts, Kwarteng was proposing both tax *cuts* and increased *spending*. The Budget document had rhetorical commitments to 'fiscal discipline' and 'keeping spending under control', but no concrete proposals were forthcoming on how to do this.[12] What Kwarteng did promise was that 'a Medium-Term Fiscal Plan' would be outlined in due course, 'setting out our responsible fiscal approach more fully'.[13]

Afterwards, Kwarteng repaired with Matt Sinclair and other advisers to the Two Chairmen in nearby St James's for a pint. That afternoon, he and Truss headed to Ebbsfleet in Kent for a visit to new housing developments. She later wrote in her memoir, 'that afternoon was probably my happiest moment as Prime Minister. We had managed to deliver what we said we would.'[14]

Soon, the first non-partisan assessments on the Mini-Budget came in. Paul Johnson, the director of the Institute for Fiscal Studies, the leading economic think tank, commented, 'Today, the Chancellor announced the biggest package of tax cuts in 50 years without even a semblance of an effort to make the public finances add up.' He accused Kwarteng of borrowing large sums 'at increasingly expensive rates', putting government debt 'on an unsustainable rising path', and being 'willing to gamble with fiscal sustainability'. He went on to say that Kwarteng was 'willing to shrug off the risks of inflation', and 'pulling in the exact opposite direction to the Bank of England'. If that wasn't bad enough, 'we heard nothing on public spending... Mr Kwarteng is not just gambling on a new strategy, he is betting the house.'[15]

On the following morning, the papers delivered their verdict, with enthusiastic early responses from the *Daily Mail*, the *Daily Express* and the *Daily Telegraph*. This was the moment that many on the right had been longing for since Brexit; indeed, since Thatcher. 'The boldness and courage of Kwasi Kwarteng's debut budget is seismic,' wrote Alex Brummer in the *Daily Mail*. 'By taking a hatchet to taxes and placing growth front and centre of economic policy, the Chancellor has produced a genuine Tory package elbowing to one side the Treasury's fiscal conservatism which restrained his predecessors. The scale of the package is mind-boggling. Liz Truss and her Chancellor have turned their backs on the doomsters in the think-tanks, in the civil service and on the political Left to launch a revolution.'[16] 'AT LAST! A <u>TRUE</u> TORY BUDGET', screamed the headline. 'With one move, Britain's competitiveness, its investor friendliness and its attractiveness to top talent has been hugely amplified,' wrote Allister Heath for the *Telegraph*.[17]

'This is not a plan for growth, but a plan to reward the already wealthy. It is a return to the trickle down of the past. It is back to the future, not a brave new era,' said Shadow Chancellor Rachel Reeves in her reply to Kwarteng.[18] 'A budget for the rich,' said the *Guardian* the following day.[19] These comments were to be expected, but much more significant was the response from two less partisan sources; no amount of criticism from the Truss team could eradicate their sting.

The *Financial Times* accused Truss and Kwarteng of acting capriciously, changing the direction of economic policy on which the Conservatives had been elected in December 2019. The new plan 'wasn't just clear. It wasn't just bold. It was kamikaze – or should we say, kami-Kwasi. Less Britannia Unchained, more Britannia Unhinged.' Particular ire was directed at the removal of the bankers' bonus cap (which they could spend on 'cheaper champagne' achieved by 'shorting the pound'). The Mini-Budget was seen as the fourth major change in direction of economic policy since 2010, with this one appearing 'the most reckless metamorphosis yet'.[20]

Then, *The Economist* ripped into the economic illiteracy of the Mini-Budget, which, it argued, sought to introduce Reaganomics without comprehending the conditions that enabled the Reagan economic transformation in the 1980s. For example, a strengthening dollar was essential to its success, yet in Britain 'the pound has slumped by 16% against the dollar in 2022'; to date, 'The pound has fallen… because it is perceived as a riskier asset than [other] currencies and investors are worried about global growth.' An expanding and relatively youthful workforce was equally important to the Reagan boom, but 'Britain is ageing and its economy is still adjusting to Brexit.'[21] Reagan, it might be added, also had the world's largest economy, and the vast natural resources of the American continent, on his side. These were all points that Truss either didn't know about, or chose to ignore.

Almost from the moment Kwarteng sat down in the Commons, the value of the pound began to fall. By the end of the day it stood at the lowest level against the dollar since the 1980s. The FTSE 100 had its worst daily fall since the height of Covid, as traders sold off UK assets, and borrowing costs on five-year bonds experienced the largest increase in a single day. The markets hadn't expected, and had received no forewarning, of the 45 per cent income tax change, and they were surprised by the generosity of the energy support package.[22] Indeed, even in the Treasury, there were raised eyebrows. 'It was a surprise to me. The sense in the Treasury was "that's quite punchy, not because of the money but because of the signal that it's sending, on top of everything else they're doing",' one senior official said.

Late that afternoon, a worried Simon Case, whose job as Cabinet secretary was to be the nation's chief worrier, sent a message to the Treasury to say the market reaction to the Chancellor's statement was already 'outside expectations', even taking into account that markets across the world were falling. By Friday evening, sterling was weakening and sinking further, and long-term gilt yields were rising quickly, causing the value of these government-issued bonds to drop.[23] Anxious calls were coming into the Bank of England, with particular concerns about pension funds, which were heavily invested in gilts. Bank officials became increasingly concerned: in response to the shock, selling was continuing, which led to prices falling. They stayed watching the markets in the USA, which were open till 10 p.m. UK time, and were in regular contact with their opposite numbers in the Treasury. Kwarteng was difficult to contact that evening but the Bank and Treasury representatives eventually agreed jointly that there was no need to react yet.

For its part, the Bank had been, according to one senior figure, 'completely blindsided' by the contents of the Mini-Budget. It had been briefed by the Treasury on the Wednesday before. But there had been no suggestion of the cuts in stamp duty and the abolition of the 45p rate, because the Treasury was apparently unaware that Truss and Kwarteng had taken those decisions.

Truss was phlegmatic, at least on the surface. But her team had already started to ask why the Bank and the Treasury had not indicated there might be serious market disruption. The best answer they could come up with was that it was as much a reaction to the personalities of Truss and Kwarteng, and concerns about what the government might do next, as the substance of what had been announced.

On Saturday morning, a worried Case called Bank Governor Andrew Bailey. 'What on earth is going on?' he asked. A short while after, the No. 10 Private Office called a senior official at the Bank to ask the same question: 'For God's sake, explain what is happening. We don't understand.' Downing Street was now in regular touch with the Bank's leadership. They sent the same message back: 'The markets are losing confidence *quickly*.' Case then messaged Catsaras to say 'The reactions are worse than the Treasury was expecting. The Bank are watching very closely.'

To restore stability, the Bank advised that the government bring forward the timing of its plan in order to show it still believed in the fiscal framework and that it had a proper financial plan. Bailey advised Case to tell them to stop badmouthing the OBR too. There needed to be some indication of fiscal responsibility not least before the next MPC in November. It was clear that Kwarteng needed to go public the following day and say *something* to steady the markets.

On Sunday morning, it was agreed that Kwarteng would be a guest on Laura Kuenssberg's BBC flagship politics show. An insider at the programme said, 'We had asked for Kwarteng to represent the government because of the market meltdown during the week,' not expecting him to accept so readily. During Kwarteng's private briefing by his media team beforehand, 'a carefully apologetic line, and talk about robust action to put us on a more secure footing' was agreed, said one special adviser. The aim was that Kwarteng would 'reduce the pulse rate, calm it down'. But then, fatally, Kwarteng spoke to Truss shortly before he went on the show. And she suggested that he double down on their agenda. She had spoken to her advisers, and decided, according to one of those advisers, that 'we don't think that he should be too apologetic'. She suggested he utter four words that have become among the most consequential in modern economic history: 'there's more to come'.

On air, Kwarteng did not say anything about the intention of producing a costed plan, or a long-term framework, later in the autumn. He defended the government's policy and direction. 'We are very focused on making sure that people keep more of their own money,' he told Kuenssberg. He defended the Mini-Budget and rejected her arguments that it was pushing in the opposite direction to the Bank of England's counter-inflationary policies. He told her that as a result of conversations, 'I've said that I will see the Governor twice a week and we share ideas… but… there was no way we were going to get more growth by simply increasing taxes and taking more of people's money.'

After a few minutes, Kuenssberg argued that the government was reducing taxes on the wealthy. Kwarteng responded with the rationale for his decision, and then uttered those famous words: 'There's more to come.' He continued, 'We've only been here nineteen days. I want to see over the next year people retain more of their income because I believe that it's the British people who are going to drive this economy.' When challenged on this, he reinforced what he had said: 'The only way we are going to pay for our public services in the future, the only way we are going to have the kind of economy and society we want is by growing this economy, and that is what I, the Prime Minister and the government are 100 per cent focused on.'[24]

One of Truss's advisers, watching with surprise, shot off a text message to a fellow special adviser: 'Did we know he'd say this? It's a totally crazy thing to say!' The response came back quickly: 'It was almost off the cuff, bombastic. That is his style.'

Kwarteng had intended his remarks to convey Nelsonian sangfroid and reassurance. He hoped that sending out a message that the government was not about to change course would deliver all the confidence that the markets required. But that was not how the four words were received. Instead, the markets wondered how *much* more was to come – what, how and when? Did this government, which had removed Tom Scholar and sidelined the OBR, have any sense of fiscal responsibility? Where were the tax cuts going to come from? Where, exactly, was this going?

At least one economist believes that Kwarteng's television appearance that morning was the critical moment in the Truss premiership: 'The markets had stabilized by Friday evening, and the weekend should be the time when the Chancellor took stock and got on top of the messaging.' Had there been a more confident team at the top of the Treasury, or perhaps a long-standing permanent secretary who knew the terrain, things might have been different.

'The Chancellor says on Sunday that the government plans more tax cuts and the fiscal credibility of the government detonates,' one of the Bank of England's leadership recalled. He had been receiving worrying signals all weekend. That Sunday afternoon, one Bank economist spoke to a trader on one of the East Asian markets, to be told that 'everything British had to be sold and the markets would be testing the resolve of the British government'. Then, on Sunday evening, the directors of the Bank of England held a conference call. The mood was bleak. Sterling was already falling in East Asia and there were rumbles in the gilt markets. There was indeed 'more to come', just not as Kwarteng intended. Looking back, Kwarteng reflected, 'Yes, it was a foolish thing to say.'[25]

Meltdown: 26–30 September 2022

Twenty minutes after the gilt and currency markets opened in London at 8 a.m. on Monday 26 September, a critical call took place between Bailey, the Deputy Governors and other key market figures at the Bank. There was a lot to discuss, and strong opinions were expressed. Did the Bank need to put out a statement that the monetary framework was secure? Did the Bank need to make clear to the markets that it would raise rates by as much as necessary to bring inflation back to target and offset the inflationary impact of the Mini-Budget? Would it do whatever was needed to stabilize prices through the use of interest rates? Had the time come to announce an extraordinary meeting of the Monetary Policy Committee? If so, it would be the first such since the emergency meeting during Covid, and there was a risk that if they did convene one, there'd be no alternative but to raise interest rates. Some argued that an emergency meeting might have precisely the opposite effect of reassuring the markets. Moreover, several commentators had fuelled the speculation that there would be an MPC meeting, increasing the pressure. Despite this, there was little support for convening the MPC, and instead they agreed a reassuring statement should be put out at 10 a.m.

At this point, Treasury officials intervened to inform the Bank that the Chancellor wanted to put out his own statement at the same time, fearful that a unilateral statement by the Bank would expose him.

No. 10 had been in meltdown on Monday morning. The expectation in the Truss camp had been that the markets would play up, but fairly soon calm down. That transparently wasn't happening. Case walked into No. 10, grabbed a couple of Truss's staff and said, 'You two guys come with me to see the Prime Minister.' She was resolute: the message she wanted to give out was 'all is well'. Indeed, she didn't want Kwarteng to put out a statement at all: 'The markets will have to learn that this is the way that we're going to be doing policy from now on', was her adamant position.

Her apparent serenity – which struck some as completely detached from reality – surprised officials at the Treasury and the Bank. Fraught conversations ensued, concluding with Kwarteng saying he would agree to a *joint* announcement being issued. 'No way', was the swift response from the Bank. All the time, those involved in the discussion were nervously watching their television screens as sterling fell, reaching an all-time low against the dollar at $1.03, its lowest level since decimalization in 1971. The nightmare scenario was it would sink below $1 (though it recovered to $1.10 by the end of the week).

Kwarteng fought Truss hard to let him make a statement, and while that struggle went back and forth, the Bank was told to hold fire on releasing its own 'because Kwarteng's office continued to argue that it would look very bad if it made an announcement before the Chancellor', said an official.

The air cleared after lunch, when Kwarteng's statement eventually went out, pledging what he had planned to say on television the day before: he would deliver a Medium-Term Fiscal Plan on 23 November and the OBR would be asked to produce a forecast.[26] This proved a major concession as it involved having to balance the books five years out. 'This was the moment when the process of realizing that there would have to be some very serious and project-changing cuts began,' said an official. The Bank made its own statement at 3 p.m.: 'The Bank is monitoring developments in financial markets very closely in light of the significant repricing of financial assets.'[27] For all the fraught back and forth about the statements, neither was to make much difference to the markets.

Truss spoke to Treasury officials at 8.30 p.m. and, one recalled, they 'explained to her that the position we were in was much more serious and it needed to be stabilized'. Teams at No. 10, the Treasury and the Bank sat up late debating what further action might be required. That evening, concerns about Liability Driven Investments (LDIs) began to trouble the Treasury and Bank of England. 'A message came through that they'd been hearing worrying news from LD investors,' said one Treasury official. 'The great worry was that LD firms would have to offload gilts rapidly in the morning and that would create a huge market reaction.'

The outlook on the morning of Tuesday 27 September seemed better; for a while it looked as if enough had been done to calm the markets. There was momentary relief in the Treasury. But then banks and building societies started to withdraw mortgage products as a result of concerns about a possible increase in the interest rate. Virgin Money and Skipton Building Society stopped mortgage offers altogether for new customers.[28] News then broke that, in a rare public attack on the government of a prominent country, the International Monetary Fund (IMF) had launched a stinging criticism of Truss's government. It called on No. 10 to reconsider tax cuts to prevent them stoking inequality, saying the measures risked undermining the Bank's efforts to tackle inflation and that they would worsen the cost of living crisis.[29]

By mid-afternoon, conditions were deteriorating badly. At this point a new term began to be heard in the corridors of Whitehall: 'LDIs'. Staff in No. 10 turned to their computers to look it up. One witness said, 'There was huge ignorance about them across the system really, absolutely no one knew about them.' It was like twenty-one years before when, in the immediate aftermath of 9/11, flummoxed staff were sent from Downing Street to buy books about the Taliban and Al Qaeda.[30] The only person who seemed to understand them was the Treasury's chief economic adviser, Clare Lombardelli, who had worked at the Bank earlier in her career and was the main conduit of conversations between both institutions during the crisis. 'She started talking to us about them: we had never heard about them,' said a Cabinet Office official. Liability Driven Investment is a long-term investment strategy used by pension funds. They are designed to ensure that the investor has income-generating assets to satisfy their financial obligations, which is vital for organizations that have to make regular payouts. Many UK pension funds had adopted a liability-driven investment strategy and had borrowed heavily to invest in UK gilts to meet future needs. These funds held capital cushions against risk, but as yields rose rapidly, and prices fell sharply, they needed to post more capital as collateral but many lacked the cash to do so and risked default.[31]

Fund managers started telling the Bank that if the trend continued, LDI funds were likely to fall into negative asset value and they would have to begin winding up on Wednesday morning. This meant that a large quantity of gilts, held as collateral by LDI funds, would likely be sold on the open market. The Bank's executive convened a meeting to brief the Financial Policy Committee about the fear of a 'self-reinforcing spiral... threatening severe disruption of core funding markets and consequent widespread financial instability'.[32] Truss later admitted that she had never heard of LDIs. 'The Treasury should certainly have warned us about them, as should the Bank,' she said. She was also angry that the Bank announced the sale of £80 billion of gilts the day before the Mini-Budget.[33] 'I could never introduce the measures I wanted against such institutional resistance.'[34]

It became clear to the Bank that it would have to intervene. But how? The difficulty was that it needed to tighten monetary policy by interest rate rises and selling gilts, while at the same time buying gilts to enhance financial stability, a contradictory position the Bank had not found itself in before. All Tuesday evening and through the night Bank staff, in close collaboration with Treasury officials, worked out the details of the plan, which was agreed by the Bank's Executive early the next day.

On Wednesday morning, Kwarteng was briefed on the details of the scheme by Lombardelli and the Treasury team. It would have to be indemnified by the Treasury, which he would have to approve. Truss was briefed on the plan by Case, and she too agreed with the Treasury support. Kwarteng then phoned Bailey and gave his approval; the Bank of England was cleared to act.

Hence its statement late morning on Wednesday 28 September that as the 'repricing' had become more intense on Tuesday, particularly affecting long-term government debt with its risk to UK financial stability, the Bank was acting to reduce risks from contagion to UK households and businesses. To achieve this, it would carry out temporary purchases of long-dated UK government bonds at whatever scale was necessary to achieve market stability. The operation would be fully indemnified by the Treasury and would be explicitly time-limited, ending on 14 October.[35] One Bank insider later said that 'the problem was essentially one of time; the gilt price moves after the Mini-Budget were so sharp and fast that the normal mechanisms for recapitalizing the asset management funds could not work.' Hence the Bank's intervention was designed to buy time. The message that the Bank was prepared to buy up to £65 billion of long-dated gilts to prevent the market rout was designed to overawe the markets with the Bank's 'fiscal firepower'.[36] It worked, and, ultimately, the Bank spent £19.3 billion in doing so (with all of the gilts sold back to the market between November 2022 and January 2023).[37] The immediate response was encouraging: there was a 100 basis point fall in thirty-year gilt yields (effectively, their prices were returning to normal).[38] Good for the Bank's credibility but not for the government's.

Thursday 29 September saw an irate Truss berate her team. 'You should've communicated the Mini-Budget better in the first place,' she thundered to a small group of advisers huddled in No. 10, as one recalled. 'The communications have been a total s**t-show.' A long pause ensued before Simon McGee, her director of communications, mustered his courage to speak: 'Prime Minister, we hadn't heard about key elements of the Mini-Budget even twelve or fourteen hours before. You can hardly blame us.' A silence followed.

'You're right. It's my fault,' she said.

That morning, Truss broke her self-imposed public silence. 'From the moment she had stepped into No. 10 until this point, she had her blinkers on. She had no idea what the Conservative Party was thinking. No idea what the nation was thinking. She had refused to read the newspapers. Now she suddenly changed direction,' said one of her team. As if on an adrenaline rush, she gave no fewer than twenty-four live interviews from No. 10. These were with local radio and television stations, deemed to be a safer way of getting her message across than through the national BBC. It proved a humiliation; the local radio presenters were well informed and confronted the Prime Minister bluntly. Rima Ahmed from BBC Radio Leeds asked, 'Where have you been?', pointing out that nothing had been heard from Truss over the previous four days of chaos.

'Are you ashamed of what you've done?' posed Anna Cookson, presenter for BBC Radio Kent. 'I think we have to remember the situation this country was facing...' Truss ventured before Cookson said, 'And you've made it worse!' There was no let-up from other parts of Britain. 'Are you cleverer than the IMF, the economists and bishops who all slammed the Budget?' one asked, then, 'Have you taken the keys to the country and crashed the economy?'[39] Worse than any response that she offered was her tone – robotic, rote and lacking in empathy towards people suffering in the crisis. She didn't seem to know what she was doing.

The strain was beginning to show. Later that day, during a study session for her conference speech, she briefly lost her composure and wept, according to one who was there. 'The speech writing isn't that bad,' said one of her team, trying to cheer her up. 'Yeah, just feeling emotional,' she responded. 'Great speech. Twenty-five-year anniversary of your first conference – you were arguing then against the NICs [National Insurance contributions] rise,' they added. 'It's making me emotional, honestly,' she said. She recovered after a minute or so and the session continued.

At the heart of Truss's strategy was positioning herself to beat Labour in the general election. She wanted to win her own mandate and then have five years to cement her project properly. The strategy wasn't going to plan. That week, the contrast with Keir Starmer could not have been starker. His conference speech in Liverpool on Tuesday had been powerful, castigating 'the Tory trickle-down fantasy' and promising that 'Britain will get its future back'. Never in his wildest dreams could he have imagined being gifted a better launchpad for his keynote: 'The government has lost control of the British economy – and for what? They've crashed the pound – and for what? Higher interest rates. Higher inflation. Higher borrowing. And for what? Not for you. Not for working people. For tax cuts for the richest 1 per cent in our society. Don't forget. Don't forgive.'[40] A YouGov poll for *The Times* on Thursday reported Labour now had a 33-point lead, the biggest gap between Labour and the Conservatives since the 1990s. This was accompanied by reports of mounting pressure on Truss to rethink her entire policy.[41]

It was at this point, before Truss's own conference speech, that Conservative MPs gave up on her and started to openly discuss what could be done. 'It was also the time, three weeks in, when officials in No. 10 concluded that she was never going to make it,' said one insider. 'But to their credit, they never let up or let on. They continued to serve her till the end with a loyalty she didn't always deserve.'

Truss realized that she would have to go further still and parley with the enemy. On Friday 30 September an announcement was released that she would meet the OBR's Budget Responsibility Committee to discuss their forecast intended to accompany Kwarteng's Medium-Term Fiscal Plan scheduled for 23 November.[42] She hated to do it but realized she would have to trim her sails if her project was to remain seaworthy. So, through gritted teeth, she asked her office to contact the OBR: 'The Prime Minister would like to meet you,' its very surprised chair Richard Hughes was told. He duly trooped into

Downing Street with his senior colleagues, under no illusion that this was anything other than a PR exercise to show the world that 'the OBR was back in town'. True to their remit, the OBR team costed the policies that had been announced, and put a revised forecast to Kwarteng privately, meshing in work that the Treasury had already done on costings for the Energy Price Guarantee. It was the only time Hughes met Truss.

She continued to hate the OBR and the 'blob' with a vengeance. The departed Tom Scholar remained a figure of dark suspicion, blamed for encouraging the IMF to utter its damning verdict midweek.[43] Such a claim is indicative of the state of her and her fellow travellers' mindset at the time. It would also have been news to Scholar himself, who was walking the coast-to-coast Wainwright trail across Northern England and was not in contact with anyone in the financial community. Others close to Truss believed that 'Conservative MPs allied to Sunak phoned their friends in the City to tell them to create havoc'.

'Nonsense,' says Charlie Bean, the Bank's former Deputy Governor. 'It was naïve if they did believe that because that's not how the financial markets work. They are made up of thousands of individual actors and foreign banks. The idea that individuals could somehow collaborate together and conspire against the government is wrong-headed.'[44] A senior Treasury official said, 'Liz Truss brought down Liz Truss. It was the speed in which she acted, the nature of her decisions, and her not using the institutional framework.' They observed that had the Bank of England wished to bring down Truss, it might have done so simply by not buying up the gilts to stabilize the markets. This would have generated exactly the sort of crisis that would have caused Truss's government to collapse.

The Verdict: Avoid Major Policy Failures?

The Mini-Budget most certainly qualifies as a major prime ministerial policy error; indeed, it is the greatest example of its kind in modern history. Despite that, it didn't necessarily mean the end of the Truss premiership. Kwarteng's admission to Laura Kuenssberg of 'more to come' was another axe blow to her premiership. But even that didn't spell the end. Truss believed she had been unlucky – the economic climate and the death of the monarch, compounded by institutional resistance – and, ever the optimist, she believed her luck would change. After the Mini-Budget, Kwarteng had said to Truss that 'We will only have two months, unless you move more slowly.' Even that was optimistic; in just twenty-two days' time, she would throw in the towel.

The Mini-Budget might have worked earlier in the year, but not with inflation running at 9.9 per cent and the expectation of it rising to between 11 and 12 per cent. Economic growth was low, with many bodies including the independent National Institute of Economic and Social Research believing the UK had already entered recession.[45] Following the MPC's rise in interest rates two days before to 2.25 per cent, the expectation was that they could rise as high as 5 per cent, and that was *after* twelve months of sharp increases.[46] The Energy Price Guarantee had been generous – too broad some thought, as it supported the affluent as much as the poor – and made a major hole in any headroom. Public sector net debt stood at 96.6 per cent of GDP in August, 1.1 per cent higher than the OBR had predicted in March.[47] Against this economic backdrop was much political uncertainty, with a new and volatile Prime Minister and Chancellor, the death of the Queen (and consequent growth-reducing bank holidays) and the sacking of Scholar. All of this, coupled with the dismissal of the OBR forecast, created huge anxiety in the market; the certainties that underlay the British economy and public finances no longer applied.

To make matters worse, interest rates were rising worldwide and the dollar was strong against most major currencies, which made sterling's decline look bleaker than it was. The increased use of LDI strategies by some pension funds exacerbated the rise in UK government gilts, which triggered the vicious spiral of sales, driving up yields further and ultimately forcing the Bank to step in. Even that might have been manageable, but for the turmoil in the mortgage markets. This proved the final straw. 'No one in No. 10 knew about the worries about gilts or LDIs,' said one of Truss's senior colleagues. 'Either Treasury officials did, and deliberately decided not to tell her, or no one saw the gilt reaction and knew how to react.' In fact, the Financial Policy Committee of the Bank had flagged up the LDI vulnerability a year earlier to the Treasury. The one person who might have had the knowledge to warn about the impact and counsel how to deal with it was persona non grata.

For Truss to survive, she needed above all to restore the credibility of her growth plan. The Bank's intervention on Wednesday 28 September had brought stability. Would it be enough?

Rule Number Eight: Maintain a reputation for economic competence.
Truss, her credibility in tatters, announces the departure of Kwarteng
at an excoriating press conference on Friday 14 October

8

MAINTAIN A REPUTATION FOR ECONOMIC COMPETENCE
30 September–12 October 2022

Overseeing national finances was the Prime Minister's personal responsibility for the first 120 years of the office's existence. Indeed, until Robert Peel separated the Prime Minister's job from the Chancellor's in 1841, the Treasury at the end of Downing Street was the PM's own office. The importance of maintainig a reputation for financial competence has been etched into the cranium of every Prime Minister since the post's inception. That was, until a management accountant who had been Chief Secretary to the Treasury stepped across the threshold of No. 10: Liz Truss.

The Annual Party Conference: 30 September–5 October 2022

'It's Tom Scholar and his f**king mates at the IMF who are responsible for all the fuss,' she told aides on Friday 30 September. The Conservative Party's annual conference in Birmingham was due to begin the following day. 'The package is absolutely fine. It's just a communications problem: we simply haven't explained it clearly enough.' Truss was bouncing between two states of mind, from full-scale denial to believing all kinds of conspiracy theories. 'She was inhabiting a tiny bubble. She had cut herself off completely from what the media was saying and what her MPs were talking about,' lamented one of her senior advisers.

'We're not having newspapers in the office any more,' she had told officials at the start of her premiership. In a sense, they found this a welcome change from Johnson, who would fume over critical stories and fire off angry messages. But Truss went disastrously far in the opposite direction: no Prime Minister since 1945 has shown such disregard for what the media, the PM's window on the world, was saying. Unlike most Prime Ministers, she never listened to Radio 4's *Today* programme: 'typical BBC', she would say. To compensate, her team prepared a daily digest for her of the key news stories including what was happening to the pound and on the markets. 'We put it into her box every day, but our suspicion was that she never worked her way down that far,' one recalled. So while her staff across Downing Street were glued to the television screens reporting the latest news on sterling and gilts, their boss was nursing pet theories out of touch with reality. 'Truss, Kwarteng and Sinclair, together with their friends, were not living in the real world but were just talking to each other in an echo chamber, constantly banging on about how right they were,' said an aide. 'It's just hedge fund managers buggering around', was Kwarteng's verdict at the end of the week.

Friday 30 September was a balmy day. Truss had wanted to convene a staff meeting in Downing Street before they packed up and left for the annual conference in Birmingham. Delays to an overseas phone call at No. 10 meant she shifted the meeting to her suite in Birmingham at the Hyatt Regency Hotel. When they gathered, they found her in a highly excitable state, her mind focused on her conference speech ('How's it reading? What do you think? Am I saying the right things?'). Nothing was going to spoil the conference's focus on growth and the economy. Word had gone out to the private offices of Secretaries of State across Whitehall with the emphatic message: 'The Prime Minister doesn't want there to be any policy announcements at conference.' The majority of her ministers were still working their way through their letters of appointment, and were content to do as asked. But not all. Some were thinking of their own futures.

Home Secretary Suella Braverman and Work and Pensions Secretary Chloe Smith had either not read the directive or chose to ignore it. Truss was exasperated when she found out: 'What don't they understand? Ministerial policy announcements never work at party conference: nothing must take away from our focus on growth!' she shouted. Then when Braverman submitted her speech talking about further legislation to reduce migration, Truss exploded. The Home Secretary was summoned to explain herself. But reluctant to haul her over the coals, Truss was all sweetness and light, leaving Braverman with the impression that she had got what she wanted. 'It was typical Liz. She never wants to be the bad guy, ever – she always wants other people to break the bad news,' said one of her advisers. So it was left to her staff to explain that the Home Secretary was to edit out anything that could be construed as new policy. Braverman did not forget that the Prime Minister was not strong willed enough to deliver this reprimand herself.

Truss spent some of Saturday out and about greeting MPs and having conversations, as she loved to do, with journalists. The more she listened, the more it dawned on her that holding to Kwarteng's pledge to remove the 45p rate of income tax on those earning over

£150,000 would be unsustainable. 'She was learning as if for the first time that MPs were unhappy with the economics of the Mini-Budget – she thought that they would be delighted and she was shocked. So by early evening she was beginning to rethink things,' said an aide. Reports began to filter into her that former ministers she had excluded from government, especially Michael Gove and Grant Shapps, were on manoeuvres. The first to launch an attack had been former Chief Whip Julian Smith, who had been furious and attacked the Mini-Budget publicly as 'wrong' on the day it was given.[1] 'It's a completely barking policy,' he angrily WhatsApped a government minister. The intelligence seeping up to her suite through the day incensed and stunned her. It was not a bit as she had imagined. For too long she had listened to those who had said MPs would love it when a Prime Minister finally enacted tax-cutting measures. Somehow she had managed to unite a broad coalition of MPs, disunited over many things but all believing she was getting it badly wrong. It was becoming clear that a rebellion of Tory MPs over the cut to the 45p rate would threaten the passage of the Mini-Budget legislation through Parliament.

Sunday 2 October was to prove one of the pivotal days of her short premiership. Early that morning, her senior team had met and concluded that Truss wouldn't budge: Adam Jones briefed the media accordingly that 'the Lady is not for turning'. In her morning briefing before she went on BBC1's *Sunday with Laura Kuenssberg* she was palpably unsettled and edgy; she seemed to be in a strange mood, according to one adviser. Her 'we're sticking with the policy' appearance was followed, within moments, by Gove launching a sustained broadside on the Mini-Budget. He alleged that it was 'not Conservative' to fund tax cuts from borrowing, and said that the financial plans marked a betrayal of the party's 'One Nation' 2019 election manifesto.[2] Shapps came out with his own extraordinary attack later in the day, bluntly telling the BBC that the legislation would not pass the Commons: 'I don't think the House is in a place where it's likely to support that.' Disgruntled MPs, growing in number by the hour, said they would vote against the legislation, despite Party Chair Jake Berry saying they would lose the whip.[3]

'That snake' (Truss's standard moniker for Gove), she hissed when out of earshot of the television crew. 'She knew what Michael was like. But she was surprised because she never thought he would knife her so brazenly: she imagined her first party conference would be one big happy Conservative gathering with everyone supporting each other,' said an aide.

She was particularly perplexed because she had held a confidential conversation with Gove late morning on Tuesday 27 September. Acting on advice that he was biddable and that she should bury the hatchet, especially before the conference, he was called in. 'I'm not quite certain why I got the summons. It was very nice of her, but I was rather perplexed by what she was trying to say,' recalled Gove.

No meeting in the forty-nine days was odder; polar opposites, Truss now sat before the man she felt had patronized her when she was his junior minister at Education. They spent three quarters of an hour in a state of confusion, opposite each other in No. 10's Terracotta Room, no one taking notes. Fullbrook sat outside on a chair, keeping guard. According to Gove, he told Truss why he disagreed strongly with the 45p tax change. 'But there are some matters on which we agree, for example Israel,' she interjected. They shared similar views on Benjamin Netanyahu, and both supported moving the British Embassy from Tel Aviv to Jerusalem, recognizing the city as Israel's capital, as the United States had done in 2017. Gove began to feel that she was sizing him up to become British ambassador to Israel, which rankled him because he didn't like to think he was being bought off. Not wanting to rebuff her altogether, he said, 'You never know, Liz, after the general election, things might be different.'[4]

After Gove left, she had bounced up to her two top aides, saying, 'He's fully on board! His one condition is that we find room for "his boys".' This was her term for his tight-knit group of special advisers with whom he had worked for several years. Fullbrook and Porter exchanged knowing glances. 'To them, it looked like a suicide pact,' said a third party. 'A lifeline for Liz, maybe, but at the expense of embedding Gove and his lieutenants deep into her government.' 'She never imagined he would betray her, especially not with his nuclear bomb less than a week later,' said an aide. 'I didn't see how she possibly could have concluded that she had won me round,' Gove himself said of their meeting.

All Sunday she brooded. Perhaps she would have to bow to the inevitable. 'Nick, I'm thinking of dropping the 45p rate change. What do you think?'

In moments of high tension, Truss always turned to Catsaras. Now he was about to demonstrate just how dependable he could be.

'Yes, of course I think you should do it, Prime Minister.'

'Are you sure?'

'I think you should ditch the bankers' bonus too.'

'No, no. That's an EU thing. I won't do it.'

'So you are just going to ditch the 45p rate?'

'Yes, I think so.'

All day, she had been messaging different members of her team saying, 'Come up for a glass of wine.' It was clear that she was on a journey, realizing she had a full-scale rebellion brewing, and a limited concession would be sensible if she was not going to lose control of her agenda. So at 7 p.m., when her team had dispersed to attend various dinners and events, they each received a WhatsApp message from Sophie Jarvis to say 'Liz might want us all to meet up', followed rapidly by a text from Truss herself demanding, 'Where are you? Come to my room now.' When the team had gathered – Porter, Sinclair, Stein, Jones, Hope and Jarvis – she went around each one and asked what they thought about abandoning the plans. 'Stick to your guns,' Porter said. Sinclair was even stronger: 'Hold your nerve.' Not all agreed. 'If you're going to make the change, do it early and don't hang around,' said Stein. The others were more nuanced but thought that if the economics and the politics were not stacking up, a change of course was right. Truss listened carefully and dispatched everyone back to their engagements, only for another summons thirty or so minutes later. This time they found she was joined by Chief of Staff Mark Fullbrook, Director of Strategy Iain Carter and the Chancellor.

Kwarteng was having dinner at the Malmaison Hotel with the cream of the country's bestselling paper, the *Sun*. Victoria Newton, the editor, was holding court with past and present political editors Trevor Kavanagh and Harry Cole. They were awaiting their main course when Cameron Brown, Kwarteng's media adviser, saw that Porter was calling him on his mobile so he stepped away from the table to pick up. 'The Prime Minister wants to see Kwasi at once to discuss dropping the 45p rate,' she told him. 'He's having dinner with the editor of the *Sun*. It will be very awkward if he slips away.

Can't it wait?' he whispered. 'No, the Prime Minister wants to see him now.' Further protestations about how damaging it would look proved unsuccessful. But how could the young special adviser prise Kwarteng, in full flow, away from three of the most powerful forces in the British press? Out of the line of sight of the others, so he thought, he raised four fingers, then five to Kwarteng to indicate the topic. But Cole spotted it and quickly surmised what might be happening.[5]

Kwarteng was visibly unhappy at being dragged away from the dinner, and when they arrived at Truss's suite, they found Fullbrook holding the floor. 'The Prime Minister and I have been discussing the matter of the 45p tax rate,' he told them.

'I think we have to do something about it,' Truss said, giving the clear impression that she had made up her mind on one of the Chancellor's flagship policies and that her team fully agreed.

'I am not sure about it. I think we should tough it out,' Kwarteng replied.

'I'm sorry, Kwasi, but I've come to the conclusion we have to go for it.'

'But why the change now? If we do, it'll overshadow the entire conference.'

'It's already overshadowing the conference,' she shot back at him.

'I think we are exaggerating the problems. We can sort out the mathematics, we can't let ourselves be dictated to.'

'I'm sorry, but we have to do it. It's our best way of keeping the initiative.'

Those present noted how their conversation fell into the usual pattern, with Kwarteng putting up a fight and making his case strongly, then backtracking and conceding to her. After ten minutes, they had agreed that the U-turn would have to be made, that he would announce it in his speech and that the press lobby would be briefed in the morning. He left the room apparently happy enough and even smiling, and she gave him an affectionate touch on the arm.

Truss then rushed down to attend a drinks party hosted by Graham Brady for the 1922 Committee, and another given by the ConservativeHome website at a nearby bar. But it became clear that speculation was already spreading fast, and a story was inevitably going to appear on the *Sun*'s website saying that the 45p tax rate abolition was being reversed.[6] Truss was told the news had leaked out and she would lose the initiative. If she didn't act, Tory MPs who had spent a week defending the policy in public would learn about the change from the *Sun*. So thirty minutes later, she spoke to Kwarteng on the phone. This time, his frustration and anger were evident to all on the conference call.

'Kwasi, we're going to have to announce it tonight.'

'Why?'

'It's about keeping control.'

'This doesn't make any sense to me at all. First we agreed that we were going to do nothing but stick it out. Then we agreed we were going to make the announcement tomorrow. Now you tell me you want to make it tonight.'

'I'm sorry, Kwasi.'

'This is totally shambolic and chaotic and we should not be doing this.'

He left the call far from happy.

At this point, tensions that had long been bubbling under the surface exploded into the open. 'What the f**k is this all about? We can't carry on with this frenetic policy-making,' one of his team said after the Chancellor had hung up.

'We're being forced into it,' one of Truss's team responded.

'No we're not. We're letting ourselves be bounced around from one opinion poll to another,' they responded.

The atmosphere was awkward. No one knew what to say. Truss's team was already divided, and now they were falling out with Kwarteng's team.

'I've had enough. I'm heading off to bed,' said the Prime Minister.

Rumours then reached the team that the *Daily Mail*, which had been markedly supportive of Truss, was going to run a front-page defence of the 45p tax rate decision. 'We can't let them do that,' one of her team said. So they instructed Kwarteng to speak to the editor, Ted Verity, to say 'you must do as you think fit, but if you run with that story, you're going to look rather silly because the policy is going to change'. The deed done, McGee, Stein and Jones debated how to tell the lobby at large. 'Going from full-on endorsing the 45p policy to abandoning it twelve hours later shows how impossible doing communications is for Liz,' they concluded. When they reached the ground floor, the doors opened onto three journalists who were following the emerging story with intense interest. All of them – Harry Cole, Ben Riley-Smith and Tim Shipman – would go on to write books about the events. 'You couldn't have made it up,' said one of Truss's team later.

'We get it, and we have listened,' Kwarteng tweeted at 7.30 a.m. on Monday 3 October.[7] Hopes the announcement would regain the initiative took a bashing when Gove let it be known he'd still vote against any plan involving a real-term cut in benefits.[8] Worse, former Cabinet ministers Damian Green and Esther McVey joined him in the criticism.[9] Truss now found herself under attack from supporters of Johnson (troubling given that his support had propelled her into Downing Street) as well as Sunak supporters.

In Kwarteng's conference speech, described as 'brief and abashed' by the *Guardian*, he admitted it had been 'a tough day'.[10] Abolishing the 45p rate of income tax, he said, had become 'a distraction' from the other policies in the growth plan. He also took a swipe at Sunak for presiding over 'slow, managed decline'.[11] After Kwarteng's speech, Truss escaped back to her room to concentrate on her own speech, ignoring what was happening nearby on the conference floor.

It wasn't just politicians who were worried: back in the Cabinet Office, Simon Case had been holding conversations with the Treasury and the Bank of England. 'The 45p tax rate reversal made little difference as the markets are effectively priced in already,' said a Treasury official. Case was being told that 'more needed to be done to calm the markets'. A second U-turn thus followed in the form of advancing the date for the Medium-Term Fiscal Plan (to include cuts in spending) from 23 November to late October, and announcing it would be accompanied by a new forecast from the OBR. This was all designed to help restore market stability.[12] But even this didn't do enough to quell rebellion. 'The market still didn't have confidence in the government,' said an official. Additional political concerns were coming to the fore over how cuts in spending would hit benefits, which Kwarteng refused to rule out. Mel Stride, Chair of the Treasury Select Committee, then weighed in saying that further measures still might be needed 'to unwind' aspects of the Mini-Budget.[13]

The conference was falling apart in front of the whole country. Truss's supporters were livid. According to Jake Berry, 'It was appalling the way that Gove went around whipping up people against her. Together with Grant Shapps, they machine-gunned Liz. They would never accept that Liz had won. Then, it was utterly incredible that Mel Stride came out slamming the Mini-Budget. You can't overstate how ruthless these people were and how well tuned into the media.'[14] Stride was regarded with deep suspicion in the Truss camp as he was a well-known Sunak supporter – they wouldn't accept that he might be acting with anything other than a fratricidal motive.

Tuesday 4 October brought little relief. The sense grew that Truss had lost control, with Cabinet ministers, including Braverman, openly speaking off message. 'Here in Birmingham, there is a pervading sense that the damage has already been done,' wrote Charlotte Ivers for the *New Statesman*.[15] 'Four weeks into her reign it feels as though the party is already over', was the verdict of Camilla Cavendish in the *Financial Times*.[16] 'The conference was awful... the worst start to any premiership, I think, in recent history – perhaps even in all British history,' wrote historian Dominic Sandbrook.[17]

What was missing, oddly but devastatingly, were the voices of Conservative parliamentarians of authority. Where was her Foreign Secretary, her Home Secretary, her Defence Secretary? Where were the former Prime Ministers like Johnson or Cameron? Where were the former party leaders who still carried weight like Duncan Smith, Howard or Hague? Where were her rivals in the leadership contest, Sunak, Mordaunt and Badenoch?

When Major was under pressure in the build-up to his leadership re-election in the summer of 1995, the party grandees Michael Heseltine (DPM), Douglas Hurd (Foreign Secretary) and Ken Clarke (Chancellor) closed ranks around him. Chief Whip Alastair Goodlad and the Leaders of the Commons and Lords respectively,

Tony Newton and Lord Cranborne, deployed their considerable influence bringing people into line.[18] This time? Total silence.

Truss's DPM, Party Chair and Chief Whip let it be known they were angry with the critics, but it was 'sound and fury, signifying nothing' because none were weighty figures in the party. 'The vacuum showed just how paper-thin her support in Cabinet and party was: it was transactional only. They had backed her for personal gain. They were now re-evaluating their investment,' said former Chief Whip Gavin Williamson. 'You can't expect mercenaries to throw away their lives in battle.'[19]

Truss channelled all her anger into her speech. In one of the practice sessions her mind went back to how she had been defeated in the West Yorkshire constituency of Hemsworth in 2001. But she also remembered how, despite the former mining constituency's strong anti-Tory tendencies, the local people had liked her 'Save the Pound' stance: 'Those patriotic people were moving our way. And we won some of those seats in 2017, even under Theresa May. No offence to our great former leader.' Her team laughed. Pumping herself up, her mind went back even further, to the 1980s. 'We are in a similar position to then where we're making tough decisions that aren't necessarily popular that will deliver for the long term. I don't think it's necessarily a bad thing to hark back to that. If you want the best example of the policy prescription, it's Thatcher and Reagan between them. I wonder if we mention Reagan?'

'I wouldn't. It's a bit tired,' Stein volunteered.

'It's basically the same thing. The policies were said to be mad then too.'

'Everyone always calls Prime Ministers, Cabinets, policies – everything – mad,' Stein said, encouraging her.

Her state of mind was evident when she railed against pampered elites and the 'blob': 'They don't understand aspiration... They don't want to set up a business... They don't understand what's paying their f**king left-wing journalist wages... Have they ever been outside North London? And now, thanks to Zoom, they never need to leave!'[20]

The actual speech was just as forthright, if less profane. It contained a passionate attack on the 'anti-growth coalition' holding back the country: 'I will not allow [them] to hold us back. Labour, the Lib Dems and the SNP, the militant unions, the vested interests dressed up as think tanks. The talking heads, the Brexit deniers and Extinction Rebellion... The fact is they prefer protesting to doing. They prefer talking on Twitter to taking tough decisions... From broadcast to podcast, they peddle the same old answers. It's always more taxes, more regulation and more meddling. Wrong, wrong, wrong.' The party membership loved it and sat ever further forward on their seats as she spoke. 'My friends, does this anti-growth coalition have any idea who pays their wages? It's the people who make things in factories across our country. It's the people who get up at the crack of dawn to go to work. It's the commuters who get trains into towns and cities across our country.' The response was euphoric, the clapping going on and on.[21]

'We didn't expect it. She didn't expect it. You can see that in her face,' said an aide. 'This was the members delivering a very clear message to the MPs. This is the leader we want,' said another. It was, in that sense, a repeat-run of the leadership contest: the MPs didn't want her, the party in the country did. Something would have to give. But when?

Full Speed Ahead on Truss's Growth Agenda: 5–7 October 2022

'Press ahead. I don't want to hear any f**king objections,' a post-speech Truss told a meeting of her staff on Wednesday 5 October. She was acting as if the party conference had been a triumph. She had almost found herself talking to an empty room. 'I want us to meet up immediately when I'm back. I've got much to say,' she had told her team as she left the conference at midday on Wednesday, not appreciating they'd struggle to get back from Birmingham as quickly as she did in her traffic-clearing police convoy.

The 'hopper' (her 'super secret' announcement list) was the focus as they gathered around Truss at the Cabinet table. Truss had coined the name herself, inspired by the way in which her team fed material into a master document, and how it came out the other side in polished form, just like an industrial hopper. This was the growth agenda and supply-side revolution that she intended would dominate the autumn and beyond, and which she hadn't wanted her Cabinet ministers to foreshadow or upstage at conference. The hopper was going to be her secret weapon for regaining the initiative, wresting back the attention of the fickle media from their obsession with sterling and financial markets. Her three priorities – investment zones, changes to planning and regulation, and broadband – she fondly imagined would amount to a revolution akin to Thatcher's.

Urgency was dictated in part by her needing to be in Prague the following day for the first meeting of Macron's European Political Community. She could have done without it, especially as the very idea of it sounded fishy to the ERG. 'This is not about moving closer to Europe,' she had been at pains to stress in public, but rather about working with Europe 'on issues that we all face'.[22] Urgency was also dictated by her knowing that in forty-eight hours there might be bad news from the OBR. 'We all knew it was coming, but she didn't want to talk about it,' said an aide.

For the remaining two weeks of her premiership, she exhibited manic and, some felt, unhinged energy pushing forward her growth agenda. A stream of announcements came from No. 10 focused on three priorities. 'She was infuriated by "nimbyism" and believed passionately that you have to allow construction if growth was to be stimulated,' said an aide. 'She didn't want to accept any limitations or problems.' The height of phone masts on public buildings created a particular furore when Coffey told her that MPs were objecting. 'I don't care how high the masts are – push ahead. Stop worrying about these things, Thérèse,' she said, according to an aide. One broadband initiative she was shown would cost £150 million, another £20 million, while another was cost-free but would require primary legislation to pave the way. 'We don't have time: we must pay for it.' 'But Prime Minister, this will need money, and I just don't think we're in a position to spend it,' said economic adviser Shabbir Merali. 'I don't f**king care. Press on,' she replied. 'It was all totally shambolic. The official machine was trying to help her, but it couldn't work at the speed and in the way she wanted,' said a senior adviser.

A Very Big, Very Black Hole: 7–9 October 2022

'Knock before entering', was the uncharacteristic message that the economics team pinned on the door of their office in No. 10 on Friday morning, 7 October. A short while before, they had gone over to No. 11 to receive a briefing about the OBR's forecast. They were told not to share what they had heard with anyone at No. 10 apart from Porter and Sinclair. They knew it would be a problem. There would be a big gap between spending and revenue: the only question was how big.

The Treasury and the Bank of England had been in close conversation all week, very worried by the interest rate markets and the foreign exchange markets. They had been debating what interventions the Bank could make, and whether it could move beyond buying the conventional gilts it normally traded in to buying index-linked gilts.

No. 10 was focused on the more immediate issue of the size of the budgetary black hole. The expectation among the staff was that it would be large but manageable: the Resolution Foundation think tank had estimated it might be £36 billion.[23] But when Kwarteng was told the figure on Friday of £72 billion, caused by the largesse of the Energy Price Guarantee, the tax cuts and the slowing growth outlook, it was beyond worst expectations.

A top secret meeting was convened in the Cabinet Room. Truss and Kwarteng were fuming. 'We must send out people to attack the f**king OBR and the IMF at once,' they said. 'Who at No. 10 have the Treasury and the OBR been speaking to?' 'Why didn't they speak to us?' 'The OBR is just another example of a failed institution – they are in danger of losing the plot.' The atmosphere was described by an adviser as 'ugly, menacing even'. 'The comments were very nasty in private, and for a time there was a real risk that the bile would seep out in public,' said one who had been in the room. The rage was not without reason because the OBR projections of the future were unnecessarily pessimistic. As an aide said, 'The precise moment the dream went wrong was after the OBR demanded eye-watering cuts. That was when the project ended, when it was game over.'

The financially literate knew what the politicians didn't: this was one of the most serious fiscal predicaments in Britain's recent financial history and the scale of spending cuts needed if the interest on debt incurred was not to damage the country would be extremely difficult to find, and all but impossible to achieve in one fiscal event. 'I'm not so worried. We can achieve it through spending cuts,' Kwarteng said. 'But £72 billion is just an estimate: what happens if the hole increases to £80 billion?' interjected one of the team. 'The OBR forecast doesn't take full account of growth. If we make the supply-side reforms, the black hole will shrink. We must forge ahead with our supply-side reforms,' responded Truss.

It was a dialogue of the deaf. 'Listening to Kwarteng and Truss talk, the officials and economic advisers concluded that they had neither insight nor understanding about how economic growth occurs; no understanding about economics, nor financial markets, nor that you can't cut £72 billion in one sweep,' said an aide.

Saturday 8 October was spent examining options for cuts. Any hopes of a day off on Sunday after the frenetic conference week were rudely interrupted by a message that the Prime Minister wanted to see her team at Chequers on Sunday morning. A small political meeting preceded the main event, consisting of the PM, the Chancellor and special advisers. The atmosphere was a million miles from the optimism and exuberance of Chevening just six weeks before.

Rather than a conversation focused on the £72 billion and how to address it, much of the time was spent talking about parliamentary business for the week ahead, and, even more puzzlingly to some present, whether the PM should host a reception at No. 10 for the England women's football team who had won the Euros during the summer (the decision was to meet them on Tuesday at their training ground).[24]

For the main meeting, they were joined by senior Treasury officials. 'The markets frankly were looking pretty grim – both exchange rates and interest rates,' recalled an official. One described it as the most anxious moment of the whole Mini-Budget crisis aside from the hours leading up to the Bank's announcement on 28 September to make its time-limited intervention.

As they all sat around the table at Chequers, their focus was the 'Treasury spreadsheet', which listed a range of remedial measures including windfall taxes and reversal of the Mini-Budget initiatives. Truss seemed to favour savings in departmental spending and cuts to capital projects, but the conversation ended inconclusively, with participants wondering what the plan was. The officials left for London without answers.

Truss asked her political team to stay back for a side meeting to debate whether Kwarteng should go to the IMF for its autumn meeting in Washington DC. Given the delicacy of the current financial climate, Truss thought he should stay in the UK, but he argued that this was the key annual meeting for finance ministers, and it would create more uncertainty if he did not go, that it should be business as usual. Reluctantly she agreed. The timing of the forthcoming fiscal event was then discussed. Monday 31 October had been the date agreed earlier in the week. Should it be moved even earlier? There were concerns of it being linked to Halloween with the prospect of endless lurid headlines, but more significantly, it was argued there was no time to lose for reassuring the markets that the government had a plan. A lack of urgency continued to worry some present, not helped by an unwillingness to pin down precise dates and figures.

Part of the problem was that the Treasury still did not have a permanent secretary to provide robust leadership and demand answers from Truss and Kwarteng. Cat Little and Beth Russell were providing gallant leadership, but they lacked the authority of established leaders, especially after it had been made clear that the full-time appointment would go to an 'existing permanent secretary', thereby knocking both of them out of the running. In the absence of a leader, Treasury officials were apprehensive about challenging Kwarteng and Truss head on. They were working on a strategy of incremental persuasion to bring them round to the realization that more urgent and drastic action was needed. But special advisers in both the Prime Minister's and the Chancellor's camps were beginning to realize that they might have to take action into their own hands.

The Abandonment of Truss's Daring Treasury Plan: 5 September–10 October 2022

Of all the institutions that Truss and Kwarteng disliked, the Treasury came top of the list. 'I had no problems with Treasury officials per se: I'd worked with them before. It was Treasury orthodoxy I couldn't stand,' said Truss.[25] They contemplated, if not seriously, dismantling it altogether. But history was not encouraging: the last Prime Minister to dismember it was Harold Wilson, who created the Department of Economic Affairs in 1964. Five years later, it was reabsorbed back into the all-powerful Treasury. This was not a fight that Truss and Kwarteng wanted to have with the crazy timetable they had given themselves. Instead, they envisaged a remodelled Treasury operating under a permanent secretary who would approve of their commitment to radical thinking, organizational innovation and growth.

The person they both wanted was Antonia Romeo, an official with whom Truss had worked at the Department for International Trade between 2019 and 2021. There they had struck up a fruitful professional relationship. Romeo was exactly the kind of 'can-do' permanent secretary that Truss liked. Kwarteng held a similarly positive view of her and was equally irritated as Truss by the Treasury. When he had been Business Secretary under Johnson, he had repeatedly clashed with the Treasury over what he saw as its overly cautious attitude to growth.

Axing Scholar and putting in Romeo was all part of the same plan. To their irritation, however, they were told by Case they had to go through a formal application process. 'Liz and I just had a general understanding we were going to go for Antonia,' said Kwarteng. 'We felt the Treasury was simply too controlling and we needed a different operation. We both liked her and thought she was the person to sort out the Treasury and make it a growth department.'[26] Romeo duly came out the winner of an official appointment process, and it was briefed that she was to start work shortly. But the meltdown on the markets changed everything.

Case spoke privately to Truss and told her there may be unrest in the department if Romeo, who had not worked in the Treasury, was brought in, and that the markets would also not be reassured to see a Treasury outsider appointed. So on Sunday 9 October when they were at Chequers, Truss told Kwarteng she was sorry, but she thought it too risky, she would play safe, and appoint someone they had initially discounted as being 'continuity Scholar'. This was James Bowler, whom she had liked when he had succeeded Romeo as International Trade permanent secretary, and who had held a series of senior positions at the Treasury, as well as the crucial job of principal private secretary to the Prime Minister (to Cameron in the Coalition government). Kwarteng was far from happy and thought him too 'Brownite', arguing strongly to keep with the Romeo appointment. It took her two attempts to persuade him the switch had to be made. Bowler's appointment was announced on Monday 10 October.

The collapse of the plan to make the Treasury the new UK growth department with Romeo at the head was a huge blow. It made a mockery of all the stick Truss had taken over the sacking of Scholar. The Treasury growth plan was effectively now dead.

So too was her plan to buy long-term gas supplies from Norway, having gained a fixed price from Equinor, the Norwegian state-owned energy company, at a cost of £130 billion. Kwarteng had the temerity to stand up to her on this, backed by some strong official advice. 'I am going to sign up for it regardless,' she said. But he steadfastly refused to let it go ahead. His advice indicated that the price was too high and it would almost certainly fall. Locking Britain into a gas deal at inflated prices would not help anybody. Sure enough, it was one of Kwarteng's few decisions to be fully vindicated and the price fell dramatically over subsequent months. The previous two weeks had toughened him. He would not let himself be pushed around again, he told himself. That wasn't the kind of Chancellor Truss had wanted.

A Revolt from Below: 10–12 October 2022

When the markets opened for trading on the morning of Monday 10 October, predictions of a collapse of confidence were widespread. Kwarteng spoke to the Bank early that morning to ask it to do more to provide cover by extending support for UK gilts beyond the declared date of Friday 14 October, just four days away, but to no avail. He was livid, as he later recalled: 'Why did our growth project fail? Because the Bank of England refused to extend the support beyond 14 October. It's no surprise the markets went into meltdown on 17 October.' Andrew Griffith, then Financial Secretary to the Treasury, recalled, 'My own experience of markets taught me you just don't reveal your hand publicly like that. Tapering it off gradually would have been a better way to do it.'[27] The Bank was taking further action, which was helping to bring stability at the start of the week, including buying index-linked gilts. Bank officials were told by pension fund managers that this had significantly helped solve their LDI problem.

On Tuesday 11 October, to Kwarteng's fury, Governor Bailey repeated on stage at the IMF that intervention to support market function would end at close of business on Friday 14 October, saying the Bank never intended that bond-buying would become a permanent backstop.[28] One Bank insider said that the Governor had 'repeated the cut-off date to force the funds to sell gilts to the bank and recapitalize'. Bailey had become deeply concerned by what he had been hearing at the IMF, with talk about a major loss of confidence in Britain among the G7. 'He had very senior people in the IMF and World Bank community telling him that Britain was letting down the G7, and if a major crisis was to be averted, it needed to put its house in order,' said a Bank official. Bailey worried that if he extended the purchasing beyond 14 October, it would jeopardize the Bank's status as an independent institution, and he also believed that the immediate LDI crisis would have been resolved by then. After all, the heart of the crisis was not about LDIs, but a loss of confidence in Britain's fiscal architecture.

'Nothing that Andrew Bailey said on that Tuesday was out of line with what he had said all along,' said one of the Bank's senior leadership, who argued that the time-limited decision on the intervention was taken not by Bailey alone, but by the Bank's senior leadership as a whole. Turbulence was magnified, the Bank believed, by a rogue article in the *Financial Times* suggesting that the Bank's intervention might continue after 14 October. 'We could only speculate about [their] motives,' said a Bank source.[29] Tuesday continued to be a very difficult day with market turbulence. 'The basic issue was the credibility of the government: the markets no longer had faith they had the will or capability to do what was needed,' said a Treasury source.

Truss's economic adviser Shabbir Merali, who had been gaining ground against Matt Sinclair, had been regularly talking about the sterling and gilt crisis with his opposite number in Kwarteng's team, Adam Memon. Conscious of the almost total ignorance in No. 10, the Treasury and Cabinet Office about how financial markets actually operated, the two decided they should speak to a wide range of people in the City and beyond about what had caused the crisis and how best to respond. That Monday and Tuesday, they started making phone calls. Robert Stheeman, long-standing head of the Debt Management Office, an executive agency of the Treasury, impressed on them his concerns about what might happen to demand for gilts: with the Bank of England intervention finishing on 14 October, there was a potential risk of a 'doom loop scenario' with a gilt sale failing altogether, which would have been perilous. Traders told Merali and Memon that the UK was at risk of heading towards a sovereign debt crisis. A regular message they heard was that the best way to restore confidence would be to reverse the corporation tax change. 'The Treasury knew it made sense, but they were still not advising the Chancellor to reverse it because of the fear of saying anything critical about a central plank of their policy,' said an aide. 'Despite good interim leadership after Scholar left, it was evident that there was a vacuum in leadership till his successor was in post,' said another. The Treasury, in part as a result of negativity from recent PMs, had lost confidence in itself and some of its best minds. No. 10 too was critically short of senior figures with expert economic and financial knowledge, or a Treasury background (for good reason the PM's principal private secretary traditionally had been a Treasury official but not since May and Johnson).

Wednesday was a bruising day for Truss in Parliament. She had PMQs at midday, where Starmer accused her of 'a kamikaze Budget' and asked, 'Who voted for this?' At one point, he asked her whether she still stuck by her pledge not to cut public spending. 'Absolutely,' she replied. Truss then defended her plans, telling the House that she 'will make sure that, over the medium term, the debt is falling, and we will do that not by cutting public spending but by making sure we spend public money well'.[30]

Conservative MPs were unimpressed by her performance. Later that day, she was confronted by Tory MPs in a 1922 Committee meeting. The atmosphere was extraordinarily tense.[31] MPs asked how exactly she planned to pay for the tax cuts without spending reductions. Another MP asked her what would happen to promised infrastructure projects, a question that she struggled to answer. 'It obviously just dawned on her that these things are going to need more money,' an MP told the *Observer*.[32] In one intervention, Robert Halfon accused her of having 'trashed' the work of Conservative leaders to win over working-class voters. 'It was embarrassing,' he later said. 'MP after MP lined up to denigrate her.'[33] Outside the room, Tory MPs told reporters that the meeting had been 'funereal' and that she had been 'just appalling'.[34]

Back at No. 10, the more they heard, the more Merali and Memon became worried. 'We thought we had a week for government to come up with a financial framework that would convince the markets. We were told that the markets were already pricing in that the government was going to reverse Mini-Budget measures, and if it didn't, there would be a double blow,' said one. By Wednesday afternoon, with two days left before the Bank intervention ended on 14 October, they concluded that there was no viable route out of the predicament without major policy reversals, and that they didn't see the plan being advocated by either ministers or officials. Among the latter, they were aware of Case's concerns, but were not sure how quickly the newly appointed Bowler would be able to seize the reins. They worried too that, puzzlingly, 'the centre of government, bar a few isolated voices in the Treasury and in the Cabinet Office's Economic and Domestic Affairs Secretariat, was not really on top of all that was happening in the markets'.

Jamie Hope, despite being Truss's head of policy, had been excluded from the economic developments, and invited neither to review the documents nor attend meetings. He was becoming 'terrified' by watching what he had seen unfolding on the No. 10 television screens. He shared his concerns that afternoon with Merali: 'I'm worried about all this. We really need to talk about it.'

'Let's do so. So am I,' Merali replied. 'We've been speaking to traders who work in the financial markets and they're telling us that if nothing happens, they're going to start betting against us when the markets open next Monday.'

'There's no urgency round here. It's f**king weird,' Hope said.

'We've been hearing that the financial markets have got no confidence in Liz. No confidence in the economic policy.'

'What can we do?'

'Someone's going to have to tell the Prime Minister. She won't like it but she needs to know.'

At that point, they were joined by fellow special adviser Alex Boyd, who was told that Truss and Kwarteng were thinking they could still sort out the black hole with severe cuts. 'We've been told that they're looking at stopping cancer treatment on the NHS,' they told him.

'Is she being serious?' Boyd asked.

'She's lost the plot,' they replied. 'She's shouting at everyone – at us and officials that we've "got to find the money!" When we tell her it can't be done, she shouts back, "It's not true. The money is there. You go and find it."'

A note to Truss laying out their collective concerns seemed the best way forward. Merali thought they should bring in Memon, who suggested they write the note in No. 11 for privacy. Finding £72 billion was a tall order: they estimated that Osborne in his austerity drive from 2010 to 2015 'only' made cuts of some £30 billion in total.

'It's not going to happen, is it?' concluded one.

'Even if the cuts were announced, the markets won't believe them and our position would only weaken,' said another.

'And they would never get cuts that size through Parliament,' said another.

'There'll have to be some change of personnel. The markets won't believe it if Kwarteng announces the cuts: he'll never be able to stand up and reverse them.'

This was the elephant in the room.

'But if he goes, her authority goes with him. And she will go too,' said Hope.

A long silence followed.

'How long does she have?' one of them asked.

'As long as Christmas,' Boyd said.

'It's all over, isn't it?' said another.

The question did not need an answer. For a while, the four sat around the table silently taking in the magnitude of what they had been saying.

'Come on. Let's get the note written,' said one. On Merali's laptop they hammered out the document for Truss, just two pages of A4. The first part had the evidence from conversations that Merali and Memon had been having with the market experts about why they thought a meltdown could happen on Monday 17 October, and the second part, a list of options for the Prime Minister to decide.

The document presented to Truss has come to light and is one of the most remarkable documents ever penned by a Prime Minister's advisers. It lists the points tersely on both sides of a single crumpled page.

It begins with a summary of 'trusted market feedback received':

1. The market wide view is if the MTFP [Medium-Term Fiscal Plan] on 31 Oct is not credible there is a serious risk of a financial/sovereign debt crisis.

2. Markets will not believe that we will be able get through this level of spending cuts. They don't believe that we won't reverse course in the face of NHS pressures etc and that we will be able to get this through the parliamentary party.

3. They assume that we have no choice but to reverse corporation tax at the very least they say, if we are to do it, sooner is better than later.

4. 31 Oct is a very long time away, and there is a serious risk of extreme market volatility before then. It's not clear that we will last that long before we are forced to act on account of deteriorating market conditions.

It advised a 'pivot' because 'our overriding objective is growth. The way yields are rising, there is no route to growth without financial stability. A financial crisis would choke off growth for several years and lead to long term financial scarring'.

The document then went through a list of options for tax rises, including reversing the cut to Corporation tax and several other mini budget policies. It listed the amounts of money this would raise. All told, these measures would raise some £36 billion, but that was still not enough.

It then proposed several ways to reduce spending by £36 billion. These included focusing 'cuts on non-growth measures' in departmental expenditure, as well as reviewing the triple lock on pensions, the state pension age, the winter fuel allowance and child benefit. It concluded that the next steps were to 'Reverse cuts.

Calm markets. Deliver credible MTFP. Supply side reform. Increase headroom for March forecast.'

The question now was who should deliver the memo to Truss. The obvious person was Kwarteng, but he was in Washington and they worried he would try to dismiss their concerns. 'Our worry was that if he got to her first, he would convince her that the threat of a sovereign debt crisis wasn't real and that the problem would go away,' said one adviser. 'If that happens, it may take years to recover,' said Memon. Who else then should break the news? The next obvious person was Coffey in her capacity as DPM, but she was discounted because they didn't believe that she grasped the complexity of what was at stake financially. They were running out of options. Where were the grown-ups? Hope suggested Fullbrook who, as chief of staff, was the next most senior. He was at a reception in the Drawing Rooms upstairs. Hope sidled up to him sheepishly at about 8 p.m.

'Can I have a minute?'

'Sure.'

Out of earshot of the guests, Hope told him, 'I think you need to come to the Chancellor's dining room, Mark. We need to talk to you urgently about the economy.'

'Give me fifteen minutes, and I'll be with you.'

He showed up shortly afterwards, 'which seemed like an interminable time when the economy was starting to resemble Venezuela's', as one recalled.

Merali and Memon at once launched into telling him about their conversations with traders, the debt crisis and the consequences for the economy.

Silence. They had absolutely no idea how he might respond.

'Well, she's f**ked then, isn't she?' they recall him saying, quick as ever to assess political reality. Fullbrook might not have been the finished article as No. 10's chief of staff, but his political nous was peerless. 'Why doesn't she realize how bad it is?' he enquired.

They replied that the Treasury were not telling her fully what might happen: the position was a lot more serious than they or No. 10 appreciated.

'Well, I will see that she's told about it. Even if she says I don't care, there's a moral duty to tell her,' he told them. There were murmurs of agreement across the table.

'This is one of those moments that you remember for the rest of your life,' he said, and he whipped out his phone to take a photograph with the conspirators.

The time on the image was 8.45 p.m.

It was agreed that the note should be presented at the team meeting the following morning. Pizzas were ordered at 9.30 p.m., and Merali and Memon were left polishing the wording of the brief note for Truss until almost midnight.

Elsewhere in the heart of Whitehall a parallel discussion had been taking place. Prime ministerial administrations can be dysfunctional, but none have been more dysfunctional than those overseen by Johnson and Truss. Often one part of Downing Street didn't know what the other was doing. Not since the modern centre emerged under Lloyd George with the creation of the Cabinet Office in December 1916 had it been more chaotic. Case had remained on a state of high alert ever since the first weekend after the Mini-Budget. He recognized the country was in a potentially dangerous predicament. The Chancellor was out of the country, the Treasury was in an unsteady position with its change of leader, and he was incensed by a leak to the press about possible changes in government policy. The worrier-in-chief wasn't yet contemplating talks with the warrior-in-chief, Chief of Defence Staff Admiral Sir Tony Radakin, but that moment might come. Certainly Britain's intelligence services were monitoring the developing financial situation and the potential hazards.

Earlier that Wednesday Case shared his concerns with Stein. 'The market position is very, very volatile,' he said, 'and I am concerned the PM is losing control of the party.' They talked about how she could strengthen her government: replacing Chief Whip Morton with Coffey, and bringing in Shapps as the Health Secretary were top of the agenda. They discussed the leak – Stein confirmed he thought it had come from the Treasury.[35]

Merali and Memon arrived in the Thatcher Room at 9 a.m. on Thursday 13 October to find it already full of senior staff – Porter, Fullbrook, Stein, Sinclair and Jones. Several of them later recalled what was said. They reprised their arguments from the evening before, and repeated that if decisive action wasn't taken, they feared they could find themselves in 'a very bad position with no choices left'. Sinclair had already made known his deep scepticism about the scale of the danger and thus the disproportionality of their response. Porter asked searching questions, but was brought round by the end of the meeting. Stein, fresh from his conversations with Case, immediately understood the import of what was being said, and asked for more details. The meeting concluded with Porter saying that she would talk to Truss, who had already been spoken to by Fullbrook.

There was still a nervousness among the special advisers about whether the urgency had fully registered. Truss had been chatting with them first thing that morning. 'I hear you were busy last night talking to Mark about the economy. You're not supposed to be working on the economy, are you?' she said scornfully to one. She was clearly rattled and 'smirking unaccountably'. 'We were just trying to come up with some ideas to get out of the impasse,' they replied. 'I'm not cross with you if that's what you're worrying about,' she said, confusing them all, because evidently she was.

Hope searched out Catsaras and told him bluntly, 'The Prime Minister has got to reverse the corporation tax policy now.'

'There has to be a basis for doing so. It can't just be that you guys have now changed your mind,' he responded.

'Nick, you have got to tell her. You will get through to her.'

Several of Truss's aides had worked with James Bowler at International Trade, liked him and now pinned their faith on him.

So Catsaras called Bowler, now on his fourth day in the illustrious Treasury permanent secretary's office, and explained the urgency of the position as No. 10 saw it and the belief that reversing the policy on corporation tax would address it. 'Can you come urgently to talk to the PM in No. 10?' This was highly irregular, and they both knew it – the Treasury permanent secretary owes their primary allegiance to the Chancellor. The predicament tested the unwritten constitution to the very heart. 'Because we were worried the Treasury might leak Bowler's visit, we kept it confidential and basically smuggled him into the building,' said an aide. When he arrived at 10.30 a.m., Truss was sitting at the Cabinet table with senior staff.

'Prime Minister, the position is dire. We think you must listen to what James has to tell you,' said Stein.

'Prime Minister, it is highly unusual for the Treasury permanent secretary to brief the Prime Minister without the Chancellor present,' Bowler opened. 'In any previous administration if the permanent secretary to the Treasury spoke to the Prime Minister without the Chancellor present, it would be a sackable offence. I'm feeling extremely uncomfortable. But it seems your special advisers want me to tell you that you need to reverse the corporation tax policy.'

'I know what *they* think. What do *you* think?' she shot back at him with her intense stare.

Bowler shifted uncomfortably on his seat. He found himself in a near impossible position with his new masters; the Prime Minister and her Chancellor were clearly wedded to one policy, but his instincts told him the opposite. She sensed his discomfort. She turned to Merali, whose advice she was minded to rate above Sinclair's.

'Shabbir, what do you think?'

'I think that we must change the policy, Prime Minister,' he said.

At that point, Bowler spoke out: 'Prime Minister, the reason I'm here is because the people round the table believe you should change policy on corporation tax.' Without expressly saying it, he indicated he saw the sense in the change. Those present describe it as 'a really remarkable moment'.

The meeting broke up shortly afterwards. Truss's team huddled together and apologized to Bowler for putting him through the ordeal. 'It's OK, let's see what happens,' he said before shooting back to the Treasury. After he left, Porter and Stein spoke to Truss in the Cabinet Room. 'Do you think they are right?' she asked them. 'How can we know?' they replied. 'The problem is, they were probably right about the Mini-Budget too, and I didn't listen,' she said, in a rare moment of vulnerability and honesty.

Truss was unhappy and she tried to get Kwarteng back from Washington a day early. 'No, I can't come back, Liz, because if I do so, it will cause more turbulence,' he told her. He was worried that it would be worse 'if one panics and overacts in a crisis', he reflected later. 'This was deeply baked into me. Second World War veterans in my constituency used to say that if you're going to die, keep calm to the end.'[36]

Catsaras spoke to Case, who was himself rapidly getting up to speed with what had been happening that morning. The leak that corporation tax would be reversed had led to the markets calming, but also an expectation that Truss would make the change. She was in torment. In one ear, almost her entire team at No. 10 advised her to junk the policies as quickly as possible, as did figures such as Rupert Harrison, former right-hand man to Osborne; in the other ear, she had the old guard urging her to revert to Fortress Liz mentality. The revanchists appeared to be winning.

'She swatted the idea away and said it was ridiculous,' said an aide. They had played their James Bowler trump card, and it appeared to have failed. So Catsaras said to Case, 'We need to work out if this is a genuine problem or not, and do so face-to-face.' Case insisted the outlook was potentially so grave he should contact Bailey at the Bank of England. 'Andrew,' he said, 'I need, for the record, to ask your advice on the state of the markets.' The Governor told him there had been significant volatility not least in the last couple of hours in the UK gilt markets, and if the corporation tax change didn't go ahead, given the assumption it would, things could be 'very bumpy'. After the call, Case told Catsaras he was going to write him an official letter laying out the substance of the conversation. He wrote that Bailey thought there would be 'significant evidence of volatility if the change didn't go ahead and that the underlying improvement of the bank's market operations would also be jeopardised'. Catsaras then showed Truss the letter at 5.30 p.m. They were alone in the office at the end of the Cabinet Room.

'Nick, you are organizing a Bank and Whitehall conspiracy against me,' she told him in that ambiguous tone of voice that is either teasing or menacing.

'You need to read the letter first, Prime Minister, before you dismiss the judgement.'

She did, but she was still leaning towards not changing direction. The Brexit Praetorian Guard – including John Redwood and Bill Cash – were telling her to hold her ground. Redwood said that he'd spoken to friends in the markets and there was nothing to worry about – that it was all the fault of the Bank of England. They warned of the political risks of a U-turn. Chief Secretary to the Treasury Chris Philp, who, in Kwarteng's absence abroad, was her most senior finance minister on the ground, also counselled sticking to her guns. One of her ministers wrote to her saying that there was no risk of a run on the pound, and that pension managers would make their decisions on Monday, not Friday. He thought that there was no need to panic, and a U-turn would not significantly alter the market reaction. Hold the line. 'Treasury officials were doing strange things behind Kwasi's back. Liz was panicking and pivoting on the back of a sixpence, having been wound up by his officials,' one minister later said.

The Verdict: Maintain a Reputation for Economic Competence?

The country faced the most precarious financial position since the global financial crisis of 2008. The risk was that, if Truss didn't change direction, the markets would have started melting down when they opened in Asia on Sunday evening, with sterling being sold alongside government debt, and a full-scale crisis unfolding. But whatever she did now, any reputation she, or her party, had for economic competence was long gone.

Truss had spectacularly failed on the eighth requirement for a successful premiership: financial and economic competence. There were just seven days before she was to announce her resignation.

Then, at nine o'clock that evening, Catsaras received a summons to the No. 10 flat.

Rule Number Nine: Avoid major U-turns. Jeremy Hunt shreds the mini budget to restore market confidence, Monday 17 October

9

AVOID U-TURNS
13–17 October 2022

'OK, I'm going to do it,' Truss told her startled senior advisers who had just rushed up the stairs to the PM's flat on the evening of Thursday 13 October. 'I'm going to reverse it.'

'Very well, Prime Minister.'

'And... that's not all I'm going to do.'

U-turns and Prime Ministers

Liz Truss was just about to initiate the quickest U-turn on a major policy in British prime ministerial history. Changing course is always painful for leaders. While flexing on a position in the light of fresh circumstances can be seen as courageous leadership, reversing direction on a major policy quickly or repeatedly makes them look weak and indecisive. People think either the leader made the wrong decisions implementing the policy in the first place or they failed to have the grit to stick by it under pressure. Those who supported the policy in public feel betrayed.

Thatcher knew this in her bones, another stark contrast between her and Truss. One year in from election victory in 1979, she was under great stress with her economic policy, and her monetarist

Chancellor Geoffrey Howe was out of step with most economic commentators and many Tory MPs. With unemployment reaching an unprecedented 2 million, a level not seen since the 1930s, the atmosphere was tense. She was under pressure to change course within her own Cabinet from the 'wets'. Even former Prime Minister Harold Macmillan wrote to her in private that summer advocating a return to 'consensus politics'. He did not receive a reply.[1] But, on 10 October 1980, Thatcher's conference speech was defiant, and in a deliberate snub to her predecessor as Tory leader, Ted Heath, who had changed direction, she famously told delegates, 'You turn if you want to. The Lady's not for turning.' A few months later, she reshuffled her Cabinet, leaving it more sympathetic to her policies. But it was the speech, and these words, that became the anthem of every blue-blooded Conservative: true leaders do not U-turn.

Prime Ministers who have U-turned since 1945 have not fared well. In the early 1970s, Ted Heath carried out a significant U-turn: at the general election of 1970, he promised spending cuts, but faced with unemployment rising above 1 million for the first time since 1947, in 1972 he changed direction and started pouring money into the economy. It didn't help, and he was still defeated in the 1974 general election.

The Prime Minister can survive a U-turn with little damage if it's reversing a policy introduced by a predecessor, even if of the same party. Hence, after he came to power in November 1990, John Major abandoned Thatcher's deeply unpopular poll tax, which imposed a level taxation system, with the exact rate set by local authorities, replacing it with the council tax, based on property values. Major went on to win a general election in April 1992.

Tony Blair, though, became unstuck when he U-turned on one of his own policies. In the run-up to the 1997 general election he campaigned on a platform of promising not to introduce tuition fees for students in higher education. But the following year, he did exactly that, allowing universities to charge tuition fees up to £1,000 a year (later increased to £3,000 in 2004 then £9,000 after he stood down). His reputation for honesty suffered significant damage.

Theresa May managed almost to normalize U-turns, being responsible for nine significant *volte-faces* in her first year alone, on topics as diverse as Brexit, Hinkley Point nuclear power station, workers on corporate boards and ruling out an early general election.[2] Then in the general election, she made her most spectacular about-face on her policy on social care laid out in the manifesto. Her series of U-turns played their part in the loss of confidence that led to her standing down as Prime Minister after just under three years.

Prime ministerial history, distant and recent, provided a clear message for Liz Truss: don't launch a policy unless you're absolutely confident that you can see it through.

Dropping the Chancellor: 13–14 October 2022

By mid-afternoon on Thursday 13 October, Truss had begun to think she would have to concede on corporation tax. Or not. Messages had been pouring into Downing Street that she needed to go even further: a change of personnel might be needed too. At 6 p.m., she convened a meeting of her top party figures around the Cabinet table including Thérèse Coffey, past and present Party Chairs Brandon Lewis and Jake Berry, and Deputy Chief Whip Craig Whittaker, flanked by her senior special advisers. One by one, she went round the table and said, 'I'm going to have to change gear on corporation tax. Do I need to go further?' Lewis and Whittaker backed each other up agreeing 'someone's got to go'. 'Really? Who?' she asked. The latter announced boldly, 'Kwasi.' Others quickly jumped in to protest. Whittaker, who was being seen as the Chief Whip in all but name, responded, 'If it's not him, it'll be you, Prime Minister.' When Lewis backed him up she really started to listen. The strongest voice on the other side were the advisers, worried that if Kwarteng fell, it would be 'too explosive' and prove the end not just of the 'Truss project', but her as well. And them. Truss listened carefully and concluded, 'I'll go away and have a think.' Most present felt she had still not made up her mind.

At 10 p.m., up in the flat, she told Catsaras, 'I'm going to do more than scrap the corporation tax change. I'm going to change the Chancellor as well.'

'That's your decision, Prime Minister, but I don't think it's absolutely necessary.'

'Senior ministers have advised me he has to go,' she replied, not wanting to divulge the names.

Later that evening, about 10.30 p.m., Simon McGee, who as Truss's joint director of communications was responsible for breaking news stories, became aware of Kwarteng's likely dismissal. 'This is a great mistake,' he told those still left in the Private Office. 'Why?' 'Because it is absolutely bloody obvious that he has done her bidding.' McGee was troubled. 'Let me see her to see if I can help her to rethink the decision,' he said. 'She's made up her mind and there's no point now in trying to change it,' they responded.[3] Not for the first time he was left thinking why on earth he had accepted doing a job that she made it impossible to do. It was left to Fullbrook to tell it like it was: 'It was absolutely obvious: either she had to go, or he had to go. It was that simple. Someone had to take the hit.'[4]

After a night worrying about whether she was making the right decision, Truss saw Fullbrook early the next morning to tell him and then she saw Catsaras. The deed must be done! 'A judgement call. I decided that given that I was having to reverse everything I'd done, it would've been very hard for him to do it with conviction,' she said later.[5] Dismissing any senior Cabinet minister is a big deal, far more so if it's the Chancellor of the Exchequer and it's in the middle of a major financial crisis. As the PM's principal private secretary, Catsaras had to inform the Palace, the Cabinet secretary and prepare the whole system for the massive imminent electric jolt.

Truss had three immediate headaches: telling Kwarteng he was fired; choosing an alternative; and working out what to do if her first choice declined. She knew that any of these three going wrong could break her.

Kwarteng had been picking up some concerning messages on Thursday 13 October at the IMF conference in Washington. Lynn Davidson, former special adviser and friend, rang him to say, 'Watch out, Kwasi: there's a rumour circulating that you're about to be sacked. Sajid to take over.' Another special adviser, Cameron Brown, then called him to say Truss has been talking furtively to MPs about who might replace him. 'Resign, Kwasi, walk away, apologize and take the hit. It will be better for you and better for the government,' his young media adviser said. 'No need,' he replied breezily. 'She won't be so stupid as to sack me because she knows that if I go, she will have to go too.' He saw himself as her 'Kevlar body armour', and if that was stripped away, there would be nothing to stop the bullets hitting her.[6] So he was still a reasonably confident Chancellor when he boarded the last flight out of Dulles Airport on the Thursday evening, bound for London.

He landed at Heathrow at 10.30 a.m. on Friday 14 October, 'the first time I had a motorcade waiting for me on the tarmac, and the last,' he recalled. When he switched on his phone, his messages were not encouraging. As the car was setting off to whisk him to Downing Street, fellow passenger Celia McSwaine, another of his advisers, called one of Truss's aides: 'What's going on? Kwasi has asked me to call.' 'What has he heard?' 'There is speculation all over the media. He wants to know – is he on the road just to come in to be sacked?' At that point Kwarteng himself grabbed the phone. 'She's going to sack me, isn't she? I want to know the truth. What the hell's happening?' he demanded. 'I agree it's mad,' said the adviser. McSwaine took back the phone while Kwarteng, demonstrably in a deep rage, chuntered away in the background for the rest of the call. He had already tried ringing Coffey. She hadn't picked up as Truss had sent out the instruction to her inner circle not to tell or speak to anyone. He felt as if he had already become persona non grata.

It was 11 a.m. and an atmosphere of deep gloom had enveloped the back of the car. As the convoy glided round Chiswick roundabout still twenty minutes from Downing Street, Steve Swinford of *The Times* released some jaw-dropping news. He had earlier on tweeted that Truss was on the verge of junking parts of the Mini-Budget. 'No. 10 then went into full submarine mode, which is always a sign that something is in the offing. Within minutes of tweeting that news, a trusted source got in touch, confirmed by a second source who had never been wrong, telling me it wasn't just the Budget measures that were going – Truss was sacking Kwarteng as well,' Swinford said later.[7] McSwaine broke it to her boss that she had just picked up Swinford's latest tweet. It said: 'I'm told that Kwasi Kwarteng is being sacked as Chancellor as Liz Truss prepares to reverse the mini-Budget. Not clear who will be replacing him. Events moving very, very quickly this morning. No. 10 not commenting.'[8] 'If Steve tweeted it, it will be true,' McSwaine said, even though for an hour and more, no other media outlet covered it. Kwarteng concurred. They assumed that either Stein or Porter had briefed it. 'Just doing their jobs. Looking after top dog. It's what they do,' he thought ruefully. Others close to Truss thought that the leak came from Case himself to ensure that there would be no going back, a view strongly denied.

Truss herself was highly emotional and conflicted. One of her closest allies described her as 'very, very upset at the imminent sacking of her closest and oldest ally and replacing him by someone who would reverse her policies'. As she sat waiting in the Cabinet Room, the corner of her mouth froze, as it could do in moments of high tension, and she spoke from the other side. 'She couldn't sit still: she got up, she sat down, she walked around feverishly trying to burn off energy,' recalled one present. Regular updates were given of the progress of Kwarteng's car: Hammersmith flyover, Cromwell Road, Hyde Park Corner, closer and closer the Chancellor came. As she paced around, she repeatedly shook her shoulders and balled both fists. Up and down she went at an increasing tempo. After what seemed like an interminable wait, the diary secretary popped her head round the door to say, 'The Chancellor is going to be here any minute.' Someone said, 'Can we give the Prime Minister the room?'

The Chancellor's car drove into Downing Street at 11.35 a.m. He dropped his bags inside the door of No. 11 and walked straight into

No. 10, down the long corridor and into the Cabinet Room at the end. The PM was on her own, visibly emotional, tears in her eyes. 'You've got to go,' she blurted out, choking.

'I know, I saw it on Steve Swinford's Twitter,' Kwarteng replied.

'I'm very sorry you saw it like that. You can come back in a year.'

Kwarteng was lost for words, thinking the whole predicament was insane, not least her even imagining she would still be Prime Minister in a year. He stood in front of her in total bewilderment. He considered arguing against her, but he could see that there was no point: her mind was made up.

'It's been a really difficult time. Graham Brady says you have to go,' Truss told him.

'Who replaces me?'

'Jeremy Hunt.'

'I'm very surprised.' He had assumed it was going to be Sajid Javid.

'Would you like to see the text of my statement I'm going to be making?'

'Yes, I would.' He spent three minutes reading it. 'The first question you will get asked by journalists is why you are getting rid of someone who you campaigned with on these policies.'

'I know.'

'They will come for you.'

Truss looked at him blankly, alternating between silence and words that were not entirely coherent. After twenty minutes the meeting broke up.

'So, good luck. Watch out,' he said when leaving.

'They are already coming for me.'

Kwarteng walked out numb. The thought kept running through his mind that coups happened when Presidents were abroad, as sometimes happened in West Africa where his parents came from. He mulled over who might have been responsible for his departure: the Treasury? Simon Case? The 1922 Committee? 'He wasn't certain, but it felt like the establishment reasserting itself,' said an aide.

Rishi Sunak was one of the first to call him when the announcement was officially made, saying, 'Kwasi, I'm so sorry to hear this terrible news.' He appreciated the words, but he also surmised this was Sunak's way of sniffing out how long he thought Truss had before she collapsed altogether. Hunt called on Saturday, a courtesy call, uttering no words of significance; they were not buddies, but had a respectful relationship. Kwarteng resolved to keep his own counsel, but a careless comment to a *Times* journalist resulted in the headline in the print edition that went up promptly online: 'Kwasi Kwarteng thinks Liz Truss will be gone in weeks'.[9]

The loss of a Chancellor so quickly was devastating and historically unprecedented. While Iain Macleod, Heath's intellectually brilliant Chancellor, served a shorter period at just thirty days, chain-smoking had combined with a war wound to shorten his life: he had a heart attack while in No. 11 and died an hour later, depriving Heath and the country of a masterful politician who might well have obviated the need for the fateful U-turn two years later. Kwarteng with thirty-eight days was the shortest-serving Chancellor to leave office alive in the 300 years since the PM's office was created. Comment since Truss fell has concentrated on her own transience: in reality, the brevity of the Chancellor, and the combination of both, were remarkable as well. Nadhim Zahawi came next on the list, serving sixty-three days in Johnson's twilight zone over the summer of 2022. Next up was Javid who served 204 days, and only then do figures from further back appear again:

Stanley Baldwin (307 days) and Peter Thorneycroft (358 days). All other Chancellors served at least a year.[10]

Hunt for the New Chancellor: 14 October 2022

Truss's second and third problems were who to appoint in Kwarteng's place, and what happened if she couldn't find anyone, a serious possibility.

Before she took the plunge and removed Kwarteng from his post, her team had prepared a shortlist for her. The most obvious candidate was Javid, who had declared for her in the leadership contest, and hence was at least nominally on side. He had the credibility to stabilize the markets as a former Chancellor, albeit for only nine months and never delivering a Budget. 'Had I been offered it, I would have accepted for the very same reasons of public service that Jeremy Hunt did, as was the case when I took Health Secretary,' he later said.[11] Despite widespread speculation on Thursday, Truss never asked him. Neither Porter nor Stein were keen on him, but the decision against was totally the PM's. There was no love lost between them and she thought his declaration of support had been skin deep at best. Ideologically and temperamentally, they were miles apart.

Zahawi was briefly considered as he too had been Chancellor and the chemistry worked better. She would have hated to lose him as her man overseeing delivery in his role as Chancellor of the Duchy of Lancaster – she had great faith in him and he had proven himself on the Vaccine Task Force – but she would have gone with him were it not for the downside. He had only been Chancellor for nine weeks in the dying days of Johnson. Questions were asked: would he really have the credibility and experience to provide the reassurance that the markets sought? Alok Sharma, most recently president of COP26, and a former Business Secretary, was on the list; but again, he was felt to lack credibility with the markets, and Truss did not get on well with him. So it was back to the drawing board.

Any former Chancellor might theoretically have fitted the bill. But who else was there? Zahawi's predecessor was Sunak, who would have been a humiliation too far even for her, even if he accepted it. Before him was Javid, already ruled out, and before him Hammond and Osborne, neither still in the House of Commons. A Chief Secretary to the Treasury might just possibly have had the credibility, but neither Philp nor his predecessor Clarke had the gravitas, and none of those before were in tune with her. That left Jacob Rees-Mogg, who for all his hunger for the job was not considered because he was known to be an even more devout believer than Kwarteng, and far less biddable. John Redwood was a name that put a twinkle in her eye. 'I'd have liked Jacob or John,' she admitted, 'but the truth is that the markets wouldn't have gone for either of them. Neither of them would have signalled a change and the economic establishment wouldn't have approved.'[12]

That left one person who had not supported her, but who had been in Cabinet continuously from May 2010 until Johnson failed to give him a job in July 2019 – Jeremy Hunt. Truss immediately warmed to the idea when her aides proposed him. On the upside, she respected him as an accomplished minister who had always been straight with her; he had credibility because of the posts he had filled including Foreign Secretary; and he would help bring on side the centre left of the party. They also agreed on some things, such as increasing defence spending and taking a tough line against China. On the downside was the inconvenient fact that he had voted for

Sunak in the leadership election. In discussions with her advisers, she had been wont to describe him as 'boring', and regarded him as the leader of the 'wets', as she termed them. But the clinching argument in his favour was that he was deemed to be the most credible bet to steady the markets, and to help bind the party together. 'It was really quite calculated: she thought the perception of Jeremy was that she wouldn't be able to push him around, as she had Kwarteng,' said an aide. But would he agree?

Having alighted on him, Truss relaxed a little for the first time in days. She knew she could only sack Kwarteng if she was 100 per cent sure of a credible successor. What could possibly go wrong? She leaped into action, summoning an official into her office: 'We have the plan now. I'm going to sack Kwasi.' 'Right, Prime Minister. Do you have a plan on who to appoint as his successor? He will need to be locked in before you sack him.'

'I do. Jeremy Hunt.'

'Does he know about it?'

'He's in Brussels with his wife apparently.'

'Does he know it's coming? Has he said yes?'

'I am going to speak to him this morning, but we've been sounding him out.'

'And are you sure it's going to work out?'

The truth is that she wasn't, but she explained that Porter had used a back channel to contact an ex-aide of Hunt's and alluding to Truss 'wanting him for a senior role and would he be willing to take the time out to take her call'.

'Liz Truss here. Please call.' Jeremy Hunt was still in his bedroom at the Amigo Hotel in Brussels with his wife Lucia getting ready for the day ahead when the reception called with the message at

9.30 a.m. local time (one hour ahead of the UK). At that point, Kwarteng was still in the air, two hours from landing at Heathrow. Hunt was irritated, thinking it a hoax, and wondered how he had been tracked down. Then his mobile phone started vibrating: 'No Caller ID'. Assuming it was a journalist, he promptly declined it. But then Edward Jones, the former special adviser whom Porter had contacted, called him to say 'No. 10 are trying to get hold of you.' Still suspicious, he called the No. 10 switchboard, saying, 'It may be a hoax, but I've had a message that in five minutes the Prime Minister wants to speak to me.' 'She does indeed, Mr Hunt, but she's on the other line.' He waited, speculating why she wanted to get hold of him. Whatever it might be, he thought, it didn't merit disturbing him on holiday.

'Hello, Jeremy, it's Liz here.'

'Thank you for calling,' he replied politely.

'Things are not going as well as I hoped.'

'And how can I help, Prime Minister?'

She replied in just one word: 'Chancellor.'

Hunt was stunned. As an aide said, 'Jeremy had a perfectly cordial relationship with Liz, but he was no admirer.' He had no idea how to respond. 'Can I have half an hour to think it through and talk to the family?'

She responded again with just one word: 'Fine.' The line went dead.

He was in a complete quandary with no idea what to do. So he spoke to the two people closest to him, first Lucia, and then his younger brother Charlie.

The conversations clarified for him what was at stake: if he accepted, he would have to resign as Chair of the Health and Social

Care Select Committee, a role he greatly valued, and might not get the position back. The government might not last long and he might be dragged down with it. Was he being set up as the fall guy? On the other hand, he saw the opportunity to do something of national significance. His mind went back to his battles with the Treasury in his seven years as Health Secretary. He thought, 'I'm out of office now: I might not have another opportunity, and this is in the national interest.' So twenty minutes later, he called her back to accept her offer. 'Thank you,' she said, giving away very little of how she was feeling.

Had he said no, there was no Plan B. Javid was the only possible show in town, and she'd already vetoed him. She would have fallen that morning with the news that Kwasi was going had she had no one to replace him, the country on the verge of a financial catastrophe on the coming Monday. So in accepting the job, a significant shift in power was immediately apparent. Like William Pitt the Elder or Lord Palmerston when they experienced their own career-changing moments, Hunt had, in a heartbeat, become the most important person in the government.

When he woke up that morning, he was an ageing politician on his way down; suddenly, he alone was propping up the Prime Minister in the midst of what risked becoming 'the worst market crisis since 1976' according to Nick Macpherson, former Treasury permanent secretary.[13] Could the odd couple ever have lasted together? 'We had absolutely no plan to junk him after a certain time. Heavens. If someone lends you a lifeboat, you're not going to sink the ship,' said Fullbrook. 'It was never going to save the Truss project. It was only designed to stop the project hitting the rocks there and then.'[14]

Back in Brussels, Hunt broke the news to Lucia that their holiday was over, and that she might not be seeing much of him for quite some time. They took the first Eurostar to St Pancras, and then a taxi to No. 10. By then, the news of Kwarteng's sacking was breaking. 'Thank you for appointing me Chancellor', were his opening words in his short meeting with the Prime Minister. 'You have a completely free hand to do anything you think you need to do,' she told him again. He hadn't expected to be given quite that degree of carte blanche, and was relieved and impressed. 'Jeremy was struck that she appeared to have no cunning plan of her own, but was genuinely in total survival mode,' said a Treasury aide.

That evening, Hunt went to the Treasury for the first time to take up the job he had long craved. 'I'm going to reverse most if not all of the Mini-Budget, as I said to the Prime Minister,' he told the assembled company after he had been clapped in by the Private Office, as is the custom for incoming Chancellors. 'I want you all to help me work out how far I should go, and when I should make the announcements,' political adviser Adam Smith recalled him saying.[15] As he settled down between 5 and 7 p.m. at the large table in the Chancellor's office with his senior officials and aides, he knew he had just forty-eight hours before the Asian markets opened on Sunday night, and with the Bank's support ending this very day, market turmoil and even meltdown was the fear.

Hunt had never held an economic portfolio and was aware he was not in a strong position technically, given the urgency, to query the advice from officials. Officials found themselves in uncharted waters, but how unequivocal should they be? None had a closer grasp of markets than Clare Lombardelli, who, given the Chancellor's invitation to speak out, felt she should not hold back. 'My strong advice is that you reverse all the measures and do it on Monday. That will be the most effective way to resolve it: do the measures quickly,' she told him. 'She was worried that unless he acted very decisively and strongly, given the failure of the adjustments so far to make much impact, the instability in the markets could just go on and on,' said one present.

Since the phone call from Truss that morning, he had been reflecting deeply on what to do. Two of the figures who were to influence him most to go far and fast had been at the heart of Cameron's No. 10, the Treasury's chief economist Clare Lombardelli (who had been Cameron's private secretary for economic affairs), and Osborne's chief of staff, Rupert Harrison.

The latter had been in regular communication with Stein since the day before. They spoke at 4.30 p.m. 'What would you advise?' Stein asked. 'You need to junk most of the package and signal very clearly that you get it,' said Harrison without a moment's hesitation. They texted at 9.30 on the Friday morning. 'Gilt yields are plunging – shows the impact you can have. Does mean a fair amount of the u-turn is now getting priced in... if expectations now get disappointed markets will react pretty badly,' Harrison messaged him, warning that they would need to go further still if they were to avoid a potentially catastrophic reaction on the markets.

'Congratulations, Chancellor!' were his opening words to a surprised Hunt who called him at 11 that morning before any official announcement had been made of personnel changes at No. 11. 'I put two and two together: Kwarteng suddenly flying back from the IMF, and Jeremy calling me out of the blue. It could only have been that he was to be the new Chancellor,' Harrison said later. 'You will have to go further to reassure the markets,' he advised Hunt on that call.

'I was telling him that he'll never be in a more powerful position nor have more leverage than in that first forty-eight hours, that he will need to move quickly and kill off the vast majority of the unfunded package. My worry was that if the markets were still not reassured by the change to corporation tax and by the change of Chancellor, then much better to get ahead of the curve than be forced into it later, which he inevitably would be.'[16]

While Hunt was talking to his new team on Friday evening, a story broke on Bloomberg that Truss had secured agreement from Hunt that there would be 'no further U-turns'. The story spooked those pressing for a wholesale Mini-Budget reversal because they knew that when the markets reopened, they would react badly to the notion that there was still life in the 'Truss project'. If the leak had been designed to put a stop to the rot, it had the opposite effect: it made Hunt and all of the same persuasion determined to go for broke.

The End of the Project: 14–17 October 2022

For Truss, the torture of a press conference in the No. 9 Downing Street press briefing room came next. Adding to her vulnerability was the absence of her political team who had left for Adam Jones's wedding in Yorkshire the next day. The remaining team planned the event to make her time on stage as short as possible to avoid the risk of particularly damaging questions and her own composure being exposed. Highly volatile and close to the edge as she was, her team were worrying whether she could hold it together.

Her statement, which lasted just four minutes, was designed to justify her continued presence at the helm. 'My conviction that this country needs to go for growth is rooted in my personal experience,' she started. But she accepted that Britain was suffering from global factors and 'it is clear that parts of our Mini-Budget went further and faster than markets were expecting'. Then came the three bombshells of keeping the increase in corporation tax, sacking Kwarteng ('I was incredibly sorry to lose him') and appointing Hunt, 'one of the most experienced and widely respected government ministers and parliamentarians' (which begged the question why she hadn't appointed him to her Cabinet originally).[17]

'As Prime Minister I will always act in the national interest,' she said at the end, while admitting, in one of her best lines, 'I want to be honest, this is difficult.' She then selected questions from the media beginning with two newspapers she thought most likely to be friendly to her, before turning to the BBC and ITV, which normally take precedence. First up, Ben Riley-Smith from the *Telegraph* asked her, 'Can you explain to the public why you think you should still be Prime Minister?' The directness of the question took her aback. Because she was 'determined to see through what I have promised,' she replied. Second, Harry Cole from the *Sun* asked why, as she and Kwarteng had designed the Mini-Budget in lockstep and often in secret, 'how come you get to stay?' Again she reeled. If these questions were from two friendly journalists, what would happen when the neutrals started interrogating her? BBC political editor Chris Mason didn't disappoint: 'Excuse the bluntness, Prime Minister, but given everything that has happened, what credibility do you have to continue governing?' Finally, ITV News political editor Robert Peston quoted Philip Hammond at her, who had said she had 'totally trashed the Tory party's election winning reputation for economic competence', and asked her, 'Will you apologize to your party?' Three times in response to the questions she repeated that her goal was to maintain economic stability: she argued that had she quit, with further uncertainty of a leadership election compounding the financial instability, the result could have been dire. After four questions in four minutes, she left the stage to shouts of 'Aren't you going to say sorry?'[18]

She managed to retain a composure of sorts, but the event singularly failed to make the case for her continuing as Prime Minister. Given that she was reversing key planks of her leadership platform, and jettisoning her closest political ally, the press conference was never going to be anything other than deeply damaging. She never contemplated apologizing to her party as Peston had asked, and most of her answers appeared as if she was dissembling and not engaging with the reality of her position. No one in or outside No. 10 thought she had acquitted herself well. But no one told her. She knew it.

That evening at seven o'clock, his two-hour meeting concluded, Hunt's immediate concerns 250 metres away at the Treasury were being briefed for Radio 4's *Today* programme the following morning, and for *Sunday with Laura Kuenssberg* on BBC1. He was back in the building early on Saturday working with James Bowler and officials unpicking the Mini-Budget. 'It was taken for granted he couldn't delay decisions till the Autumn Statement that Kwarteng had promised for the end of October, two weeks away,' said one present. But could it even wait one week?

One of his first moves was to replace Chris Philp as Chief Secretary. He initially wanted to promote the like-minded Mel Stride in his place, but Truss did not care for Stride and vetoed his appointment: 'Absolutely not.' Hunt then suggested Osborne's former adviser Rupert Harrison, but he was neither an MP nor a Peer, and it would be politically difficult. Finally, he settled on

MP Edward Argar, who was destined to hold the role for only a week.

The senior team at the Treasury worked separately throughout Saturday morning while Hunt did several interviews, and a pre-recorded interview for Laura Kuenssberg's Sunday morning show, giving the clear message of reassurance that there would be further measures to ensure stability. Courtesy calls had to be made as well, primarily to Bank Governor Andrew Bailey and Richard Hughes at the OBR. He reassured Bailey, who was still in Washington, that stability was the priority, and they were still working out exactly what to say and when to say it. He spoke to Bailey again on his return to the UK the following day.

Hunt reconvened the team at 2 p.m. for two hours to work through all the Mini-Budget measures one by one. Bowler let Lombardelli do the talking about the state of the markets; she was equally emphatic as the night before. Hunt made his sensitivity to the feelings of the Prime Minister clear, but nevertheless announced that almost everything was to be reversed except National Insurance, which the Commons had already voted on, and stamp duty. 'Jeremy was insistent that radical action was needed and that was why he would need to reverse most or all of the Mini-Budget,' said one present. 'The point he drilled home was we have to reassure the markets and that we must do whatever we need to do.' By mid-afternoon, the task was complete. Hunt then worked through a shortlist of people he wanted to talk to, to confirm what he was doing, including former Tory Chancellors Hammond and Osborne. Subsequently, he spoke to an earlier generation, including Major's two Chancellors Norman Lamont and Ken Clarke. Nigel Lawson's frailty alone prevented Hunt from speaking to Thatcher's radical Chancellor, now aged ninety and who died six months later.

In the car on his way home on Saturday afternoon, Hunt called Javid, an old friend, whose advice he sought not least because of his experience in financial markets. If Javid had indeed wanted the job, there was no trace of bitterness or regret. 'How worried should I be about the markets opening tomorrow night in Asia?' Hunt asked him. 'I think you should be very worried,' Javid replied.

As a result of the conversation with Javid, Hunt called Bowler. A witness recalled their conversation: 'Do you think we should advance the timing of my announcement?' 'I am not sure, Chancellor. I'd like to get some advice and talk to others. I'll find out,' the new permanent secretary told him. After Hunt arrived home in Surrey, his phone rang. It was Bowler. 'Chancellor, I have been speaking to people and my advice is there *is* a risk. We will need to announce the measures on Monday morning. We cannot wait till an Autumn Statement.' A conference call with officials followed at 8.30 p.m. to discuss whether the announcement should be made first in Parliament. Hunt was sensitive to MPs liking to be the first to hear important news, but as Parliament wasn't meeting till 3.30 p.m. on Monday, the consensus was it was too late. 'I need to deliver something earlier,' he said and the discussion moved on to how this could be done without offending Parliament, and the best means of him giving the message. The conclusion was that before the markets in London opened on Monday morning they should put out a pre-recorded video by him from the Chancellor's office in the Treasury to calm the markets ahead of his announcement that afternoon in the Commons.

Truss's power was slipping away from her by the minute. So, like Tudor monarchs displaying their riches to show off their status to their subjects, Truss used the grandeur of Tudor country house Chequers on Sunday 16 October to remind her guests who was in charge. Case was surprised to find himself summoned to breakfast with her, and still more surprised when, rather than the heavyweight argument he had anticipated and feared, the conversation was chit-chat about family topics including children and the length of school half term just beginning. But they did refer to the impending meeting. Case told her, 'Jeremy is going to come up with a plan and you are going to have to accept it,' according to one present. At 10 a.m., she chaired a meeting in the Long Gallery. Party discipline was the topic of the day. Party Chair Berry pressed her to stamp her authority over wayward MPs, with news that Crispin Blunt and Andrew Bridgen were about to call for her to resign and an Opinium poll forecasting a 411-seat Labour landslide.[19] CCHQ was equally infested by those who were no longer loyal to her, reported Berry: Johnson's right-hand aide Ross Kempsell was one he wanted fired.

Indicative of crumbling regimes everywhere, they had their guns aimed at most people apart from themselves, including the Chief Whip and the director of communications at No. 10. The old canard reared its head: 'the message isn't being heard clearly enough'. Former Vote Leave director of communications Paul Stephenson was favoured as a replacement for the latter, but was thought to have no interest in leaving his public affairs business, Hanbury. Truss refused to accept that he wouldn't succumb to an invitation. 'Liz, he's not going to be interested,' said an aide in a jaded voice. 'Just ask him, will you,' she replied tersely. Macer Hall, long-standing political editor at the *Express*, was another name mentioned. But before any decisions could be taken, Truss had to break up the meeting because guests were assembling downstairs for the main event at 10.30 a.m., a discussion of financial measures urgently needing her ratification, chaired by her, with Hunt, Case, Treasury officials and political aides from No. 10 and No. 11 all in attendance. Before it formally opened, Hunt had a private word with her, anxious that she shouldn't be humiliated or blindsided in the open meeting. According to an observer, Hunt adopted his most solicitous bedside manner to tell her, 'Prime Minister, I'm afraid I'm going to have to be reversing 90 per cent of what was laid out in the Mini-Budget.'

In the entire history of relations between the Prime Minister and their Chancellor, never before in an open meeting had the former so deferred to the latter on issues of such major economic importance.

Hunt went clinically and systematically through the plan that had been agreed on Saturday morning in the Treasury. He did leave in what one present described as a 'catnip', namely not revoking the cut in National Insurance. 'He felt the issue was totemic for her, it wasn't that significant financially, and he wanted to spare her some dignity,' said one present. 'The atmosphere was just extraordinary: Liz was visibly shaken and quite passive. The dominant thought I had was "Jeremy is now the Prime Minister",' said another. 'Liz wasn't really there,' said yet another.

When it finished shortly after midday, officials and aides departed to get on with the statements and actions required for the following day while she was left to comprehend the gravity of what had just happened, trying to think through where she stood in this totally changed world. To help her, she embarked on a series of short talks with her closest advisers as they walked around the Chequers garden.

According to one adviser, her husband Hugh asked, 'Do you think you should resign?'

'Jeremy is the Prime Minister,' Stein added.

'Well, I've still got the outriders [police motorbikes],' she snapped back with either flippancy or bitterness – perhaps both. 'What else could I do?' she said, believing that she had been outplayed, a belief to which she still holds.

The principal private secretary to the PM has the task of ensuring the smooth operation of the office. Losing a Prime Minister at any point, above all in a crisis, is the last thing they want to happen. According to a witness, they talked briefly:

'What will you do now, Prime Minister?' Catsaras asked her.

'I'll carry on.'

'Very good, Prime Minister.'

'I've been thinking about it. Jeremy will do the domestic side and I'll do the foreign.'

'Are you sure about that?'

'Yes, I am. I want to tie things up with the EU.'

'All right, Prime Minister, we can make that work.'

Fullbrook, Porter and Stein huddled together after Truss went indoors and agreed there was still a real possibility that she might chuck it in when the reality fully dawned that, very evidently, she was no longer in charge. Porter, who thought that the PM was edging her way towards the departure lounge, left and Case and Fullbrook were now alone together. They walked to their cars and agreed that they needed to stay in close contact to minimize the fallout if Truss decided to call it a day. Case challenged Fullbrook on his own priorities as her senior adviser. 'As her chief of staff I will look after her to the end. But my priority is equally now minimizing the damage to the country of whatever comes next,' Fullbrook replied. They looked at each other, the significance of what was said sinking in. They shook hands and drove their separate ways out through the Chequers front gates.

Lunch for the two families alone in the formal dining room was not the most spontaneous of occasions. For Hunt, his decision to accept her invitation to become Chancellor forty-eight hours before had been fully vindicated. She had been true to her word in giving him carte blanche in charting the new course. He found unravelling someone else's errors was not difficult; indeed, it was rather exhilarating. For Truss, in contrast, her whole life's ambition and reputation were being smashed to pieces.

The conversation was stilted until both sets of children started to talk about their favourite series on Netflix, which produced a heated argument and a welcome distraction. The Hunts left for home soon after and an exhausted Truss spent the afternoon and evening on and off her phone, flicking through the news and messaging the party's big-hitters for advice while she weighed her future. Theresa May counselled being honest about the mistakes, and being more businesslike in her manner and appearance. 'Apologize and bring in fresh blood,' advised George Osborne.[20] 'Fight on,' messaged a beach-bound Boris, 'the people who plotted against one PM are now trying to bring down another.' Less supportively, Biden's 'I wasn't the only one that thought [the Mini-Budget] was a mistake' comment at the ice cream parlour made the news at this time, and further riled her.

Early on Monday 17 October, as agreed on Saturday, Hunt's five-minute video was released. Because of 'the volatility in the markets', Hunt said that he had agreed with the Speaker to release this short statement now, followed by a detailed statement to Parliament that afternoon with an opportunity for MPs to ask questions. Then he delivered the bombshell: 'We will reverse almost all the tax measures announced in the growth plan three weeks ago.'[21]

That afternoon in the Chamber, with a listless Truss by his side, he provided the details, saying that the need for stability and reducing damaging speculation dictated the changes to the Mini-Budget being announced now, rather than waiting until the Medium-Term Fiscal Plan in two weeks' time. As had been announced on Friday, the government would not be proceeding with the cut in corporation tax. He had now decided that the cut to dividend tax rates, the cut in the basic rate of income tax, the VAT-free shopping scheme, the freeze to alcohol duty rates and more would all be ended. Together with the rollback of the 45p tax rate, he said these measures were the equivalent of reversing £32 billion of the original £45 billion in unfunded tax cuts.[22] As expected, the markets reacted positively: the pound rose against the dollar, and the yield on UK bonds fell, making government borrowing less expensive.[23] 'As Jeremy was talking, we were being sent screenshots of Bloomberg screens showing the pound rallying and the market stabilizing apace,' said economics adviser Adam Smith.[24] 'Reaction from markets good, from colleagues good, the most that can be expected,' Hunt messaged his team at 8 p.m. that night.

In his speech, Hunt announced the creation of the new 'Economic Advisory Council' to assist the government as it sought to repair the damage caused by the Mini-Budget, chaired by Rupert Harrison and Karen Ward, who had advised Hammond when Chancellor. For personal reasons Harrison had turned down the offer to be 'minister for financial stability' with a seat in Cabinet, but was delighted to serve in this capacity. A Council of this nature had been discussed at Chevening, but had been aborted. The idea then was that it should be peopled by economists of sound mind who would prevent Truss and her ministers being swallowed up by the groupthink of the economic 'blob' they would encounter in power. Now, though the commitment to 'independent economic advice' was the same, a very different kind of economist and financier sat on it. Truss did manage to veto one of the suggested members: economist Kate Barker, who had served on the Bank of England's Monetary Policy Committee under Labour, and was thought by No. 10 to be 'politically unsound'.

The Verdict: Avoid U-turns?

An interpretation was rapidly gaining widespread credence on the right, tacitly encouraged by Truss herself: Hunt, a non-economist, had been manipulated and bounced by Treasury officials determined to reinstate orthodoxy as they had always wanted. They and the Bank had panicked Hunt into the U-turn, they believed. Particular ire was reserved for the Governor's 'cliff-edge' statement of the end of the Bank of England intervention, as planned, on Friday 14 October which had been unnecessary, while predictions of a 'run on the pound' the following Monday were ungrounded. Here was visible evidence of the 'deep state' in action, as Truss had long warned.

The Bank in contrast believes that 'the markets might indeed have melted down on Monday had the swift action not been taken', with sterling sold along with government debt, with disastrous consequences. It asserts that Bailey had only two choices, neither desirable: either announcing it was not the job of the Bank to buy up gilts and save the government's humiliation, which would have created a bloodbath in the markets, or announcing an extension of its intervention by going back into the markets on Monday to buy gilts in large quantities. This latter course of action would have spooked the markets even more, and fatally lost credibility for the Bank as an inflation-fighting and independent institution.

It is also possible that such an intervention would have failed entirely. One of the Bank's leaders dismissed the idea that further Bank action would have proved effective: 'My strong view is that it would have lasted a day or two before the markets forced Truss into a U-turn on fiscal policy. It was fiscal policy and the attack on the institutions that drove the crisis and until that changed there could be no solution.'

The ninth rule of premiership says that the Prime Minister must not U-turn on a major policy. Whether or not she was right to do so, and this book believes that she had no option but to do it, is beside the point. She implemented the biggest U-turn in modern prime ministerial history and it didn't work for her.

She had just four more days left as Prime Minister before she announced her resignation.

The financial markets might have been steadied, but the political marketplace was still in frenzy. Hunt brought her economic stability, but against her expectations it came at the price of political instability. 'It might've been done to appease the centre, though they'd already made up their mind on her, but what it did was explode Project Truss and lost her the right of the party,' said Gavin Williamson.[25] Confidence in her was further undermined when Leader of the House Penny Mordaunt, rather than Truss, answered questions in the House of Commons on the replacement of the Chancellor, not least when she had to deny that the PM had been hiding 'under a desk'.[26] 'It was evident to all: Jeremy was the Prime Minister in all but name,' said Kwarteng, a view echoed by many.[27] Thatcher had not U-turned when under massive pressure in 1981. The Tory right asked: why had Truss allowed herself to do so now?

The *volte-face* in her policies did not win the City round to Truss either. By Monday, several senior figures, including Tory peer Stuart Rose, private equity boss Guy Hands and former chair of Land Securities Alison Carnwath all called on her to resign.[28]

Had Truss studied her history more closely, she would have appreciated that Thatcher was able to resist a U-turn in 1980 because she had spent eighteen months preparing her ground. Truss had no choice but to U-turn almost forty-two years to the day later because she had spent eighteen days completely failing to do so herself.

The premiership was still not dead, though. As long as her MPs were prepared to back the new dispensation, she could survive till Christmas; and, who knows, even beyond.

Rule Number Ten: Truss failed to retain the confidence of the party. Here at PMQs on Wednesday 19 October

10

RETAIN THE CONFIDENCE OF THE PARTY
17–20 October 2022

If you rise to become Prime Minister, you no longer have to worry about people above you sacking you because, once the monarch lost that power in the nineteenth century, there is no one above you. Instead, you have to worry about people *below* you, because they hold your future in their hands.

'Don't divide the party'

What is surprising is how often in history Prime Ministers have forgotten this truth that constitutes the tenth and final rule of premiership. If a Prime Minister retains the confidence of colleagues in the parliamentary party, they may remain at No. 10 for years. But once that confidence is lost, they will be gone within weeks or even days.

The first Prime Minister to lose their party's confidence in the post-1832 Reform Act era was Robert Peel. During the 1840s, he decided on the repeal of the Corn Laws, protective agricultural tariffs that boosted the profits of landholders, many of whom were represented on the Conservative benches. It would be Benjamin Disraeli who rallied the backbench rebellion, arguing that free trade would ruin the finely balanced 'territorial constitution' of England. Peel won the fight, with the help of Radical and Whig MPs, but left his party irrevocably divided and was forced to resign in 1846, consigning the Conservatives to almost thirty years of opposition, and a few short-lived minority governments, before they were returned to Downing Street with a decisive majority, led by Disraeli. The lesson that Peel taught to subsequent Conservative leaders and that has reverberated down into the twenty-first century could not have been clearer: keep the party together, whatever the cost.

The outstanding example in modern times is Margaret Thatcher, who ultimately fell because she lost her parliamentary party. Her steadfast refusal to change course on the poll tax, her combative attitude towards the burgeoning European Union and her stridency despite plummeting opinion polls alienated her parliamentary colleagues. In November 1990, the challenge from Michael Heseltine led to a ballot of MPs, and dramatic scenes in Parliament. Diarist and Tory MP Alan Clark wrote, 'The whole house is in ferment. Little groups, conclaves everywhere… in the corridors it is all furtive whispering and glancing over shoulders.'[1] Though she won the first ballot, it was not by enough and a second was required. Her Cabinet then almost unanimously gave her the same message: 'I will support you if you stand, but you cannot win.'[2] She announced her withdrawal from the leadership ballots the following day and thereby paved the way for John Major's victory. When she left No. 10 on 28 November 1990, as Prime Ministers have all done, in public or in private, she left in tears.

This century, May and Johnson fell after they lost the support of their MPs. The former had a deep love of her party, the latter anything but. Openly scornful of it, Johnson preferred to see himself as a presidential figure with a personal mandate gained in the 2019 election. He shunned multiple attempts to ingratiate himself to his tiresome MPs, believing at heart, like Truss, that his support derived from the party in the country, which continued to love him, rather than the parliamentary party, which no longer did. But it was the parliamentary party that he had to work with, and it was they – fed up with months of scandal and humiliation – that finally brought him down in July 2022.

The one factor that can keep an ailing Prime Minister alive after they have lost the support of their MPs is the absence of a successor, a 'Prince over the Water' who would clearly be a more convincing leader to the electorate. In September 2022, there was one. By mid-October, a second was beginning to stir. Rishi Sunak had never gone away, and now Boris Johnson was pondering coming back. Backers of both men began, in these fraught days, stealthily to move onto the front foot. One of Truss's sovereign errors, not accepting that the parliamentary party had always preferred Sunak and doing nothing to heal the divide, now came back to haunt her with a vengeance. True, many Conservative MPs, for a mixture of economic, political and personal reasons, continued to loathe Sunak, but he had strong and influential backers. Her Cabinet, which had only ever had a handful of loyalists and had now lost the most prominent, Kwarteng, were beginning to stick their noses into the headwinds and decide which way they would jump.

Monday 17 October: Delusion

On the surface, Monday 17 October was not a bad day for the Prime Minister. She survived the low points of Hunt delivering his

Commons statement that tore up her growth plan, and Mordaunt standing in for her at the despatch box. Against the background of Twitter speculation that she was resigning imminently, she was herself having a short meeting with Graham Brady, Chair of the 1922 Committee. Truss surprised him by telling him, 'Kwasi has let me down and I have been dealing with his mistakes,' adding, 'I have no intention of resigning,' recalled an observer. She left, as was her tendency, with a more positive interpretation of a difficult meeting than her interlocutor. 'It was a very good conversation. There's no immediate concern from members,' she told her team. Indeed, she was 'jubilant', telling them, 'The news about Jeremy has gone down very well. The party has been brought back together.'

No. 10, as part of the refresh discussed the day before at Chequers, had been reorganized that Monday with a fresh sense of purpose. Long-term party adviser David Canzini, to general surprise but widespread applause, had pitched up early in the morning to inject vigour into the operation. Canzini was widely respected as a strategist. He was exactly the kind of no-nonsense organizational and party wizard who Truss had needed all along: she had wanted to appoint him at the start, but Wallace had objected. 'F**k Ben Wallace,' one of her Cabinet heavyweights told her. 'You're still the f**king Prime Minister.' So in he came. A 'War Room' was set up in the Pillared Room upstairs in No. 10 with a square of desks in the middle, a nascent communications and policy grid, and a procession of MPs and aides striding purposefully in and out. To old Johnson hands, it was reminiscent of 'operation save big dog', the rearguard action fought in his final months and weeks to keep him in power.

Truss knew that her greatest hope of survival rested on the lack of any viable successor. That Monday, she thought she was safe enough.

Those who had always wanted Sunak to succeed her were no closer to a breakthrough, with Hunt seeming to spike their guns, while Johnson was still egging her on with encouragement, the dream of a return still, he thought, far away.

Meetings with her Conservative MPs also buoyed her spirits. Sophie Jarvis was back in favour with Truss and being asked to do what she did best: sweet talk MPs. All day on Sunday at Chequers, having come back through the night from Adam Jones's wedding, she had been on her phone talking to members of the European Research Group and the One Nation Conservatives group, persuading them that they should get behind the PM, and that the party had no alternative candidate or choice. Truss's meeting with ERG members on Monday went particularly well: 'They were electrified to see Canzini with her,' said one present. 'There was a sense in the building on Monday that it might work,' said Simon McGee, her comms director.[3] For a few hours Truss was full of hope about her plans for a slimmed-down growth plan, and thoughts of leadership on the international stage. A question from one of her aides brought her crashing down to earth: 'Are you not disappointed about the reversals under Jeremy?' 'It is what it is,' she replied, her mood suddenly becoming icy.

Tuesday 18 October: Denial

The nosedive in Truss's premiership was precipitous. Tuesday's newspapers were dire. Talk of fresh rail strikes were secondary to withering attacks on her leadership. 'Truss: "I'm sorry… We went too far and too fast"', 'Hunt rips up PM's plans in an astonishing U-turn on tax' and 'Hunt takes charge as PM fears the exit' were the headlines in the *Daily Express*, the *Guardian* and the *i* newspaper respectively.[4] 'By lurching from crisis to self-inflicted crisis, the Conservatives risk irrevocable damage to the party,' said normally loyal *Daily Mail*. 'It's time for the wise men and women of the Conservative Party to decide whether the loss of confidence in Miss [sic] Truss is terminal. If it is, they must come to a solution – and fast.'[5]

Support was still coming from Johnson and allies, deeply worried about Sunak taking over. That day, he sent her a message with ideas for the case she should be making. He told her to 'Get out on the front foot' and contrasted recent strikes to 'the heroes... who keep our country moving' and who built for the future. He finished his message urging her to say she is 'delivering future growth and gains in productivity. I say to politicians across the country. It's time to get off Twitter and on with the job.'

Truss still banked on being safe from a challenge from her own MPs. The final weeks of May's and Johnson's premierships had been plagued by daily news, often speculative, of letters coming into Graham Brady in his capacity as Chair of the 1922 Committee, requesting a vote of confidence be held in the Prime Minister. Conservative MPs, for decades deep into the twentieth century the epitome of loyalty to their leader, could now not resist grandstanding on submitting letters, calling cards for a hoped-for successor. The threshold for triggering such a vote is normally 15 per cent of Conservative MPs, i.e. fifty-four letters. But as Johnson had suffered such a vote in June 2022, she thought she would be safe because the rules prevented another confidence vote for eleven months unless half the parliamentary party, a staggering 179 MPs, declared that they wanted one.[6] Independent sources confirm that the letters started trickling in soon after the Mini-Budget, and from Friday 14 October, the tempo increased dramatically. By early the following week, Brady gave up even trying to count the letters because it was obvious that there were more than enough.[7]

Cabinet that Tuesday morning only just managed to paper over the gathered ministers' barely concealed sceptical disdain and dis-appointment towards their leader of ministers sitting around the table. Where the axe would fall in the Autumn Statement later that month was the principal question under review. Even after Hunt's announcement the day before, many billions of pounds of savings still needed to be found. The Chancellor outlined some thoughts. A moratorium on new prison building had been high on the list: Truss wanted to cap it but Justice Secretary Brandon Lewis told her that it would require changes to sentencing because there was insufficient space to house all those being sentenced. 'Does that mean MPs will have to vote for softer sentences?' an adviser enquired. 'Yes, I fear it will.' 'Well, we can't do that then!' Truss responded brusquely, quickly changing course.

The policy choices were bleak indeed. Over a decade after being elected on a platform of austerity, the government now discussed… even more and deeper austerity. There were no easy decisions and public services would get worse, not good news with the general election no more than two years away. There was no exciting growth agenda to stir Tory blood any more, no more hopes, no more dreams. Just grim reality.

Lewis was one of the very few loyalists left in Cabinet alongside Cleverly and Coffey, who, for all her intense frustrations with her capricious leadership, stayed loyal to the end. Ideologists like Clarke and Rees-Mogg who had liked her championing the free market had become disenchanted. The latter, whose anger that he had not been made Chancellor was reinvigorated when Kwarteng U-turned, was pushing for progress on fracking legislation, which was shortly to unravel badly. Berry and Zahawi backed her still largely out of loyalty to Fullbrook. A dwindling band of party loyalists who accepted that she had won the leadership election and their duty was to support her included figures such as Anne-Marie Trevelyan and Tom Tugendhat. But early that week, the balance in Cabinet tipped towards those such as Braverman who had never liked or rated her, and only backed her leadership bid because they judged she would beat Sunak.

Wallace, the man who would most likely have won the leadership had he come forward, was chief among those who had never been enamoured with Truss. Dislike of Labour alone was keeping him in the tent. But Hunt's talk of spending cuts and the prospect of her imminent collapse forced him out into the open, along with his Minister of State James Heappey, saying they would resign if the pledge to raise defence spending to 3 per cent of GDP by the end of the decade was scrapped.[8] Wallace carried huge influence and his stand was widely noted by MPs.

Above all, a Prime Minister in difficulty needs to demonstrate calm proficiency and to offer a steady direction around which the party can unite. The more acute the difficulty, the more stable they need to be. But in three separate episodes involving her Home Secretary, a former Chancellor and her Chief Whip, Truss was to display the exact opposite.

Before Tuesday ended, Truss was to trigger the loss of Braverman. Heavy duty resignations, as Johnson discovered, can be far more damaging across the parliamentary party than a PM in their No. 10 eyrie can imagine.

Braverman had been a reluctant convert to Truss, the only senior figure explicitly offered a Cabinet job as a condition for her support during the leadership election among MPs. Immigration had been a divisive issue between them from the very first Cabinet, and Truss's attempt to slap her down on the topic at the party conference still rankled with her. On Tuesday afternoon, Truss asked her to announce that immigrants were welcome in key employment sectors including science and IT, in part to placate the OBR, which thought the Home Office's rejection of additional visas, and Braverman's aim of reducing immigration by hundreds of thousands, would dampen growth by reducing firms' ability to hire. No. 10 got wind the following day that Braverman had sent a draft written ministerial statement on immigration from her personal email to one of her most loyal MPs, John Hayes. She also sent it to Tory MP Andrew Percy by mistake, who reported it to the Chief Whip. Though it was initially briefed out that the information was secret and market sensitive, Braverman would later defend herself by saying that the documents were not marked in that manner.[9]

Officials in Downing Street were alarmed and told Truss, 'This action has broken the ministerial code. She has forwarded government material from her personal email to an MP... You could try to mount a defence but it would be hard to see how it would work, not least because she is the minister responsible herself for Security.' According to an aide who was in the room, Truss replied, 'Very well. Please speak to Sue. She will need to resign.' But Braverman refused to resign when Case met her in the House, and so she was summoned to the Cabinet Room.

'I'm sorry, Prime Minister, but I don't think I've done anything wrong,' she said in her defence, as an aide recalled.

'I'm sorry too, but what you have done is not OK, Suella,' Truss replied.

'This is not classified material. I am merely asking for a view from parliamentary stakeholders.'

'It is market sensitive information, and regarded by No. 10 as affecting the OBR's economic forecast at a sensitive time,' Truss replied.

'I do not agree and do not see why it is regarded as a sensitive issue,' Braverman persisted, denying that the information was market sensitive.

'I'm sorry, Suella. I don't think that you can remain in office having done this. I think you will have to go.'

'I think that's totally unfair. I've been very clear with you. I agree with your growth plan, but doing it via immigration is not the right way. MPs won't wear it. You'll never get support for it,' Braverman countered.

'Yes we will. We will do it in conjunction with Rwanda,' Truss said emphatically, referring to the plan to process and resettle asylum seekers who enter the UK illegally in Rwanda. 'I'm very sorry about this. We will send you a draft of my letter so you can read it over before it is released.'

Braverman left shortly afterwards, clearly very displeased.

Aides drafted the letter, but while they did so, Braverman released her own, acidic letter: 'The business of government relies upon people accepting responsibility for their mistakes. Pretending we haven't made mistakes, carrying on as if everyone can't see that we have made them, and hoping that things will magically come right is not serious politics. I have made a mistake; I accept responsibility: I resign.' The furious letter concluded with a challenge to the whole direction of

Truss's government: 'Not only have we broken key pledges that were promised to our voters, but I have had serious concerns about this Government's commitment to honouring manifesto commitments, such as reducing overall migration numbers and stopping illegal migration'.[10] The aides promptly went back to work to amend the PM's glowing letter to something more robust.

Truss was content to lose Braverman, if not so acrimoniously. She had never wanted her as Home Secretary, and now more than ever she needed this plum job to offer elsewhere. Key to the survival strategy was to bring in senior figures from the Sunak camp, as Osborne had counselled when she'd called him a couple of days before. 'I went through prominent names on the Sunak wing, and told her it had to be dramatic, or it wouldn't be noticed,' he said.[11] Shapps was the name who had frequently been mentioned as the man to broaden her Cabinet.

Here was the holder of the parliamentary spreadsheet with its to-die-for information on the motivations of all Conservative MPs. She knew he was a serial agitator against her. But she knew too he was after a big job involving his great love, security and secrecy. Unsure if even this bait would entice him, she had a backup plan to shift Cleverly to the Home Office and to offer Shapps Foreign Secretary if he played hard to get. Concerns that he might be an enemy within were silenced by the argument that 'once Ken [Ken McCallum, director general of MI5] gives Grant his first security briefing, he will quickly fall in behind us', said an aide. Shapps duly accepted the job, becoming, with just six days in office, the shortest-serving Home Secretary in history. Records were tumbling so quickly barely anyone noticed. Had he not accepted the bait, he might have become the shortest-serving Foreign Secretary instead.

As far as Truss was concerned, on the face of it a dangerous flare-up had been resolved rather nicely.

Rumbling on throughout Tuesday, and Wednesday morning too, was the second time bomb: Javid's displeasure at reading disparaging words about himself from No. 10 in *The Sunday Times*. The source, key comms adviser Jason Stein, knew at once he had gone too far in his desire to trash the story that Hunt wasn't the first choice as Chancellor, which might have undermined his credibility and that of his rescue package. As a result, Stein went too far in the opposite direction to trash Javid's character, whom many had speculated was the alternative candidate.[12] Equally, the adviser knew that Truss had his back: 'I've been told about the Saj stuff. Hilarious,' she had texted him on Saturday evening. But Truss was also keen to douse down the story, so she called Javid at eight o'clock on Sunday morning. One witness recalled the conversation that followed.

'It's been brought to my attention about the article. I want to say it's nothing to do with me. I never said it,' she told him.

Javid was unimpressed. 'Thank you for saying that, but *The Sunday Times* would never have printed it if it hadn't come from someone in your circle very close to you,' he replied.

Javid had been told by an insider that Stein had planted the story. 'I want you to find the culprit at once.'

'I will, but I'm not certain who actually said it.'

'Well, I'm not certain you will last the week and certainly not if you don't fire him because I will make your life hell.' He hung up.

The next day, Javid passed a message to No. 10 to say that if Stein wasn't fired, he would ask a PMQ on Wednesday (he was on the Order Paper for that day as Question No. 1) along the lines of 'Does the Prime Minister value her advisers as colleagues more than her

Conservative MPs as colleagues?' Not satisfied with the response he was getting, he said he wanted a formal disciplinary process to begin to investigate the matter. No. 10 now found itself fighting wars on several fronts at the same time, with the result that it suffered significant overload. It resembled the period between December 1973 and February 1974 when Heath's No. 10 was buckling under the pressure of keeping control in the middle of an economic and financial crisis, and during which the head of the civil service, William Armstrong, had to be relieved because of excessive strain. The procedure was not clear whether the Prime Minister was able to remove a special adviser. After conversations between Catsaras and Case, Stein was removed as acting communications director and given a written warning. Tensions that had been simmering only just below the surface since August between Fullbrook and Stein now broke out into the open, with Fullbrook finding Stein's close relationship with the PM, and her reluctance to discipline him, making his own job considerably harder.

He and Porter realized how absurd and destabilizing the saga was becoming, so they both called Javid separately to try to persuade him not to proceed with his PMQ plan. 'Jason has admitted it, says he's sorry and he wants to call you to apologize. Please will you drop the PMQ?' Porter asked him. She even wrote a letter of apology on behalf of Stein. 'I totally agree with you,' Fullbrook told him. 'I can't explain why Jason has such a strong hold over Liz.' 'Look, you're the chief of staff,' Javid replied. 'You have the power to dismiss him.' 'I wish I had,' said Fullbrook.

The saga dragged on into Wednesday. 'Unless Simon Case personally confirms to me that Stein is fired, I'm going to ask my question,' Javid told No. 10. Eventually, Catsaras took Stein for a walk around St James's Park and told him he would have to be suspended pending the investigation of the allegations by the Propriety and Ethics team, as that was the only way Javid would withdraw the question. The PM hated doing it, Catsaras explained. 'It's OK, it's all done, mate. Best of luck with it. I'll see you later,' Stein told an aide as he left the building later, never to return.

At 11 a.m. on Wednesday, Javid received a call from Case. Case confirmed that Stein had been suspended. Only later did No. 10 discover that Javid had woken up with Covid that morning, and didn't plan to come into the Commons in any case to ask the question. Valuable hours and goodwill of Truss's top team had been expended on this second psychodrama. But it was to be eclipsed totally by the mortal harm that would be done by the third.

Wednesday 19 October: Division

MPs will put up with many things. But confused leadership from their PM makes them despair. It's hard to think of a day in the last 300 years of prime ministerial history more incompetently handled than Wednesday 19 October 2022. The last day before Liz Truss announced her resignation.

At the start of Wednesday, few were predicting her imminent demise. Some of the powerful forces we have described that keep a Prime Minister in post still pertained. Stephen Bush, associate editor of the *Financial Times*, while putting her chances of being removed before the next election 'at 95%', wrote, 'I am dubious that she will be removed anytime soon.' The reasons were, short of her falling on her sword, that the mechanism for removing her was fraught, with many on the right including the ERG sticking with her, while the centre/left were reluctant to oust her for fear of being labelled regicides and leaving the party even weaker.[13]

Truss, as was her wont, chose not to look at the headlines in the morning papers. But she was informed of the widespread anger they were reporting about removing the 'triple lock' on pensions introduced by the Coalition government in 2010. Under this policy the state pension must rise by whichever is higher: average earnings, inflation or 2.5 per cent; it is particularly popular among the elderly, the most dependable pro-Tory voting group in the UK, and hence liked by her MPs.[14] Cuts had to be found urgently, but she reluctantly accepted they couldn't be here. So she summoned Hunt to No. 10 in the morning to tell him that the 'triple lock' would have to stay after all.

That morning Truss, when not dealing with the fallout from the Home Secretary and Javid dramas, spent time preparing for PMQs. Her team felt she had survived largely unscathed from both. But Starmer knew he had her on the run when questions were called at noon, opening with: 'A book is being written about the Prime Minister's time in office. Apparently, it is going to be out by Christmas. Is that the release date or the title?'

'I have delivered the energy price guarantee... I have reversed the national insurance increase... and we will be taking steps to crack down on the militant unions,' she responded defiantly.

Starmer continued relentlessly. 'The country has nothing to show for it except for the destruction of the economy and the implosion of the Tory party. I have the list here [he runs over the U-turns]. Her supposed best friend, the former Chancellor, has gone as well. They are all gone. So why is she still here?'

Her response, uttered twice, came back to haunt her: 'I am a fighter and not a quitter.'[15] She didn't need to turn round to realize the widespread dismay among her MPs.

Even after Starmer's humiliation of the Prime Minister, the end still did not seem imminent. That day the words of David Frost, the Brexit supremo she had wanted as her chief of staff just three months before, were cutting: 'Truss just can't stay in office for one very obvious reason: she campaigned against the policies she's now implementing,' he wrote in the *Daily Telegraph*.[16] Hunt's appearance before the 1922 Committee brought some respite, showing that the party was not yet ready to ditch its boss. The mood was 'grim but realistic and respectful', said a Treasury aide, as the Chancellor talked over the impending Autumn Statement and the tough decisions that would be needed. Friendly MPs primed to speak to journalists as soon as the doors opened were stood down. Clear to all, Hunt had carried the room.

But then came the third swing of the axe that was finally to topple her. Business and Energy Secretary Rees-Mogg's impatience to press ahead with fracking, the politically and environmentally controversial injecting of fluid into cracks in rock fissures to access oil and gas reserves beloved by free marketeers, now exploded onto the parliamentary scene. The 2019 Conservative manifesto had effectively promised to maintain the moratorium on the practice, and had ruled out changes to the planning system to enable it. There would be no fracking 'unless the science shows categorically that it can be done safely'.[17] Many MPs had therefore felt safe to promise their constituencies that there would be no fracking on their watch, quelling strong local opposition.

But Truss supported fracking. She regarded restrictions as an unwarranted bar on free enterprise. She craved cheaper oil and gas prices for the hard-pressed struggling to pay bills, and which would no doubt help businesses thrive. Typically, she had little sympathy for her MPs who didn't agree with her. 'She never had much affinity for the Conservative Party or its MPs: she was always much more concerned to do what she herself thought was right for people in the country,' said Jarvis.[18] At issue also was Truss's presumption that she could ignore the 2019 manifesto, on which Johnson had won the majority, at will. Labour jumped on the opportunity for widening cracks in fissures in the Conservative parliamentary party and on Tuesday evening called for a motion to allocate Commons time for a debate on banning fracking.

Wendy Morton and Craig Whittaker, the Chief and Deputy Chief Whip, promptly started receiving messages from MPs concerned about how to vote on the motion. Late on Tuesday evening, Morton was becoming worried whether the government would have sufficient votes to win the next day. So she called Truss, could not get her and left a message. Relations between Morton and Truss's team had broken down weeks before: they had no confidence in her grip and regretted that they hadn't persuaded Coffey to take the job originally. 'I don't want her attending meetings,' Truss had said. 'You do realize that No. 10 are calling you Wendy Moron,' a colleague confided in Morton.

By common consent, Morton was a capable Chief Whip who had been performing her job in the genial way that anyone who knew her would have expected her to do. If Truss had wanted a bulldog, she should have appointed one. Losing confidence in such a pivotal figure in a government so quickly suggested either the PM didn't know who she was appointing, or was unsure what the job entailed. Or both.

Anxiety about the vote did not assuage overnight, so at the 9 a.m. meeting on Wednesday in the Pillared Room, Berry said, 'This is essentially a vote of confidence in the government, and we have to win it.' Morton took away that it was indeed to be a formal vote of confidence in the government, a very big deal, which weaved its way into the discussions that the whips were holding with MPs. During the PMQs on Wednesday, a planted question to provide reassurance elicited the response from Truss that there would be no fracking except if the local community agreed with it.[19] But as the evening vote approached, there was still uncertainty about the status of the vote and whether there would be enough support to get it over the line. 'I didn't know that tonight's vote was a vote of confidence,' Truss told an aide, and asked them to find out what was going on.

While Truss went off for her weekly audience with the King at Buckingham Palace, Canzini decided to bring her senior team together at 6.30 p.m. in a small room off the Cabinet Room. Still only in his third day in post, Canzini, a veteran observer of Downing Street, had been staggered by the lack of political grip in the building and the speed at which everyone was trying to move. He believed that Truss herself hadn't realized the implication of a confidence vote, a measure he considered 'a huge error for any leader in trouble because it legitimizes MPs who dislike them to cause damage'.[20] Morton joined their meeting on speakerphone from the House of Commons. 'Wendy, are you sure of the numbers?' Canzini asked her directly.

'We don't know yet. So we don't think it should be treated as a confidence vote.'

'Wendy, it *is* a confidence vote. You do realize the consequence of us losing? The government will fall.'

'It shouldn't be a confidence vote.'

'Wendy, it is.'

'Will we definitely win?' another asked her. Another pause. She and Whittaker debated the question before responding. They agreed it would probably be fine, and they had had no indication of a big rebellion, but doubt remained.

'I don't know,' Morton replied again.

Pandemonium broke out among the dozen crowded in the room until Canzini gripped the position, announcing, 'This is what we will do.' Two messages were to be sent out, he said: one to Rees-Mogg's deputy, Energy Minister Graham Stuart, to announce from the despatch box (the only place from which to annul a confidence vote) that the fracking vote was *not* a vote of confidence, and from Charlotte Owen (a hangover aide from Johnson's No. 10) to Rees-Mogg's principal parliamentary aide to tell him what was happening. For a few moments, it seemed like the problem had gone away. If the fracking vote was indeed lost, it would be an embarrassment not a disaster.

Stuart duly made his announcement when summing up the debate on behalf of the government. But it came as a surprise and shock to Tory MPs in the Chamber. Conservative MP Ruth Edwards quickly raised a point of order: 'I really need to press the Minister on this question of a confidence vote. Many of us have been told today by our Whips that if we vote for, or abstain from voting against, this motion, we will lose the Whip. Will he please confirm whether that is the case?' Stuart's response did nothing to calm frayed nerves: 'That is a matter for party managers, and I am not a party manager.'[21] Morton and Whittaker listened to Stuart's statement in horror and decided they were not prepared to be undermined by No. 10, as they believed they had been.

After Truss's meeting with the King, she had returned to Westminster to be greeted by a friendly MP who quickly told her not to go into Parliament, warning, 'It's chaos.' But she went to her parliamentary office anyway, to be confronted there by an angry Craig Whittaker who charged in to see her shouting, 'It's a total disgrace!'

'I don't know what you're talking about,' Truss retorted, in the dark about what had been happening.

'You've cut the ground from under the whips' feet,' he exclaimed.

'I have no idea why you are so worked up,' she said. It was only after he stormed off that she learned that her Downing Street team had called off the confidence vote in her absence.

Truss sent a message for her senior team to join her urgently in the Commons office. 'Why the f**k has this been happening? What the f**k is going on?' she demanded to know. 'No one was going to tell her that it was the result of her indecision,' said one present. Mid-lecture, at 6.59 p.m., she received a text from Morton: 'I've resigned'; then a second: 'With immediate effect.'[22] Prime Ministers should never panic, but at that point, Truss panicked. Reality had dawned that a PM cannot lose a Home Secretary and a Chief Whip on the same day, six days after losing a Chancellor. If this was a game of chess, she had lost a rook and a knight, and couldn't afford to lose a bishop, whatever she thought of them. 'I'm going to go off and persuade her to change her mind,' the PM announced, charging out of the door. Once she tracked Morton down, she persuaded her to join her in her inner office.

Stuck on the Chamber floor, Leader of the House Mordaunt was trying to maintain order and to make sense of it all. The Leader's prime task is to ensure government business in the House is being properly conducted; that very transparently was not the case that night. Taking the matter into her own hands, she enquired where the Chief Whip was. 'She has resigned,' the reply came back. So she slipped out of the Chamber and ran down the corridor to the Prime Minister's office to ask where the PM was. A movement of a hand gestured to the answer, so she burst into the inner office where she found Truss and Morton together 'having a heart to heart and drinking a glass of wine', as she later recalled.[23] Incredulous at 'the lack of nous', she shouted at them, 'You need to know what's happening in the Chamber. MPs are in total confusion about what you are requiring of them. You've got literally two minutes before the vote is called. Stop explaining yourselves to me, get in there and take responsibility.' On reflection, she explained, 'I didn't enjoy shouting but I thought it was necessary. They had left an experienced team without any clear instructions at a moment of great vulnerability, with no Chief Whip on duty. It seemed totally divorced from reality and a dereliction of one of the basic asks your troop make of their leader – to know what is being asked of them,' she added.[24] Morton and Truss then left to attend the vote. An aide recalled that 'she and Wendy spoke more than once. It was a mess.'

Confused MPs were not certain whether Morton had resigned or not, and, in a sign that the end was near, were being openly contemptuous of the government. Adding to the anger was the feeling among some Conservative MPs that they had been manhandled and shouted at by Truss loyalists and whips to vote the right way. An unruly crowd of MPs built up outside the 'No' lobby as Conservatives wavered, unsure of whether it was a vote of confidence or not. Government ministers tried to persuade MPs to oppose the motion, while Labour MPs encouraged them to support it. Voices were raised. On two occasions, the tellers stopped counting due to the noise level. A subsequent investigation by the Speaker found no evidence of bullying, though it did find discussion had been at times 'fraught' and 'intemperate'.[25]

The government ultimately managed to win the vote quite comfortably (326–230) defeating the Labour motion to force a vote on a bill to ban fracking.[26] But the victory had been a Pyrrhic one. The scene had been chaotic, the MPs were furious. Those who had been prepared to give Truss the benefit of the doubt concluded that her shambolic premiership could not be allowed to go on any longer.

While these scenes were taking place, another conversation between Truss and Morton was occurring in her inner Commons sanctum, as recalled by a witness. 'I'm no longer surprised to be undermined by you in this way,' Morton told her, 'which is why Craig and I are resigning.'

'I don't accept either of your resignations,' Truss replied.

'I'm sorry about all of this, Prime Minister,' Morton said, seeing how distressed Truss was.

'Well, will you continue then?'

'I will need to talk it through with the whips,' replied a very troubled Morton. So Truss and Morton walked together to the whips' office where one whip declared insouciantly, 'If they go, we're all going.' Such a collective walkout by the whips would have made the government untenable. Truss thought quickly. 'But I have persuaded them to stay,' she replied. An uneasy truce was reached whereby both Morton and Whittaker agreed to resume their posts and for a statement to that effect to be put out.

No. 10, though, was operating on the information that they had received that both had gone, and, as it is institutionally grooved to do, was swinging into action to put replacements speedily in place. As with Braverman, Truss's aides seized on the loss of someone they didn't rate as an opportunity to put somebody more useful to them in Morton's place. Whittaker would have been first choice: the previous Thursday, he'd been sent a message saying, 'Candidly, Craig, the Prime Minister thinks you are the person who is running the whipping.' But the team, assuming Whittaker had resigned too, alighted on the equable Greg Hands as their favoured replacement: they would have replaced Morton with him three or four weeks earlier had Whittaker not told No. 10, 'Sorry, if she goes, I go as well.'[27] The threat of the double resignation held Morton in place. So Hands it was. Catsaras put a call into Buckingham Palace to seek formal approval from the King for the appointment of Hands as Morton's successor as Chief Whip, a reminder that, even at times of unparalleled pressure, it is *His Majesty's* Government, not the Prime Minister's. An hour later, a call came back that the King was indeed content with the new appointment, proof that despite the chaos, some parts of the British state still operated smoothly. Then came the news that Morton had withdrawn her resignation. So the embarrassed official made a second call to the Palace to say that the appointment would not be happening after all. It is difficult to believe that the monarch was impressed by the competence of his reign's first administration.

Truss's senior staff had been told not to leave the building because she wanted an emergency strategy meeting that evening to review the position. But at 11 p.m., with confusion still reigning, the message went around, 'There might not be any meeting as we still don't know when it will all wrap up.' Her staff had had enough: voting with their feet, everyone just went home. Director of Strategy Iain Carter walked out of the building with Simon Case. 'What do you think will happen?' he asked the Cabinet secretary. 'This is still not the end. I don't think it will collapse immediately,' Case replied.[28]

Meanwhile, a formal dinner was being held at the historic Carlton Club in St James's Street, the original home of the Conservative Party before Central Office/CCHQ was established. The occasion was the hundredth anniversary of the meeting of Conservative MPs at the club that brought down Lloyd George's coalition, an ever-potent reminder of the power of MPs to dethrone Prime Ministers. Brady, one of the guest speakers, later recalled, 'It was very odd to be leaving the House of Commons in so much ferment. But once inside the club, the atmosphere was strangely calm, despite everyone knowing that a seismic event was taking place in the party simultaneously.'[29] According to Jake Berry, Brady asked him for a private word in a side room. 'This can't go on. Liz has to go,' the 1922 Committee Chair told him. Brady, for all his seniority in post (in 2022, he became the longest-serving Chair in history), was regarded by some in the party as partly responsible for the defenestration of both May and Johnson; the worry was that he might be trigger happy again. 'Be careful what you wish for, Graham,' the Party Chair cautioned, adding, 'The person who has the authority and the mandate from the electorate is Boris. We should go back to Boris.' 'That is totally unacceptable. It cannot happen,' Brady replied. Brady insisted there should be a raised bar for the number of MPs to get candidates on the ballot to avoid another lengthy multiple-round process, which Berry strongly resisted. 'Graham was desperate to do anything to keep Boris off and for Sunak to win,' he later said.[30] Brady strongly rejects any suggestion that the contest was planned in a way that would favour any one candidate, saying that 'the process was neutral'. The 100-backer threshold was to ensure speed and Johnson had as much opportunity to win as anybody else.

One hundred years on from 1922, was history repeating itself?

Thursday 20 October: Defeat

After she returned to No. 10 tired and defeated late on Wednesday evening, she cancelled a meeting with Hunt and went up to the flat instead.[31] Porter thinks that she had been toying with the idea of whether to go since Sunday: the question was now at the top of her mind. She then discussed what to do with Hugh, her closest counsellor. Like Denis Thatcher thirty-two years before, he gave the same advice to his beleaguered wife. 'The fracking vote made me realize the MPs were not with me,' she later said. 'I didn't enter No. 10 to be Prime Minister: I entered No. 10 to change things.'[32]

When she came downstairs on Thursday, though, there was still an element of doubt in her mind.

She met Catsaras in the Cabinet Room before 8 a.m. Drawing on his close relationship dating back to her appointment as Foreign Secretary just thirteen months before, he felt he could give her the unvarnished truth. 'Last night was a total shambles. You have lost any remaining authority.'

'How do you know?'

'Even David Frost is calling for your resignation.'

She had not seen Frost's article the day before. 'Is he?'

'Yes, he is, I'm afraid.'

'Do you think it's over?'

'Yes, I do.' Bar husband Hugh, there was no one whose opinion she relied on more.

A pause. She sighed.

'Get me Mark Fullbrook then,' she said. Catsaras sent a message for the chief of staff to join them. Fullbrook had missed the chaos of the previous day because he was attending his father's funeral.

'Is it all over, Mark?' she asked when he joined them.

'It's a question not of whether, but when,' he replied. She looked at him, the man who had overseen her election as party leader and her premiership. She didn't say anything.

'I mean, do you want to carry on when it's no longer your project?' Fullbrook asked her.[33] She didn't need to reply.

'Bring Simon Case in,' she demanded. The Cabinet secretary arrived a short while later.

'Is it all over?'

'Yes, Prime Minister, I think it probably is.'

A moment's silence. Then she said, 'I want to go off and talk to Hugh.'

Once she'd left the room, a debate took place on whether she should simply resign, or whether there needed to be a confidence motion. Case and Catsaras thought that it ought to be the latter because it gave the Conservative Party ownership over it, especially important given the still fragile state of the markets, and the paramount need for a legitimate and respected appointment process. Truss was back in the room. Her husband had said nothing to make her change her mind. 'Get Graham Brady in', was her next instruction. Whereas the PM visits the monarch to resign as Prime Minister, Tory MPs see the Chair of the 1922 Committee to request the Prime Minister resigns as party leader. Brady was indeed a powerful man.

Meanwhile, almost directly above the Cabinet Room upstairs in the Pillared Room, the Thursday morning meeting was not going well. No. 10 is a small place, so it's surprising how often one part of the building doesn't know what another is doing. Truss was due to be chairing it herself, but the minutes passed, and there was no sign of her. 'Where is the Prime Minister?' was the question everyone wanted answered. 'People sat around the room, staring at the floor: given the calls for her to resign, some speculated whether she had already gone,' said aide Clare Evans. 'She's not coming,' Coffey suddenly announced. 'She's up in the flat making calls. Let's get on with the meeting.' A blazing row broke out between her and Morton resulting in the latter storming out shouting, 'Just remember, I am the Chief Whip, not you, Thérèse.' Berry and Coffey kept trying to run the meeting as if nothing was awry, focusing the conversation on the communications and policy grid and what announcements would be coming up. 'Yes, there have been calls for her resignation, but these things happen all the time. It's business as usual,' Berry exhorted. 'Let's get back to our desks: we know what we've got to do,' chipped in Coffey. Many of those present were left thinking, 'This is f**king ridiculous. We won't even be here at the end of the day,' recalled one.

At the same time Brady was drinking coffee quietly at home in Battersea, mulling over the previous evening, and was preparing to call No. 10 to say that the damage made it impossible for Truss to continue. Though he had not counted the letters, he knew that the 54 threshold for a vote of no confidence had been passed. He was reaching for his phone when it began to vibrate. 'The Prime Minister would like to see you as a matter of urgency,' he was told. If not the grim reaper, there was something of the air of a well-heeled funeral director about Brady. When he arrived at the door of No. 10, it was rarely good news. To avoid the ubiquitous cameras that were building up outside No. 10 and its environs, he had taken a tube to St James's Park station rather than alighting at Westminster, which was closer. But as he strutted along the side of the park towards Downing Street to officiate at the ending of the shortest premiership in history, umbrella in hand to ward off the heavy rain, farcically a coachload of Chinese female students pulled up by him. Out they poured and each girl demanded a selfie with the face that had become one of the most recognizable in British politics. A slightly baffled Brady smiled for photographs in one of the stranger scenes to come from a turbulent era in British politics.

He just managed to slink into Downing Street by the back entrance opposite the park, and was ushered quickly into the Cabinet Room.

'Graham, how bad do you think it is?'

'I think it's pretty bad, Prime Minister.'

'Is it recoverable?'

'I don't think it is.'

'I've come to the same conclusion.'

The Chair of the 1922 Committee had witnessed the end of more premierships than any of his predecessors in the last hundred years. 'Because she was falling on her sword, I did not see any need to talk about a confidence vote,' he later recalled.[34]

The deed done, Brady was shown to a side room, given a sandwich, a cup of tea and a phone charger, and told in the nicest possible way that he was being held hostage and couldn't leave the building till the news was out there. No. 10 is also a family home for the Prime Minister. The decision taken, Hugh called their daughters' school and discussed arrangements so that the girls could come back to

Downing Street to be told by Hugh and Liz together. 'Neither of the parents wanted their daughters to hear about her resignation first on the news,' said an aide. Catsaras, meanwhile, called Buckingham Palace and arranged for the Prime Minister and the King to speak. The Palace made it clear that the King would much prefer to hear the news freshly from her, the first resignation of his monarchy. Finding a slot was difficult because, that morning, the King was seeing the President of Togo. But space in the diary was cleared, and he was told that the King would be free to speak at 12.45 p.m.

Truss asked Catsaras to summon her closest team, wanting to tell them ahead of the rest. 'I think you should see the Prime Minister. She's got something to tell you and the team,' he announced. Truss told Porter first then Jarvis, who burst into tears. 'I kept thinking that we had failed to complete the project, that the libertarian dream was over,' she recalled.[35] When Hope went in, Jarvis put her hand on his shoulder visibly upset. He sat down opposite Truss in the Prime Minister's chair at the Cabinet table. 'The game is up, Jamie Hope,' she said, and, with a spring in her voice, added, 'I'm going to resign.'

'I think that's the right thing to do,' he told her.

'Do you?'

'Yes, it's better to go before you are pushed.'

She looked at him, and tried to smile. 'I've given it all I have,' she uttered quietly. Then into the room poured senior staff from the Private Office, the Policy Unit and communications teams.

'The Prime Minister has an announcement to make,' Catsaras said.

'I've spoken to the King and told him I am going to resign. I would like to thank you all for your hard work. It's clear to me that I don't have the support of the parliamentary party. I want to thank you.'

What struck several of those present was that it was the first time that they had heard her say the word 'thank you' to them.

Then something happened that may have changed the course of history. Hunt had been watching the events of Wednesday evening with a mixture of horror and anxiety. He realized that Truss would not last many hours more. He reflected on the two months of bitter campaigning over the summer following Johnson's resignation, and concluded that another two or three months' fighting would be perilous, given the fragility of the markets. So he went to see her for a meeting that was so secret no officials were present.

'Things are not working out, Jeremy. Should I put together a Cabinet of party unity, or should I resign and trigger a leadership election?' she asked him.

Hunt was not sure how serious she was about the first suggestion, but it was very evident to him that she thought the game was up. He decided not to engage with her first question, but to home in on the second. 'If there is to be a contest, Prime Minister, I regard it as essential it should not last more than a week.'

She looked at him, taken back, unsure what to say.

He continued, 'You have acted in the national interest in my six days in office, giving me a free hand to stabilize the markets. If you are going to go, I believe you should display the same statesmanlike concern for the nation and make it clear the transition must be quick.'

'But how can that be done?'

'How? Do not make the announcement to leave until you have had confirmation from the Conservative Party that the competition should last no more than a week.'[36]

The PM gave him no indication whether or not she accepted his thesis.

After Hunt left her, he went back to his office and spoke to Brady, who was reported to be sympathetic to the plan, and then asked Berry to come and see him, who most definitely was not. Hunt had emphasized that Truss must go quickly. Brady wanted a quick election. This so soon after the last contest would likely be better for Sunak. Berry favoured Johnson, who was on holiday and would have benefited from more time. Trying to build trust with Berry, Hunt told him, 'You need to know I'm not putting my name forward or acting out of self-interest.' To allay Berry's continuing suspicions, he then asked for two Treasury officials to join them to explain more about the continuing market volatility and the risk that a protracted leadership contest might do enduring harm to the British economy. 'It went on for thirty minutes and they told me it would be doomsday for the British economy if there was a drawn-out ballot,' Berry recalled. Before leaving, he told the Treasury officials, 'I don't think it's any of your f**king business to talk about how the Conservative Party selects its leaders.' Hunt was left on tenterhooks whether the livid Party Chair would charge round to No. 10 to try to sabotage the 'within one week' proposal.

A parallel track pointing to the same destination was happening at the same time. Case's concerns for the country's economic stability and the state of its public finances over the previous days had been far from allayed by the departure of Truss. He worried greatly too that a protracted and divisive leadership election could spiral the markets out of control. He shared his concerns with Catsaras, and, independently of Hunt, decided off his own initiative to speak to Brady to see what could be done to severely cut the leadership contest.

Another conspiracy theory was being born, alongside the 'deep state' killing off the Liz Truss premiership and her growth plan. This was that Boris Johnson was poised to return in glory to Downing Street to pick up where he had left off, and lead the party into a convincing election victory in 2023 or 2024. His closest supporters, including Nigel Adams, Conor Burns and Andrew Griffith, believe that he had the momentum to have secured one hundred MP supporters (backers said they had 102 pledges), and to have made it victorious through the MP rounds. The unique Johnson magic, they thought, would power him through, a blend of his undisputed personal popularity with the electorate and the party's continuing unease with the man still blamed for vilely plotting his end just six long weeks before, Rishi Sunak. For a tantalizing few days Johnson thought he would run. 'I'm going to go for this,' he told his close ally Zahawi. Visions of returning in triumph to Downing Street danced before his eyes, Cincinnatus reborn, the plough discarded for the laurels and garlands. It fell to his wife Carrie to bring him back to earth. 'Sorry, Boris, you just don't have enough support to win,' she told him. Sensible voices around him chipped in. 'You will split the party down the middle if you stand,' they said.[37] He reluctantly accepted it was all too soon and he was not properly prepared. He still had too much baggage from office, not least the forthcoming appearance before the Privileges Committee on his conduct (held from March 2023), and in his heart of hearts, much though he relished the speculation and the boost it gave to his future income-earning potential, he knew he didn't have the puff.

Truss's decision to resign taken, she became fixated on her resignation speech. When she asked for her political team, she was told, 'Prime Minister, they are not here.' Stein was banished, Jones on honeymoon, Porter on half term, speechwriter Asa Bennett on paternity leave.

'Her resignation speech was really quite perfunctory,' said an aide. 'But she saved herself up for her departure speech five days later on 25 October.' The day before in the Cabinet Room, she batted some ideas around with her officials. 'What I want to say is that the status quo put us into a doom loop, and that I found the politics were too hard because everyone likes protections,' Truss said.

'Prime Minister, the logical conclusion of what you're saying is the status quo doesn't work, and it's really hard to take political advantage of Brexit,' volunteered one present. There was a hushed silence around the room. No one knew how she would react.

'No, that's not quite right. We might have to find some way back, but not all the way: the Single Market and the Customs Union. My view is that it's a choice between a Singapore or Norway option.'

'But Norway is the worst of all outcomes – abiding by rules while having no say in making them.'

'Yes. That's why I wanted to get EU legislation off the statute book as quickly as possible, to stop that happening,' Truss replied.

'Will you say it's Singapore or Norway in your speech today?' said another.

'No,' she said emphatically. 'Not today. But that's the choice.'

But on 20 October, her mind was much more focused and clear. At 1.35 p.m. that Thursday, she stepped out of Downing Street and walked up to the podium. 'I was elected by the Conservative Party with a mandate to change... And we set out a vision for a low tax, high growth economy – that would take advantage of the freedoms of Brexit.' But, she said, she'd been unable to deliver on that and therefore would be resigning. Suddenly, all eyes were on her final words. 'We have agreed there will be a leadership election to be completed in the next week. This will ensure we remain on a path to deliver our fiscal plans and maintain our country's economic stability and national security. I will remain as Prime Minister until a successor has been chosen.'[38]

To her great credit, at the very end, she did the right thing for the country.

The Verdict: Retain the Confidence of the Party?

The tenth and final rule is that the Prime Minister has to remember the importance of maintaining their support among their MPs. Wednesday's PMQs was when the truth began to dawn: she had lost her MPs. 'That was the moment she read the room and realized how bad it was. She was different when she came back into the building that night,' said Canzini.[39] True, she never had a mandate from a majority of her MPs from the beginning (nor indeed from the electorate). Truss came a long way second in the final ballot of MPs with just 113 votes, 24 behind Sunak's 137, and only 8 ahead of Penny Mordaunt on 105 (hence the notion that only 5 of Truss's votes needed to switch to Mordaunt for the latter to win). Less than one third of Conservative MPs voted for her. Far short of one third of the parliamentary party were believers in her: she won their vote as the candidate most likely to beat Sunak. Simmering resentment against her at party HQ didn't help her cause. 'It was dysfunctional from day one: from the moment she took over, they made it clear they hadn't wanted her and wouldn't help,' said Berry.[40] But a shrewder leader would have built bridges, reached out and tried to win MPs over.

Because the rules required 15% of her MPs submitting letters to Brady to trigger a vote of confidence it was not certain until that last week that she could be unseated. Some of Sunak's supporters undoubtedly kept up pressure on her throughout, but even Sunak himself until these last few days didn't believe he could oust her before the general election, and was thinking ahead to plans outside politics. The vast majority of her critics, personal and ideological, thought any attempt to knife her would be counter-productive. 'There was a grim determination among MPs to make it work with Liz, a sense of "we can't possibly go through that again",' said one insider. 'Let's just get through to January, then all will be OK,' Kwarteng had told her shortly before leaving for the IMF in Washington.[41]

The three dramas in the first half of the week, above all the fracking debacle, made the end inevitable, just as Johnson's more protracted dramas, over Partygate and rogue MPs Owen Paterson and Chris Pincher, did. Perhaps in an earlier era – before Brexit made MPs think the unthinkable time and time again – she might have struggled on. But an earlier era would not have made Liz Truss Prime Minister; only the febrile and frantic atmosphere of the early 2020s could do that.

The tenth rule is the least forgiving. Within hours of her losing her MPs, resignation and the end of the shortest premiership in British history was inevitable.

As Prime Minister, Truss always looked over her shoulder at what Sunak and his supporters were doing. Yet she didn't fall because of their machinations, but because of her own incompetence and unwillingness to understand the art of the possible

THE VERDICT: 'DEEP STATE' OR DEEP INCOMPETENCE?

Since leaving the office of Prime Minister, Liz Truss, in her book *Ten Years to Save the West* and in a series of public interventions, speeches and interviews, has articulated her belief that the 'deep state', i.e. powerful administrative and establishment forces, was opposed to her dynamic vision and ultimately defeated her project. Defiant as ever, she wrote, 'The economic establishment used its huge and unrivalled influence over the markets to undermine confidence in the elected government, stir up political resistance and force it to change course.'[1] To her the blame lies wholly with others. Kwarteng acknowledges his responsibility. She does not. Nor would she accept blame or apologize when her 26,000 majority was turned into a 640-vote defeat by the voters of her South West Norfolk constituency in the July 2024 general election.

Truss at 10, throughout its ten chapters, suggests that her bold vision, and she herself, fell not because her championing of growth was wrong – it was the right prescription after fifteen years of stagnation since the global financial crisis – but because of her total failure to understand the nature of leadership and the job of being Prime Minister. Every successful leader, including her admired Margaret Thatcher and Ronald Reagan, knew that they could only move at the pace at which the system they inherited was able to respond and key stakeholders be persuaded.

One by one, she broke all of the 'ten rules' paradigm for successful premierships discussed in the preface. Once in No. 10, powerful institutional and political forces come into play underpinning all PMs, however deficient in the office. To fall so quickly was careless and eminently avoidable. Only breaking all ten rules so swiftly can explain it when my earlier methodology, as discussed in the preface, failed to do so.

1 Secure the power base

She never understood that she would need a secure platform on which to build her project. She assumed like Johnson that her base was the party membership in the country, rather than her own MPs, whom she made surprisingly little attempt to bond with or win over. Unlike Johnson, who won his own mandate at the 2019 general election, she never had her own popular mandate for her project, and a failure to achieve legitimacy for her radically different policies ultimately undid her.

2 Have a clear and realistic plan for government

She had a clear plan, which was intellectually and internally consistent. But she completely misjudged both its political acceptability – no democratic mandate for radical new policy – and the economic reality – which was not at all similar to when such policies had been 'the accepted wisdom' during the 1980s and 1990s.[2] In this respect, Truss did not understand that the past is not a set of prescriptive lessons. The circumstances of late 2022 were very different to those of the 1980s when growth averaged over 2.5 per cent per annum, and even of mid-2022 when the policies were being hatched, and required political and economic adaptations that embraced those realities.

3 Appoint the best Cabinet/team

Hiring and firing the right people is an essential requirement for the Prime Minister. She failed to appoint the most capable and balanced team to Cabinet or a sufficiently experienced team in No. 10 for all the stars who might have contributed (no Gove or Javid, and only bringing in Hunt and Shapps too late in the day). Nor did she lead her ministers and her staff in Downing Street in an inspiring manner that unified and brought out the best in them.

4 Command the big events

A key skill for all Prime Ministers is to judge their historic opportunity on coming to power, to seize on the major events that arise for all Prime Ministers and turn them to their advantage. She failed to comprehend the impact of the deterioration of the economy since the summer of 2022, to understand Britain's debt vulnerability and the need to reassure financial markets, to extract full benefit from her energy support intervention, and above all to rise to the occasion and turn the death of Queen Elizabeth II into a moment to unify and settle the nation.

5 Be credible and highly regarded abroad

The Prime Minister is Britain's senior political figure abroad. At best the PM can leverage the office to achieve significant global attention to enhance their position at home; at worst, they must avoid international ridicule, such as she brought upon herself. British Prime

Ministers traditionally crave respect from the White House, but she antagonized President Biden to her detriment, prompting the most humiliating presidential putdown in modern history. She authored no international initiatives while in office, could not build on the prominence she had achieved as Foreign Secretary over the war in Ukraine and her premiership was swamped by domestic concerns before she could make a positive mark abroad. The exception was her pathbreaking work as PM towards what became the Windsor Framework in Northern Ireland.

6 Learn how to be Prime Minister

The Prime Minister is never the finished article when they arrive at No. 10. They have to possess the character that allows them to *grow* in the job. Nothing prepares a politician to be PM. Ripping out the heart of No. 10 with no historically grounded idea about how to improve it did not help her. Truss missed out, too, on the most valuable single post for learning how to do the job: Leader of the Opposition. The best PMs learn to become storytellers and teachers, and learn to act with dignity and decorum. They must learn to be communicators. Prime Ministers are leaders of their party, the government and the nation. They have to lay aside tribalism once in No. 10 and reach out to new constituencies in all three domains. They must be inclusive and act with magnanimity. Truss never made this transition. She failed as leader of party, government and nation. To the end, she was too narrow.

7 Avoid major policy failures

Prime Ministers can survive policy failures before they reach No. 10, and minor mistakes once they arrive. But early and large mistakes in office, as she committed, are fatal. May damaged her options by insisting on a hard Brexit at the outset. Prime Ministers need one quality above all: *judgement*. Truss lacked it, and she hurtled the government with unnecessary haste into bold policy announcements that were premature and ill-conceived.

8 Maintain a reputation for economic competence

The Prime Minister is the First Lord of the Treasury, and their most elemental job as head of government is to ensure the country doesn't go broke, or risk going broke. As an accountant, it is doubly surprising that she failed to understand this. She singly failed to understand the importance of gaining the trust and respect of key economic stakeholders. She displayed astonishing ignorance about how markets work. Even when warning lights were flashing crazily, she failed to heed them and take remedial action early enough.

9 Avoid U-turns

Nothing undermines confidence in a leader more than a U-turn on the central planks of their fundamental policy. If the leader has to execute one, they have to be brave enough to take the blame themselves, not pin it on others and pretend it hasn't happened, or that they were not themselves responsible.

10 Retain the confidence of the party

Since the office emerged in 1721, the Prime Minister owes their continuation in office to their base in Parliament. Lose it, and they are doomed. She never understood that a Prime Minister can never take their MPs for granted, especially necessary given she had so few allies and she was not their first choice in the leadership election. The fracking shambles destroyed what little credibility she had left. By the evening of Wednesday 19 October 2022 she had alienated her MPs to such an extent that nobody even bothered to count the number of letters of no confidence, because they had so far exceeded the 15 per cent threshold.

Was the 'deep state' to blame for her precipitous fall?

The Bank of England sale of gilts on the day of the Mini-Budget and the MPC's interest rate rise just before it might have been anticipated, but she was responsible for the failure to establish a better line between No. 10 and the Bank that would have alerted her and ameliorated the risk. The Treasury found it difficult to land warnings before the fiscal event. Chopping out its top man just before though was an act of extraordinary self-harm, from which Truss and Kwarteng were ultimately the losers. There was no coordinated 'deep state' attempt to unseat her and defeat her project. A state apparatus weakened by the Tories certainly did not perform at its peak, and it was down to officials, in No. 10, the Cabinet Office and the Treasury, to pull the country out of a nosedive that would have put the national finances in the greatest peril since the 1976 IMF Crisis.

Robert Peston has pointed the finger of blame in particular at the Bank of England's 'incompetence' for undermining the Truss project.[3] 'The Bank did not identify the risk to financial stability from LDI and neutralize it before any shock materialized – whether from Truss or elsewhere – and it did not communicate this potential risk to the Treasury for Truss and Kwarteng to be aware in their Mini-Budget planning,' he said later. He added that it was 'the structure and the timing of the end of the bailout, and the fear in Whitehall that its end would see gilt prices tank again without a complete reversal of the Mini-Budget that triggered both Kwarteng's sacking and Truss's resignation.'[4] Jon Moynihan has argued similarly the lion's share of the blame should go to the Bank of England. Do they protest too much?

The evidence in this book points to a far more nuanced conclusion. Ultimately, in any disaster, blame is always multi-causal. But in the British system primary responsibility must always rest on the Prime Minister and Chancellor and particularly when, as here, they deliberately kicked away the struts of the financial framework that in the past provided stability and predictability. She cannot escape the primary blame, nor Kwarteng for not stopping her.

The Truss premiership was expensive. The best Prime Ministers enhance the country and husband its standing. But Britain's reputation abroad suffered, and has taken time to recover. The British economy suffered, and many individuals and companies are still worse off because of what happened, as David Smith has shown, engendering a lasting bitterness. Mortgage approvals fell and rates rose. The case for free-market policies suffered because of the way in which the programme was rolled out: the future is likely to be more statist and interventionist, not less. The standing of the OBR was boosted and tax burden on high earners increased, two of the many other unintended consequences. The Conservative Party suffered directly in the July 2024 general election, with 'Partygate' under Johnson and the mini-budget under Truss prompting the biggest falls in Tory support, according to John Curtice. The Party's long-standing reputation for economic competence and cool-headed pragmatism had been severely tested since 2016, but the final thread was snapped by Liz Truss. The British state suffered from her trashing of its institutions and personnel hard on the heels of Johnson's systematic undermining of them.

To amend F. Scott Fitzgerald in *The Great Gatsby*, 'they were careless people, Boris and Liz – they smashed up things and creatures and then retreated back into their money, reveries or their vast carelessness or whatever it was that kept them together, and let other people clean up the mess that they had made'.[5] They were both gifted people with special talents and opportunities: but they spectacularly squandered them.

Britain has had a procession of underperforming Prime Ministers. They all fell short in some of the key rules of good premiership. Johnson, the subject of the previous book in the series, and now Truss, comfortably outdid them all in their wilful inability to rise to the requirement of thoughtful and responsible stewardship the job demands. One outcome of her premiership may be a cautionary tale. Robert Peel and Ramsay MacDonald taught future Conservative and Labour leaders not to risk splitting their party. She perhaps will teach them not to repeat her basic errors, not to 'do a Liz Truss' by breaking all ten rules of good premiership. In that way, if no other, perhaps her forty-nine days might at least have a gilt lining.

ACKNOWLEDGEMENTS

This book would never have happened without the insights and kindness of very large numbers of people, most of whom are anonymous. But you know who you are, and we hope you know how grateful we are.

It was written with the smallest team of any of the eight books in the series on recently departed Prime Ministers. My greatest thanks are due to Jonathan Meakin, with whom I have collaborated on over ten books, and whose intellect, historical knowledge and efficiency are without parallel. We were joined on this project late last year by Luca Boot, who worked tirelessly for over six months. They have been brilliant to work with, professionally and socially.

The methodology has remained broadly the same over the eight books since the one on John Major. We discuss the 'architecture' together, i.e., how many 'floors' (chapters) and how many 'rooms' (subheadings) on each floor. We then 'see' the book on the table between us. I then conduct the interviews, over 120 in this case. The team produces the briefings for each chapter, integrating these with other published and documentary material, and then I have the easy and fun part, writing the book. The book is then read over several times by expert witnesses for fairness and accuracy.

This book more than any other in the series has benefited from voluminous contemporary documents, some of which had to be sourced opaquely.

We were blessed with Atlantic as our publisher. Writing and publishing books on contemporary history takes the craft to an altogether different level of complexity. We reached even higher levels in this book. Particular thanks are due to the brilliant team: editor James Pulford, copy-editor Tamsin Shelton, agent Matthew Cole and pre-press director Emma Heyworth-Dunn. Thanks also to Martin Soames at SMB for his expertise and advice.

Thank you to our diligent early readers, most of whom remained anonymous. Stuart Ball, Tom Egerton, Bill Jones, John Jefferies and Lewis Baston can be mentioned though by name. We would like to thank fellow historians for their guidance and support, in particular Tim Bale, John Bew and Charles Moore.

We are so grateful for the work of other writers. Biographical works by Harry Cole and James Heale and by Ben Riley-Smith were hugely important in laying the groundwork. As always, credit to Tim Shipman, the Boswell of Brexit, for his outstanding insights.

With thanks to the club of co-authors and senior researchers on earlier PM books, who have always been ready to offer help: Chris Ballinger, Peter Snowdon, Daniel Collings, Guy Lodge, Kunal Khatri, Illias Thoms, Raymond Newell and Tom Egerton.

Particular thanks to my outstanding Institute for Government colleagues Hannah White, Alex Thomas, Emma Norris, Jordan Urban and Rhys Clyne.

The books have all been boosted by very fine reporting and commentary in the media. We also spoke to a number of people in political broadcasting. We do not think you would appreciate it if we thanked you by name here, so instead we thank you silently.

To all the anonymous and meticulous writers for Wikipedia, thank you. We guess that more authors rely on your work than is acknowledged.

This book was written when I was also the Head in extraordinary circumstances at Epsom College. My thanks go to senior team colleagues, in particular Paul Williams, Helen Keevill, Marisa Bosa, Becky Brown, Nick Russell, Mark Tobin, Richard Alton and Paul Ratcliffe; my history and politics colleagues, including Andy Bustard, James Dunn and Luke Fisher; governors, in particular Alastair Wells and Alex Russell; and incomparable EA Sophie Lawrence. Determined that I would not in any way let my attention on the school – its students, staff and parents – suffer from my writing, I invaded every spare moment to find the time to work on the book. It meant I have not been very good or present company for the last eleven months, so I would particularly like to thank my life-enhancing wife Sarah for her forbearance, and my children Jessica, Susie and Adam who saw less of their father than they should have done. In my family, friends and colleagues, my life has been truly blessed.

Anthony Seldon
July 2024

NOTES

PREFACE

1 https://www.newstatesman.com/
politics/uk-politics/2022/08/why-
liz-truss-will-fail

INTRODUCTION

1 For an exploration of this
fascinating topic see Steve
Richards, *The Prime Ministers We
Never Had: Success and Failure
from Butler to Corbyn*, London,
Atlantic Books, 2021.

2 Interview, Liz Truss.

3 Some sources record Tambroni's
tenure as 123 days. Either way,
even the shortest-serving Prime
Minister of the Italian Republic
outlasted the shortest-serving
British one.

4 https://treasury.gov.au/
publication/economic-roundup-
issue-4-2011/economic-roundup-
issue-4-2011/arthur-fadden-
treasurer-in-a-golden-age

5 Anthony Seldon with Jonathan
Meakin and Illias Thoms, *The
Impossible Office?: The History
of the British Prime Minister*,
Cambridge, Cambridge

University Press, 2021,
pp. 92–4.

6 William Hague, *Pitt the Younger*,
London, Harper Perennial, 2005,
p. 160.

7 Ibid., p. 173.

8 Margot Asquith, *The
Autobiography of Margot Asquith*,
London, Butterworth, 1922,
p. 75.

9 Harry Cole and James Heale, *Out
of the Blue: The Inside Story of the
Unexpected Rise and Rapid Fall of
Liz Truss*, London, HarperCollins,
p. 224.

10 John Colville, *The Fringes of
Power: Downing Street Diaries
1940–1955*, Volume 2,
Sevenoaks, Sceptre Publishing,
1986–87, p. 392.

11 Robert Rhodes James, *Anthony
Eden*, London, Weidenfeld &
Nicolson, 1986, p. 597.

12 Lord Owen, 'The effect of
Prime Minister Anthony Eden's
illness on his decision-making
during the Suez crisis', *QJM: An
International Journal of Medicine*,
Volume 98, Issue 6, June 2005,
pp. 387–402.

13 Gill Bennett, *The Zinoviev Letter
of 1924: A Most Extraordinary
and Mysterious Business*, London,

Foreign & Commonwealth
Office, 1999, pp. 91–2.

14 https://www.elizabethtruss.com/
news/speech-cpac-2024

15 Liz Truss, *Ten Years to Save the
West: Lessons from the Only
Conservative in the Room*,
London, Biteback Publishing,
2024, p. 252.

16 https://open.spotify.com/episode/
0hOsqQXTJycO9mKXLrvk7O

1: SECURE THE POWER BASE

1 Cole and Heale, *Out of the Blue*,
p. 236.

2 Ibid., p. 239.

3 Interview, Sophie Jarvis.

4 https://www.telegraph.co.uk/
politics/2022/07/10/liz-truss-
would-cut-taxes-day-one-prime-
minister

5 Interview, Ranil Jayawardena.

6 https://www.theguardian.com/
politics/2022/jul/12/jacob-rees-
mogg-and-nadine-dorries-back-
liz-truss-for-tory-leadership

7 https://conservativehome.com/
2022/07/12/our-latest-next-tory-
leader-survey-mordaunt-leads-
badenoch-by-under-ten-votes-in-
over-eight-hundred

8 https://www.telegraph.co.uk/
politics/2022/09/25/ben-wallace-
take-everything-putin-does-
seriously-man-without

9 https://www.theguardian.
com/politics/live/2022/jul/13/
conservative-leadership-race-
penny-mordaunt-rishi-sunak-liz-
truss-uk-politics-latest-live

10 https://www.theguardian.com/
politics/2022/jul/14/lost-to-

spam-truss-had-only-one-thing-
to-offer-it-was-still-the-convict

11 https://www.theguardian.com/
uk-news/2022/jul/09/revealed-
officials-raised-flag-over-nadim-
zahawis-tax-affairs-before-he-was-
appointed-chancellor

12 https://www.theguardian.com/
uk-news/2023/jan/20/nadhim-
zahawi-agreed-on-penalty-to-
settle-tax-bill-worth-millions

13 https://www.thetimes.com/uk/
politics/article/liz-truss-has-
the-experience-to-stand-up-for-
britain-wcrdqp6d2

14 https://www.independent.co.uk/
voices/tory-leadership-debate-liz-
truss-b2124506.html

15 'Leaked documents call Penny
Mordaunt's gender self-ID claims
into question', *The Sunday Times*,
17 July 2022.

16 https://www.independent.co.uk/
news/uk/anne-marie-trevelyan-
penny-mordaunt-b2125465.html

17 https://www.theguardian.com/
politics/2022/jul/14/david-
frost-grave-reservations-penny-
mordaunt-tory-leader

18 Interview, Jason Stein.

19 Interview, Jake Berry.
20 Interview, Penny Mordaunt.
21 Interview, Gavin Williamson.
22 https://metro.co.uk/2022/07/20/liz-truss-says-shes-ready-to-hit-the-ground-but-not-running-17038078. https://www.theguardian.com/politics/2022/jul/20/rishi-sunak-penny-mordaunt-liz-truss-final-round-tory-leadership-race
23 https://www.theguardian.com/politics/2022/jul/08/tory-members-over-60-white-male-choice-of-leader
24 https://www.independent.co.uk/voices/tory-leadership-debate-liz-truss-b2124506.html
25 https://www.theguardian.com/politics/live/2022/jul/21/tory-leadership-race-liz-truss-rishi-sunak-latest-politics-live?filterKeyEvents=false&page=with:block-62d988cf8f081aa0b140574c#block-62d988cf8f081aa0b140574c
26 https://www.theguardian.com/politics/2022/jul/23/thatcher-ministers-liz-truss-tax-cut-plans-patten-lamont-rifkind
27 https://www.theguardian.com/politics/2022/jul/23/rishi-sunak-vows-uk-crisis-footing-becomes-pm
28 Interview, Mark Fullbrook.
29 https://www.youtube.com/watch?v=mNTv06tpuSw
30 https://www.thetimes.co.uk/article/kemi-badenoch-lizz-truss-is-a-maverick-who-gets-things-done-x29d690tf
31 Interview, Mark Fullbrook.
32 https://www.theguardian.com/politics/2022/aug/19/gove-backs-sunak-and-says-truss-taking-holiday-from-reality
33 https://www.telegraph.co.uk/politics/2022/08/09/first-tory-mp-switches-support-rishi-sunak-liz-truss-leadership. https://www.telegraph.co.uk/news/2022/08/12/first-cabinet-minister-switches-support-rishi-sunak-liz-truss
34 https://www.theguardian.com/uk-news/2022/aug/13/poll-of-tory-members-gives-liz-truss-22-point-lead-to-be-next-prime-minister
35 https://www.theguardian.com/politics/2022/aug/01/liz-truss-plan-to-cut-11bn-in-whitehall-waste-ludicrous
36 Cole and Heale, *Out of the Blue*, p. 261.
37 https://www.bbc.co.uk/news/uk-politics-17815769
38 https://www.dailymail.co.uk/debate/article-11065397/I-dont-want-party-fooled-appearances-way-Cabinet-writes-NADINE-DORRIES.html
39 Interview, Jason Stein.
40 Interview, Mark Fullbrook.
41 https://www.theguardian.com/politics/2022/sep/03/the-more-tory-voters-see-of-liz-truss-the-less-they-like-her-polls-show
42 Interview, Asa Bennett.
43 Anthony Seldon, *Major: A Political Life*, London, Weidenfeld & Nicolson, 1997, pp. 117–28.
44 Anthony Seldon and Raymond Newell, *Johnson at 10*, London, Atlantic, 2024, pp. 564–8.
45 Interview, Michael Gove.

2: HAVE A CLEAR AND REALISTIC PLAN FOR GOVERNMENT

1 https://www.telegraph.co.uk/news/2022/09/03/suspect-old-friend-liz-truss-will-radical-british-prime-minister

2 For more discussion of this topic see Seldon et al., *The Impossible Office?*

3 https://www.telegraph.co.uk/politics/2022/09/05/liz-truss-speech-full-boris-johnson-rishi-sunak-deliver

4 Ben Pimlott, *Harold Wilson*, London, HarperCollins, 1992, p. 618.

5 https://www.lrb.co.uk/the-paper/v15/n02/peter-clarke/lawson-s-case

6 https://www.telegraph.co.uk/news/2022/09/03/suspect-old-friend-liz-truss-will-radical-british-prime-minister

7 For a detailed look at the thinking behind the Truss project see Jeremy Cliffe, 'Liz Truss and the Rise of the Libertarian Right', *New Statesman*, 28 September 2022, https://www.newstatesman.com/politics/conservatives/2022/09/liz-truss-rise-market-millennials-free-market-ideology

8 Letter, *The Times*, 8 August 1980.

9 https://clintonwhitehouse4.archives.gov/WH/New/other/sotu.html

10 Interview, Liz Truss.

11 Ibid.

12 Interview, Kwasi Kwarteng.

13 Interview, Liz Truss.

14 Kwasi Kwarteng, *War and Gold: A Five-Hundred-Year History of Empires, Adventures and Debt*, London, Bloomsbury, 2014.

15 Interview, Kwasi Kwarteng.

16 Interview, Shabbir Merali.

17 Interview.

18 https://dominiccummings.substack.com/p/snippets-8-the-human-handgrenade

19 Anthony Seldon and Peter Snowdon, *Cameron at 10*, London, William Collins, 2015, p. 406.

20 Interview, Adam Jones.

21 Interview, Liz Truss.

22 Anthony Seldon, *May at 10*, London, Biteback Publishing, 2019, p. 377.

23 https://www.telegraph.co.uk/politics/2018/06/25/britain-must-start-up-state-chief-disruptor/

24 https://www.gov.uk/government/speeches/chief-secretary-to-the-treasury-liz-truss-speech-to-the-london-school-of-economics

25 Interview, Philip Hammond.

26 Ibid.

27 Interview, Shabbir Merali.

28 https://www.gov.uk/government/speeches/chief-secretary-to-the-treasury-liz-truss-speech-to-the-london-school-of-economics

29 https://www.theguardian.com/politics/2018/jun/21/williamson-losing-fight-with-treasury-for-rise-in-defence-spending

30 https://www.gov.uk/government/speeches/chief-secretary-to-the-treasury-liz-truss-speech-to-the-london-school-of-economics

31 https://www.gov.uk/government/ speeches/foreign-secretary-liz-truss-building-the-network-of-liberty

32 Interview, Adam Jones.

33 https://www.gov.uk/government/ speeches/international-trade-dinner-speech

34 Interview, Adam Jones.

35 Interview, Kwasi Kwarteng.

36 Interview, Philip Hammond.

37 Interview, Charles Moore.

38 Interview, Philip Hammond.

39 https://www.theatlantic.com/ international/archive/2022/08/ tory-leadership-contest-thatcher-truss-sunak/671014

40 Richard Cockett, *Thinking the Unthinkable: Think-tanks and the Economic Counter-revolution, 1931–1983*, London, HarperCollins, 1995. https:// www.newstatesman.com/politics/ conservatives/2022/09/liz-truss-rise-market-millennials-free-market-ideology

41 Correspondence with the author, Jamie Hope, 20 March 2024.

42 Interview, Liz Truss.

43 https://www.telegraph.co.uk/ news/2022/09/03/suspect-old-friend-liz-truss-will-radical-british-prime-minister

44 Interview, Jason Stein.

45 https://www.bbc.co.uk/news/uk-politics-63442813

46 Interview, Jason Stein.

47 Interview, Simon Clarke.

48 Interview, Liz Truss.

49 https://www.ons.gov.uk/ economy/governmentpublic sectorandtaxes/publicspending/ bulletins/ukgovernmentdebtand

deficitforeurostatmaast/september 2022

50 https://www.theguardian.com/ politics/2022/may/27/rishi-sunaks-tax-rises-three-of-the-biggest-examined

51 Ben Riley-Smith, *The Right to Rule: Thirteen Years, Five Prime Ministers and the Implosion of the Tories*, London, John Murray, 2023, p. 283.

52 https://www.conservatives.com/ our-plan/conservative-party-manifesto-2019

53 Interview, Liz Truss.

54 Interview, Ranil Jayawardena.

55 Interview, Chris Philp.

56 Interview, Kwasi Kwarteng.

57 https://www.ft.com/content/ 736a695d-61f6-4e84-a567-fb92ed2a3dca

58 Interview, Gerard Lyons.

59 https://www.theguardian.com/ politics/2022/aug/05/truss-irresponsible-for-threatening-to-review-bank-of-england-remit

60 https://www.gov.uk/government/ news/chancellor-kwasi-kwarteng-sets-out-economic-priorities-in-first-meeting-with-market-leaders

61 https://thecritic.co.uk/issues/ december-january-2023/how-did-it-all-go-so-wrong-for-liz-truss/

62 Interview, Alex Boyd.

63 https://commonslibrary. parliament.uk/research-briefings/ cbp-9491

64 Cole and Heale, *Out of the Blue*, p. 270.

65 https://www.thesun.co.uk/ money/19437407/household-bills-soar-energy-food-mortgage

66 https://www.ft.com/content/
0d4e8e8c-a9f5-409b-86b8-
884304ce0568
67 https://www.telegraph.co.uk/
news/2022/09/21/liz-truss-

rip-green-planning-laws-bid-
kickstart-housebuilding
68 Interview, Liz Truss.

3: APPOINT THE BEST CABINET/TEAM

1 Andrew Blick in Foreword to George Jones, *The Power of the Prime Minister: 50 Years on*, London, The Constitution Society, 2016, p. 7.
2 Hannis Taylor, *The Origin and Growth of the English Constitution: Part Two*, Cambridge, Cambridge University Press, 1900, p. 462.
3 For further discussion of this matter see Anthony Seldon and Jonathan Meakin, *The Cabinet Office, 1916–2016: The Birth of Modern Government*, London, Biteback Publishing, 2016, pp. 1–16.
4 Interview, Kwasi Kwarteng.
5 Interview, Liz Truss.
6 Interview, Mark Fullbrook.
7 Interview, Jason Stein.
8 Interview, Daniel Johnson.
9 Interview, Adam Jones.
10 Interview, Penny Mordaunt.
11 https://www.lbc.co.uk/radio/presenters/andrew-marr/andrew-marr-truss-pm-weaker-cabinet-allies
12 https://twitter.com/GavinBarwell/status/1567045090702499840
13 https://www.theguardian.com/politics/2023/sep/01/shes-totally-lost-it-inside-story-of-the-unravelling-of-liz-trusss-premiership
14 Interview, Wendy Morton.
15 Interview, Liz Truss.
16 https://www.spectator.co.uk/article/liz-truss-s-plan-to-shake-up-downing-street
17 Seldon et al., *The Impossible Office?*, pp. 165–6.
18 Cole and Heale, *Out of the Blue*, p. 276.
19 Truss, *Ten Years to Save the West*, p. 206.
20 https://www.ft.com/content/4761449a-6353-4bf2-aa45-dfeefbbed519
21 https://conservativehome.com/2022/09/08/why-trusss-sweeping-reorganisation-of-the-downing-street-operation-could-spell-trouble-for-her
22 https://reaction.life/why-tom-scholar-of-the-treasury-was-sacked
23 https://www.telegraph.co.uk/business/2022/08/13/meet-mandarin-liz-trusss-sights-takes-treasury-orthodoxy
24 Interview, Liz Truss.
25 Interview, Kwasi Kwarteng.
26 https://www.telegraph.co.uk/business/2022/08/13/meet-mandarin-liz-trusss-sights-takes-treasury-orthodoxy
27 Interview, Mark Fullbrook.
28 Interview, Kwasi Kwarteng.
29 Ibid.
30 https://www.thetimes.co.uk/article/pm-was-right-to-sack-tom-scholar-from-the-treasury-lldjlngxj

31 https://www.theguardian.com/ politics/2022/sep/14/kwasi- kwarteng-sacking-tom-scholar- marks-shift-away-from-impartial- advice

32 https://twitter.com/ nickmacpherson2/status/ 1567907661584236545

33 https://www.bbc.co.uk/news/uk- politics-62869880

4: COMMAND THE BIG EVENTS

1 http://news.bbc.co.uk/onthisday/ hi/dates/stories/january/10/ newsid_2518000/2518957.stm

2 https://www.spectator.co.uk/ article/liz-truss-my-part-in-her- downfall

3 https://www.ft.com/content/6f48 f0ca-a6d7-11e9-b6ee-3cdf3174eb 89c

4 https://www.gov.uk/government/ statistics/public-spending- statistics-release-november-2022/ public-spending-statistics- november-2022. See section 3.1.

5 Interview, Kwasi Kwarteng.

6 Ibid.

7 https://heywoodquarterly.com/ the-mysteries-of-the-golden- triangle/

8 Interview, Liz Truss.

9 Interview, Clare Evans.

10 https://www.gov.uk/government/ speeches/prime-minister-liz- trusss-statement-6-september- 2022

11 https://www.navylookout.com/ royal-navy-nuclear-deterrent- submarines-conducting- increasingly-long-patrols

12 https://hansard.parliament.uk/ commons/2022-09-07/debates/ DC1207A6-90E7-424D-A507- 320A4E1D92EE/PrimeMinister

13 https://www.spectator.co.uk/ article/liz-truss-s-first-pmqs-felt- like-a-dress-rehearsal

14 https://www.thetimes.co.uk/ article/who-won-pmqs-liz-truss- keir-starmer-7fwmql57c

15 https://www.theguardian.com/ politics/live/2022/sep/07/liz- truss-cabinet-news-pm-therese- coffey-uk-politics-live?page= with:block-6318ca758f08aab4f 5b4cf67&filterKeyEvents=false# liveblog-navigation

16 https://www.gov.uk/government/ speeches/pm-liz-trusss-opening- speech-on-the-energy-policy- debate

17 https://hansard.parliament. uk/Commons/2022-09-08/ debates/25d439a2-1946- 4793-8022-e2a4ba8d3644/ CommonsChamber

18 Paul Bolton and Iona Stewart, *Domestic Energy Prices*, House of Commons Library, 1 March 2024, p. 9. See also 'Economic and Fiscal Outlook', Office for Budget Responsibility, March 2023, p. 57.

19 https://www.theguardian.com/ uk-news/2022/sep/08/elizabeth- ii-enjoyed-robust-health- throughout-long-reign

20 Interview, Nadhim Zahawi.

21 Ibid.

22 https://it.usembassy.gov/readout- of-the-presidents-call-with-allies- and-partners-2

23 https://www.gbnews.com/royal/ queen-news-queen-elizabeth-ii- liz-truss-balmoral

24 https://www.gov.uk/govern ment/speeches/prime-ministers- statement-on-the-death-of-her- majesty-queen-elizabeth-ii

25 https://www.independent.co. uk/tv/news/liz-truss-monarchy- republicanism-abolish-b2128076. html

26 https://www.theguardian.com/ uk-news/2022/sep/11/liz-truss- not-accompanying-king-charles- on-uk-tour-says-no-10

27 https://hansard.parliament.uk/ commons/2022-09-09/debates/

7E1BA553-600D-41B4-BAB9- 849A02B254C3/TributesToHer LateMajestyTheQueen

28 https://privycouncil.independent. gov.uk/privy-council/the-acces sion-council

29 Interview, Penny Mordaunt.

30 Ibid.

31 Robert Hardman, *Charles III: New King, New Court. The Inside Story*, London, Macmillan, 2024, p. 110.

32 'The Conduct of Sir Gavin Williamson MP', Independent Expert Panel, House of Commons, 4 September 2023, pp. 8–9.

5: BE CREDIBLE AND HIGHLY REGARDED ABROAD

1 https://www.theguardian.com/ global-development/2022/may/ 16/uk-aid-strategy-liz-truss- double-whammy-world-poor

2 https://www.gov.uk/government/ speeches/foreign-secretary-gives- keynote-speech-in-ukraine-17- february-2022

3 https://www.theguardian.com/ politics/2022/feb/12/liz-truss- instagram-diplomacy-five-photos- a-day-foreign-secretary-flickr

4 https://www.rferl.org/a/russia- ukraine-invasion-predictions- wrong-intelligence/32275740. html

5 https://www.ft.com/content/ 315346dc-e1bd-485c-865b- 979297f3fcf5

6 https://www.thetimes.co.uk/ article/liz-truss-will-declare-china- an-official-threat-for-the-first- time-3bk7jwqjx

7 Interview, Liz Truss.

8 Frost's resignation letter does not give a clear reason for his resignation, other than that it had been agreed that he'd leave in January and that the news had leaked. https://www.gov.uk/ government/publications/lord- frosts-resignation-letter-and-the- prime-ministers-response

9 https://www.telegraph.co.uk/ news/2022/03/26/liz-truss-right- now-differences-eu-seem-lot- smaller

10 https://commonslibrary. parliament.uk/research-briefings/ cbp-9560

11 Christopher Meyer, *DC Confidential: The Controversial Memoirs of Britain's Ambassador to the US at the Time of 9/11 and the Iraq War*, London, Weidenfeld & Nicolson, 2005, p. 1.

12 https://www.gov.uk/government/ publications/the-windsor- framework

13 https://twitter.com/JoeBiden/
status/1306334039557586944
14 https://www.forbes.com/sites/
roberthart/2022/09/20/they-
wouldnt-have-sat-me-back-there-
trump-scoffs-at-bidens-seating-
position-at-queens-funeral/
15 https://twitter.com/
POTUS/status/
1572218921347866624?lang=en
16 https://www.whitehouse.gov/
briefing-room/speeches-remarks/
2022/09/21/remarks-by-
president-biden-and-prime-
minister-liz-truss-of-the-united-
kingdom-before-bilateral-meeting
17 https://www.theguardian.com/
global/2022/oct/16/joe-biden-
liz-truss-tax-cuts-a-mistake-and-i-

wasnt-the-only-one-who-thought-
so
18 Interview, Kim Darroch.
19 Interview, Liz Truss.
20 https://www.politico.eu/article/
liz-truss-uk-seeks-her-own-
path-back-to-europe. https://
www.politeia.co.uk/macrons-
european-political-community-
and-britains-role-in-it. https://
ukandeu.ac.uk/explainers/the-
european-political-community
21 https://www.gov.uk/government/
news/g7-leaders-joint-statement-
on-ukraine-11-october-2022
22 Seldon and Newell, *Johnson at 10*,
p. 564.
23 https://www.bbc.co.uk/news/uk-
politics-62682448

6: LEARN HOW TO BE PRIME MINISTER

1 Dennis Kavanagh and Anthony
Seldon, *The Powers Behind the
Prime Minister: The Hidden
Influence of Number 10*, London,
HarperCollins, 1999, p. 128.
2 Truss, *Ten Years to Save the West*,
p. 203.
3 Ibid., pp. 268, 269.

4 Interview, Philip Hammond.
5 https://www.spectator.co.uk/
article/mark-field-praises-liz-truss
6 Interview, Jason Stein.
7 Interview, Mark Fullbrook.
8 Interview, Kwasi Kwarteng.
9 Interview, Penny Mordaunt.
10 Interview, Philip Hammond.

7: AVOID MAJOR POLICY FAILURES

1 Truss, *Ten Years to Save the West*,
pp. 236, 239.
2 Interview, Mark Fullbrook.
3 https://www.pwc.co.uk/services/
economics/insights/uk-economic-
outlook/september-2022.html
4 https://www.pwc.co.uk/
economic-services/ukeo/ukeo-
september-2022.pdf, p. 4.
5 Interview, Kwasi Kwarteng.
6 https://obr.uk/efo/economic-and-
fiscal-outlook-march-2022

7 https://www.ons.gov.uk/economy/
governmentpublicsectorandtaxes/
publicsectorfinance/bulletins/
publicsectorfinances/
september2022
8 https://obr.uk/docs/dlm_uploads/
Letter_to_TSC_Potential_
Emergency_Budget.pdf
9 https://committees.parliament.
uk/committee/158/treasury-
committee/news/173401/
bank-of-england-confirms-details-

of-emergency-bond-buying-in-correspondence-with-treasury-committee/

10 https://www.gov.uk/government/speeches/the-growth-plan-2022-speech

11 'The Growth Plan 2022', HM Treasury, September 2022, p. 25.

12 Ibid., p. 6.

13 https://www.gov.uk/government/speeches/the-growth-plan-2022-speech

14 Truss, *Ten Years to Save the West*, p. 242.

15 https://ifs.org.uk/articles/mini-budget-response

16 https://www.dailymail.co.uk/debate/article-11244431/ALEX-BRUMMER-Kwasi-Kwarteng-delivers-genuine-Tory-Budget-spells-end-Treasury-doomsters.html

17 https://www.telegraph.co.uk/news/2022/09/23/kwasi-kwartengs-budget-moment-history-will-radically-transform

18 https://hansard.parliament.uk/commons/2022-09-23/debates/6F82FA4B-DB6B-4E89-BA39-4ABEA1045ABF/TheGrowthPlan

19 https://x.com/guardian/status/1573416993545502730

20 https://www.ft.com/content/05a3c185-2e93-484f-bc56-380186230a1f

21 https://www.economist.com/leaders/2022/09/22/liz-trusss-selective-reaganomics-wont-work

22 https://www.theguardian.com/uk-news/2022/sep/23/kwarteng-accused-of-reckless-mini-budget-for-the-rich-as-pound-crashes

23 https://www.bankofengland.co.uk/-/media/boe/files/letter/2022/october/letter-from-jon-cunliffe-ldi-5-october-2022

24 *Sunday with Laura Kuenssberg*, BBC1, 25 September 2022.

25 Interview, Kwasi Kwarteng.

26 https://www.gov.uk/government/news/update-on-growth-plan-implementation

27 https://www.bankofengland.co.uk/news/2022/september/statement-from-the-governor-of-the-boe

28 https://www.bbc.co.uk/news/business-63041679

29 https://www.bbc.co.uk/news/business-63051702

30 Seldon, *Blair Unbound*, p. 13.

31 https://www.reuters.com/markets/europe/what-is-ldi-liability-driven-investment-strategy-explained-2022-10-04/

32 https://www.bankofengland.co.uk/-/media/boe/files/letter/2022/october/letter-from-jon-cunliffe-ldi-5-october-2022

33 https://www.bankofengland.co.uk/markets/market-notices/2022/september/apf-gilt-sales-22-september

34 Interview, Liz Truss. See also Truss, *Ten Years to Save the West*, p. 247.

35 https://www.bankofengland.co.uk/news/2022/september/bank-of-england-announces-gilt-market-operation

36 https://www.bankofengland.co.uk/quarterly-bulletin/2023/2023/financial-stability-buy-sell-tools-a-gilt-market-case-study

37 Ibid.

38 https://www.bankofengland.co.uk/speech/2022/october/current-

monetary-policy-opening-remarks-by-jonathan-haskel

39 https://www.bbc.co.uk/sounds/play/p0d3flmh. See also https://www.dailyrecord.co.uk/news/politics/liz-truss-bbc-radio-economy-28109436

40 https://labourlist.org/2022/09/british-power-to-the-british-people-starmers-2022-conference-speech

41 https://yougov.co.uk/politics/articles/43901-voting-intention-con-21-lab-54-28-29-sep-2022

42 https://www.gov.uk/government/news/readout-of-the-prime-minister-and-chancellors-meeting-with-the-obr

43 Cole and Heale, *Out of the Blue*, p. 289.

44 Interview, Charlie Bean.

45 https://www.ons.gov.uk/economy/inflationandpriceindices/bulletins/consumerpriceinflation/august2022. https://www.niesr.ac.uk/publications/inflation-fall-still-record-high?type=cpi-trackers

46 https://www.bbc.co.uk/news/business-62990423

47 https://www.ons.gov.uk/economy/governmentpublicsectorandtaxes/publicsectorfinance/bulletins/publicsectorfinances/august2022

8: MAINTAIN A REPUTATION FOR ECONOMIC COMPETENCE

1 https://www.belfasttelegraph.co.uk/news/politics/former-ni-secretary-slams-his-own-partys-mini-budget-citing-huge-tax-cut-for-the-very-rich/42012998.html

2 https://www.theguardian.com/politics/2022/oct/02/michael-gove-says-liz-trusss-tax-cut-plans-not-conservative

3 https://www.bbc.co.uk/news/uk-politics-63110541

4 Interview, Michael Gove.

5 Cole and Heale, *Out of the Blue*, pp. 291–2.

6 Ibid., p. 292.

7 https://www.theguardian.com/global/2022/oct/03/night-of-the-hurried-u-turn-how-truss-and-kwarteng-dumped-their-tax-cut

8 https://www.thetimes.co.uk/article/cabinet-split-over-mad-real-terms-cuts-to-benefits-mtspvcqfm

9 https://www.theguardian.com/politics/2022/oct/03/tory-mps-plot-to-avert-welfare-squeeze-after-u-turn-on-top-rate-of-tax-kwasi-kwarteng

10 Ibid.

11 https://conservativehome.com/2022/10/03/we-will-get-britain-moving-kwartengs-conference-speech-full-text

12 https://www.theguardian.com/politics/2022/oct/03/tory-mps-plot-to-avert-welfare-squeeze-after-u-turn-on-top-rate-of-tax-kwasi-kwarteng

13 https://www.bbc.co.uk/sounds/play/p0d49mkt

14 Interview, Jake Berry.

15 https://www.newstatesman.com/politics/conservatives/2022/10/conservative-party-conference-2022-birmingham-fear-loathing

16 https://www.ft.com/content/8dd2b237-c47e-489d-aeae-639aafeeb6c8

17 https://unherd.com/2022/10/is-truss-the-worst-pm-in-history

18 Seldon, *Major*, pp. 572–90.

19 Interview, Gavin Williamson.

20 Riley-Smith, *The Right to Rule*, p. 296.

21 https://www.spectator.co.uk/article/full-text-liz-truss-s-tory-conference-speech

22 https://www.theguardian.com/world/2022/oct/06/liz-truss-european-political-community-meeting-prague

23 https://www.resolutionfoundation.org/publications/blowing-the-budget

24 https://www.independent.co.uk/news/uk/liz-truss-lucy-bronze-olaf-scholz-leah-williamson-sarina-wiegman-b2199457.html

25 Interview, Liz Truss.

26 Interview, Kwasi Kwarteng.

27 Correspondence with the author, Andrew Griffith, 28 April 2024.

28 https://www.reuters.com/markets/europe/bank-england-buy-inflation-linked-uk-gilts-2022-10-11

29 https://www.ft.com/content/87a5b7bf-6786-427f-89d6-96b736dcb814

30 https://hansard.parliament.uk/commons/2022-10-12/debates/A4F24C85-AC0D-4BC0-BC23-EF09A009FD85/Engagements

31 https://www.theguardian.com/politics/2022/oct/16/liz-truss-lost-authority-tory-party-prime-minister-conservative-mps-kwasi-kwarteng

32 https://www.theguardian.com/politics/2022/oct/16/liz-truss-lost-authority-tory-party-prime-minister-conscrvativc-mps-kwasi-kwarteng

33 Interview, Robert Halfon.

34 https://www.theguardian.com/politics/2022/oct/12/liz-truss-in-fresh-peril-as-senior-tory-mps-round-on-her-over-economy

35 Interview, Jason Stein.

36 Interview, Kwasi Kwarteng.

9: AVOID U-TURNS

1 Daniel Collings, email to author, 28 April 2024.

2 https://www.ft.com/content/e021c208-3ede-11e7-9d56-25f963e998b2

3 Interview, Simon McGee.

4 Interview, Mark Fullbrook.

5 Interview, Liz Truss.

6 Interview, Cameron Brown.

7 Steve Swinford, email to author, 1 June 2024.

8 https://x.com/Steven_Swinford/status/1580S868S13969213
4400?lang=en

9 https://www.thetimes.co.uk/article/c0c5c3c0-4bf6-11ed-8b55-aaf85c581598

10 https://www.standard.co.uk/news/politics/kwasi-kwarteng-full-list-shortest-serving-chancellors-b1032831.html

11 Interview, Sajid Javid.

12 Interview, Liz Truss.

13 Interview, Nick Macpherson.

14 Interview, Mark Fullbrook.

15 Interview, Adam Smith.

16 Interview, Rupert Harrison.

17 https://www.gov.uk/government/ speeches/pm-press-conference-opening-remarks-14-october-2022
18 https://www.youtube.com/ watch?v=GZv9CYhppdY
19 Cole and Heale, *Out of the Blue*, pp. 30–3.
20 Interview, George Osborne.
21 https://www.youtube.com/ watch?v=BdpcveGSSQ0
22 https://www.gov.uk/government/ speeches/chancellor-statement-17-october

23 https://www.bbc.co.uk/news/ business-63278821
24 Interview, Adam Smith.
25 Interview, Gavin Williamson.
26 https://hansard.parliament.uk/ commons/2022-10-17/debates/ 54BB3823-B8E9-405D-B055-F64DC6ACE626/Replace mentOfTheChancellorOfThe Exchequer
27 Interview, Kwasi Kwarteng.
28 https://www.ft.com/content/ 38b30b44-94c2-4775-8efb-2c95b3e8c447

10: RETAIN THE CONFIDENCE OF THE PARTY

1 Alan Clark, *The Alan Clark Diaries: Thatcher's Fall*, Weidenfeld & Nicolson, London, 1993, p. 30.
2 https://www.margaretthatcher. org/document/
3 Interview, Simon McGee.
4 https://www.bbc.co.uk/news/ blogs-the-papers-63294249
5 https://www.mailplus.co.uk/ edition/comment/230362/if-pm-is-a-lame-duck-wise-tories-must-act
6 https://www.theguardian.com/ politics/2022/oct/18/dismayed-tory-mps-continue-to-plot-to-oust-liz-truss-from-no-10
7 Interview, Graham Brady.
8 Cole and Heale, *Out of the Blue*, p. 304.
9 https://www.theguardian.com/ politics/2022/oct/26/sir-john-hayes-in-lockstep-with-suella-braverman-on-immigration. https://www.theguardian. com/politics/2022/oct/19/ suella-braverman-departs-as-uk-home-secretary-liz-truss.

https://www.bbc.co.uk/news/uk-politics-63456984. https://www. politicshome.com/news/article/ suella-braverman-sent-official-documents-email-six-times. https://www.gov.uk/government/ publications/letter-to-hasc-from-home-secretary/letter-to-hasc-from-home-secretary-accessible-version. https://www.theguardian. com/politics/2022/oct/31/suella-braverman-email-four-questions-left-unanswered
10 https://www.bbc.co.uk/news/uk-politics-63320750
11 Interview, George Osborne.
12 https://www.theguardian.com/ politics/2022/oct/19/liz-truss-adviser-jason-stein-suspended-sajid-javid
13 https://www.ft.com/content/ 48d802dc-388f-4889-b5e8-08cc16f0db87
14 https://www.ft.com/content/ 52f0d575-e17d-4957-9f75-f363d4f3e30c
15 https://hansard.parliament.uk/ commons/2022-10-19/debates/

C20633EF-DAB3-4D6A-903E-
11FEDD4644D8/Engagements

16 https://www.telegraph.co.uk/
news/2022/10/19/liz-truss-
has-go-tory-party-have-chance-
recovering

17 *Get Brexit Done: The Conservative
and Unionist Party Manifesto*,
Conservative Party, London,
2019, p. 55.

18 Interview, Sophie Jarvis.

19 https://hansard.parliament.uk/
commons/2022-10-19/debates/
C20633EF-DAB3-4D6A-903E-
11FEDD4644D8/Engagements

20 Interview, David Canzini.

21 https://hansard.parliament.uk/
Commons/2022-10-19/debates/
2C2C933D-682E-439B-AA46-
096A9459F716/details

22 Interview, Wendy Morton.

23 Interview, Penny Mordaunt.

24 Ibid.

25 https://www.parliament.uk/
globalassets/investigation-report-
for-19-october-2022.pdf

26 https://hansard.parliament.uk/
commons/2022-10-19/debates/
C20633EF-DAB3-4D6A-903E-
11FEDD4644D8/Engagements

27 Interview, Craig Whittaker.

28 Interview, Iain Carter.

29 Interview, Graham Brady.

30 Interview, Jake Berry.

31 Cole and Heale, *Out of the Blue*,
p. 309.

32 Interview, Liz Truss.

33 Interview, Mark Fullbrook.

34 Interview, Graham Brady.

35 Interview, Sophie Jarvis.

36 Interview, Jeremy Hunt.

37 Private information.

38 https://www.gov.uk/government/
speeches/prime-minister-liz-
trusss-statement-in-downing-
street-20-october-2022

39 Interview, David Canzini.

40 Interview, Jake Berry.

41 Interview, Kwasi Kwarteng.

THE VERDICT: 'DEEP STATE' OR DEEP INCOMPETENCE?

1 Liz Truss, *Ten Years to Save the
West*, p. 271.

2 In her memoir, Truss wrote that
'The arguments Kwasi and I
were making were not novel or
eccentric. They'd been proved
right by the experiences of the
1970s and 1980s, and for a
time, they were accepted
wisdom. But somehow the
economic establishment had
either forgotten or repudiated
them in the years since.' Truss,
Ten Years to Save the West,
p. 233.

3 Robert Peston and Steph
McGovern, 'Who Killed Liz
Truss?', Rest is Money Podcast,
April 2024.

4 Correspondence with the author,
Robert Peston, 20 June 2024.

5 Adapted from F. Scott Fitzgerald,
The Great Gatsby, Penguin,
London, 2000, p. 170.

ILLUSTRATION CREDITS

Dramatis Personae: *Truss and Boris Johnson* (Toby Melville/ Contributor/Getty)

Preface: *Truss in Estonia* (Simon Dawson/No. 10 Downing Street)

Introduction: *Truss campaigning* (PA Images/Alamy)

1 Secure the Power Base: *Truss and Hugh O'Leary* (Pool/ Getty)

2 Have a Clear and Realistic Plan for Government: *Truss arriving at 10 Downing Street* (Imago/Alamy)

3 Appoint the Best Cabinet/Team: *Truss and her Cabinet* (Frank Augstein/Contributor/Getty)

4 Command the Big Events: *Truss at the state funeral of Queen Elizabeth II* (WPA Pool/Pool/Getty)

5 Be Credible and Highly Regarded Abroad: *Truss addresses the United Nations General Assembly* (Angela Weiss/ Contributor/Getty)

6 Learn How to Be Prime Minister: *Truss in the House of Commons* (House of Commons)

7 Avoid Major Policy Failures: *Kwasi Kwarteng* (House of Commons)

INDEX

ALSO BY ANTHONY SELDON

Churchill's Indian Summer: The Conservative Government 1951–55

By Word of Mouth: Elite Oral History

Ruling Performance: Governments since 1945 (ed. with Peter Hennessy)

Political Parties Since 1945 (ed.)

The Thatcher Effect (ed. with Dennis Kavanagh)

Politics UK (joint author)

Conservative Century (ed. with Stuart Ball)

The Major Effect (ed. with Dennis Kavanagh)

The Heath Government 1970–1974 (ed. with Stuart Ball)

The Contemporary History Handbook (ed. with Brian Brivati et al.)

The Ideas That Shaped PostWar Britain (ed. with David Marquand)

How Tory Governments Fall (ed.)

Major: A Political Life

10 Downing Street: An Illustrated History

The Powers Behind the Prime Minister (with Dennis Kavanagh)

Britain under Thatcher (with Daniel Collings)

The Foreign Office: An Illustrated History

A New Conservative Century (with Peter Snowdon)

The Blair Effect 1997–2001 (ed.)

Public and Private Education: The Divide Must End

Partnership not Paternalism

Brave New City: Brighton & Hove, Past, Present, Future

The Conservative Party: An Illustrated History (with Peter Snowdon)

New Labour, Old Labour: The Wilson and Callaghan Governments, 1974–79

Blair

The Blair Effect 2001–5 (ed. with Dennis Kavanagh)

Recovering Power: The Conservatives in Opposition since 1867 (ed. with Stuart Ball)

Blair Unbound (with Peter Snowdon and Daniel Collings)

Blair's Britain 1997–2007 (ed.)

Trust: How We Lost it and How to Get It Back

An End to Factory Schools

Why Schools, Why Universities?

Brown at 10 (with Guy Lodge)

Public Schools and the Great War (with David Walsh)

Schools United

The Architecture of Diplomacy (with Daniel Collings)

Beyond Happiness: The Trap of Happiness and How to Find Deeper Meaning and Joy

The Coalition Effect, 2010–2015 (ed. with Mike Finn)

Cameron at 10 (with Peter Snowdon)

Teaching and Learning at British Universities

The Cabinet Office 1916–2016 – The Birth of Modern British Government (with Jonathan Meakin)

The Positive and Mindful University (with Alan Martin)

The Fourth Education Revolution (with Oladimeji Abidoye)

May at 10 (with Raymond Newell)

Public Schools and the Second World War (with David Walsh)

Fourth Education Revolution Reconsidered (with Oladimeji Abidoye and Timothy Metcalf)

The Impossible Office?: The History of the British Prime Minister (with Jonathan Meakin and Illias Thoms)

The Path of Peace: Walking the Western Front Way

Johnson at 10 (with Raymond Newell)